Bharat's

MERCANTILE LAWS

with Multiple Choice Questions

Bharat's

MERCANTILE LAWS *for* CPT

with

Multiple Choice Questions

By

K.K. AGRAWAL

B.Com., DCA, MBA, LL.B., DISA (ICA), FCA

BHARAT LAW HOUSE PVT. LTD.

New Delhi

2012

First Edition 2008
Second Edition 2009
Third Edition 2010
Fourth Edition 2010
Reprint 2012

PRICE ₹ 220

ISBN: 978-81-7733-657-3

A

Printed in India

WITH THE BLESSINGS OF "MATA VAISHNO DEVI"

Published by D.C. Puliani for Bharat Law House Pvt. Ltd.
T-1/95, Mangolpuri Industrial Area, Phase-I, New Delhi-110 083.
Printed at Shanti Enterprises, New Delhi
(Phones 2791 0001-03)

Preface to the Fourth Edition

I am pleased to revise the manuscript for the publication of the present fourth edition of my book on Mercantile Laws. The previous editions received an enthusiastic response from the students. This book adopts a modern and novel approach on the subject, keeping in view the specific requirements of the students appearing in the exams of ICAI.

The distinctive features of the book are as under:

- This book is written in **teach yourself style** and provides information in **a concise manner**.
- Each topic has been arranged under **a suitable heading**.
- Objective Type Questions are set in such a manner so as to cover each and every topic of the subject. This book is a comprehensive bank of objective type questions on the subject.
- The content of the book is backed by adequate research work and is up-to-date.

All endeavour has been made to make the edition error-free, yet mistakes might have crept in, for which we are apologetic. Suggestions and criticism from the readers would be highly appreciated and acknowledged.

25th August, 2010 **K.K. AGRAWAL**

Acknowledgements

No book is the work of a single person. I take this opportunity to place on record my sincere thanks to my students for their nice efforts.

I also place my thanks to Puliani Brothers of Bharat Law House Pvt. Ltd. for their intense efforts in printing and publication of the book. It is due to their efforts that I have been able to present this book before the readers.

K. K. AGRAWAL

WITH MAA SARASWATI

Dedicated to My Parents
Sri Vishnu Agrawal
&
Smt. Vimlesh Agrawal

Contents

About the Author

- Associate member of The Institute of Chartered Accountants of India.
- Law graduate and Information System Auditor
- He has been faculty member of ICAI (Agra Branch)
- A well known author of Graduate and Post Graduate books of Agra University, Bundelkhand University and Rajasthan University.
- Presently pursuing WTO research work.
- Also presently conducting classes for professional courses
- He is in active practice of the profession.
- He can be reached at – agrawalakamal@yahoo.co.in

Maxims

(1)	*Quid-pro-quo*	:	Something in return
(2)	*Ab-initio*	:	From the beginning
(3)	*Consensus-ad-idem*	:	Parties must agree upon the same thing in Same Sense.
(4)	*Jus-in-rem*	:	A right against or in respect of a thing
(5)	*Jus-in-personam*	:	A right against or in respect of a person
(6)	*Nudum Pactum*	:	An agreement not supported by consideration
(7)	*Ignorantia juris non-exusat*	:	Ignorance of law is not an excuse.
(8)	*Ubberima fidei*	:	Requiring utmost good faith
(9)	*Caveat Emptor*	:	Let the buyer beware
(10)	*Prima facie*	:	Apparently
(11)	*Nemo dat quo non habet*	:	No one can pass a better title that what he has.
(12)	*Ex nudo pacto non oritur*	:	An agreement without consideration is void.
(13)	*Quantum Merit*	:	As much as earned
(14)	*Delegates non protest delegate*	:	A person whom authority has been given cannot delegate the authority to another.
(15)	*In pari delicto, potior est condition defendentis*	:	In cases of equal guilt, defendant is in a better position.
(16)	*Ultra vires*	:	Beyond the Authority

Doctrines

- Doctrine of constructive consideration:

  Meaning = when consideration is moved from the third party (not a party to contract)

- Doctrine of Privity of Contract:

  Meaning = Privacy of parties to enforce the rights can not be interrupted by the other parties, i.e. a person who is not a party to contract can not sue or be sued.

- Doctrine of frustration:

  Meaning = Performance of a contract becomes impossible after making it (also known as supervening impossibility).

- Doctrine of unjust enrichment:

  Meaning = Nobody will be allowed to become rich at the expense of others.

DIVISION I
THE INDIAN CONTRACT ACT, 1872

Chapter 1

BASIC CONCEPTS

☞ **Applicability:**

➤ This Act extends to the whole of India, except the State of Jammu and Kashmir.

➤ This Act comes into force w.e.f. 1-9-1872.

➤ This Act is not a complete law on all types of contract. It lays down the general principles of contract law.

WHAT IS CONTRACT?

☞ **Introduction:**

In our day to day life, we enter into a number of contracts without realising that we are entering into a contract. *For example*, when we purchase some goods from the market, we enter into '*The Contract of Sale of Goods*'. In the same way, when we leave our vehicle at a workshop for repair, we enter into '*The Contract of Bailment*' etc. Now the question arises '*what is Contract?*'

☞ **What is Contract?:**

A "Contract is—

- an agreement
- enforceable by law." —— ***Sec. 2(h)***

☞ **What is Agreement?**

"Every promise and every set of promises, forming a consideration for each other is Agreement."

—— ***Sec. 2(e)***

☞ **What is Promise?**

"When the person to whom the proposal is made signifies his assent thereto, the proposal is said to be accepted. A proposal, when accepted, becomes a promise." —— ***Sec. 2(b)***

In short, we can say that for a promise, there must be two things: first offer by one party and second acceptance by the other party. If this promise contains consideration for each other, it will become agreement and if this agreement is enforceable by law, it will become contract.

ESSENTIALS OF A VALID CONTRACT

"All agreements are contracts, if they are made—

(i) by free consent of the parties, competent to contract,

(ii) for a lawful consideration,

(iii) with a lawful object, and

(iv) not hereby expressly declared to be void." —— ***Sec. 10***

The following are the essential elements for a valid contract:—

1. Offer and Acceptance: Every contract involves two parties—one making the offer and the other accepting it. Thus, offer and acceptance are essential for every contract.

For example: Suppose Mr. A tells to Mr. B, "I offer you to buy my car for Rs. 50,000." But Mr. B does not accept the offer. In this case, there will be no contract, as there is the absence of acceptance.

2. Intention to Create Legal Relationship: Besides offer and acceptance, both the parties must have an intention to go to court, if the other party does not meet his promise. Normally, in social agreements, there is no intention to go to court. But in a commercial agreement, there is always an intention to go to court.

– Balfour vs. Balfour, 1919

Facts of the Case	Mr. A promised to pay his wife £ 30 every month as household allowance. Later, the husband failed to pay the amount.
Decision in the Case	Held, the wife could not claim, as there was no intention to create legal obligation and therefore it is not enforceable by law.

3. Lawful Consideration: Lawful consideration is the essential element of a contract. It is a general rule, "No consideration, No contract". Consideration means something in return, *i.e.* both parties must get something in return for the promise.

For example: Mr. A agrees to sell his watch to B for Rs. 500. For Mr. B, watch is one consideration and for A, Rs. 500 is one consideration.

4. Capacity to Contract: In a contract, both the parties (*i.e.* offerer and acceptor) must be capable of entering into a contract. Section 11 clearly lays down that the following parties are capable of entering into a contract:

(i) A major,

(ii) A man of sound mind, and

(iii) Every man, who is not disqualified by law to enter into contract.

Essential for a Valid Contract

1. Offer and Acceptance
2. Intention to Create Legal Relationship
3. Lawful Consideration
4. Capacity to Contract
5. Free Consent
6. Lawful Object
7. Agreement not expressly declared void
8. Possibility of Performance
9. Legal Formalities

5. Free Consent (Sec. 14):

For example: Mr. A has two cars:- one black and the other red. He agrees to sell one of his cars to Mr. B. If A is thinking to sell black car and B is thinking to buy Red Car, then A and B do not agree on the same thing in the same sense and therefore there is no contract between the two.

6. Lawful Object: The object of the contract must be lawful. It must not be—fraudulent, unlawful, immoral or opposed to public policy [Sec. 23].

For example: Mr. A agrees to give Rs. 1,00,000 to Mr. B on the condition that Mr. B murders Mr. C. In this case, the object of the agreement is unlawful, therefore it will not be enforceable by law and hence, there will be no contract.

7. Agreement not expressly declared void: The agreement must not be declared void by the law in force. There are a large number of agreements, which have expressly been declared void as these are not in public interest. ***For example***: wagering agreements, agreements in the restraint of marriage, etc.

8. Possibility of Performance: The agreement must be to do the act whose performance is possible. The agreement to do an act whose performance is impossible is not enforceable by law.

For Example: Mr. A agrees to give Rs. 1,000 to Mr. B provided B flies in the sky like birds. In this case, the agreement between A and B, is void.

9. Legal Formalities: In some cases, where the law specially requires an agreement to be in writing or registered or attested, the agreement must be so, otherwise it shall not be enforceable. For example, a promise to pay a time-barred debt must be in writing.

TYPES OF CONTRACTS

A. On the Basis of Creation

1. Expressed Contract
2. Implied/Tacit Contract
3. Quasi Contract
4. E-Commerce Contract

B. On the Basis of Validity

1. Valid Contract
2. Void Contract
3. Void-*ab-initio* Agreement
4. Voidable Contract
5. Unenforceable Contract
6. Illegal Contract

C. On the Basis of Execution

1. Bilateral Contracts-
   (a) Bilateral Contract
   (b) Executory Contract
2. Unilateral Contracts

D. On the Basis of Formalities

1. Formal Contracts-
   (a) Contracts of Records
   (b) Simple Contracts
2. Contract under Seal

A. Classification on the basis of Creation

1. Expressed Contract : The contract, which is created either by word spoken or written.

For example, if Mr. A of Agra offers to sell his car for Rs. 1,50,000 to Mr. B of Delhi by writing a letter and Mr. B accepts the offer by writing a letter. Thus the contract between A and B is Expressed.

2. Implied or Tacit Contract : The contract, which is created by the acts or conduct of parties, *i.e.* these contracts are not created either by word spoken or written.

For example—

(i) When we enter into a bus without asking the bus-conductor any question, we enter into an implied contract.

(ii) Withdrawal of cash from ATM

3. Quasi Contract : Quasi Contracts are contracts which are created—

- neither by word spoken
- nor written
- nor by the conduct of the parties,
- but these are created by the law.

For example, if Mr. A leaves his goods at Mr. B's shop by mistake, then it is for Mr. B to return the goods or to compensate the price. In fact, these contracts depend on the principle that nobody will be allowed to become rich at the expenses of the other.

4. e-Contract : An e-contract is one, which is entered into between two parties *via* the internet.

B. Classification on the basis of Validity

1. Valid Contract: A contract, which fulfills all the essential characteristics of a contract.

2. Void Contract : [Sec.2(j)] A void contract is a contract,—

- which was enforceable by law when originally created,
- but due to the happening of some events, it ceases to be enforceable by law.

As per Sec. 2(j)–

> "A contract which ceases to be enforceable by law becomes void when it ceases to be enforceable."

For example, Mr. A agrees to sell his scooter to Mr. B on 25th Jan, but unfortunately on 24th Jan the scooter catches fire and turn into ashes. In this case, Mr. B cannot file a suit against Mr. A on the ground that he did not meet his promise on 25th Jan. This is because the performance of the promise on 25th Jan is impossible.

3. Agreement Void-*ab-initio* : It is an agreement which cannot be enforced from the date they were made. *For example*, an agreement by a minor in which minor promises to pay.

4. Voidable Contract [Sec. 2(i)] : ***As per Sec. 2(i)–***

An agreement, which is enforceable by law at the option of one or more of the parties, but not at the option of the other(s) is a voidable contract.

For example, Mr. A, at knife-point, asks B to sell his scooter for Rs. 50. Mr. B gives consent. The agreement is voidable at the option of B whose consent is not free.

It is to be noted that in a voidable contract, the contract will be voidable only at the option of the party, whose consent is not free, the contract will not be voidable at the option of the party who is on guilt. In the above example, the contract will not be voidable at the option of A, as he is on guilt.

5. Unenforceable Contract : An unenforceable contract is one, which is perfectly valid, but cannot be enforced by law due to some defects, such as understamping. If the defect is removed, the contract can be enforced. *For example*, undated cheque, etc.

6. Illegal contract: The agreements which are forbidden by law. Such agreements are *void-ab-initio.*

For example: an agreement for any criminal activity.

C. Classification on the basis of Execution

1. Bilateral Contract : Bilateral contracts are contracts in which both the parties either have performed their obligations or have to perform their obligations. These are of the following two types –

(a) Executed Contract An executed contract is a contract in which both the parties have performed their obligations.

For example, if Mr. A agrees to sell his car to Mr. B for Rs. 100000, the contract will be executed if A has given car to B and B has given the agreed amount to A.

(b) Executory Contract An executory contract is a contract, in which neither of the parties has performed their obligations.

In the above example, the contract will be Executory, if neither A has given the car to B nor B has given one amount to Mr. A.

2. Unilateral Contracts : Where only one of the parties to the contract has performed its obligation, it is called 'unilateral contract.' These contracts are known as 'Partly executed and partly executory contract.'

In the above example, if A had transferred his car to B, but B does not give the sum to A, the contract will be called partly executed and partly executory contract.

D. Classification on the basis of Formalities

1. Formal Contracts : A formal contract is one, which is entered into prescribed form. These contracts may be sub-divided as follows:

(a) Contracts : of Records (*i*) *Judgment:* A judgment is an obligation imposed by the court upon one or more persons in favour of another person.

(*ii*) *Recognizance:* A recognizance is a written acknowledgement of a debt due to the crown or the state. For example, bond to appear on summon.

(b) Contracts : under Seal These are written documents signed, sealed and delivered by the parties. It is also called a Deed or Contract Under Seal. <u>No consideration is required in case of a deed.</u>

2. Simple Contract : A simple contract is a contract that is not formal. These can be made orally or in writing and must be supported by consideration.

All Contracts are Agreements, but all Agreements are not Contracts

The various agreements may be classified into two categories:

1. **Agreement not enforceable by law** : Any essential of a valid contract is not available
2. **Agreement enforceable by law** : All essentials of a valid contract are available

☞ **Conclusion:**

Thus we see that an agreement may be or may not be enforceable by law, and so all agreements are not contracts. Only those agreements are contracts, which are enforceable by law. In short,

Contract = Agreement + Enforceability by Law

Hence, we can conclude "All contracts are agreements, but all agreements are not contracts."

Distinction Between Contract & Agreement

Basis	Contract	Agreement
1. Section :	Sec. 2(h)	Sec. 2(e)
2. Definition :	A contract is an agreement enforceable by law.	Every promise or every set of promises forming consideration for each other is an agreement.
3. Enforceability :	Every contract is enforceable.	Every promise is not enforceable.
4. Inter-relationship:	A contract includes an agreement.	An agreement does not include a contract.
5. Scope :	The scope of a contract is limited, as it includes only commercial agreements.	Its scope is relatively wider, as it includes both social agreement and commercial agreements.
6. Validity :	Only legal agreements are called contracts.	An agreement may be both legal and illegal.
7. Legal Obligation :	Every contract contains a legal obligation.	It is not necessary for every agreement to have legal obligation.

Distinction Between Void & Voidable Contract

Basis	Void Contract	Voidable Contract
1. Section :	Sec. 2(j)	Sec. 2(i)
2. Definition :	A contract which ceases to be enforceable by law becomes void, when it ceases to be enforceable.	An agreement which is enforceable by Law at the option of one or more of the parties, but not at the option of the other or others, is a voidable contract.
3. Enforceability :	A void contract is not at all enforceable.	A voidable contract is enforceable at the option of the aggrieved party.
4. Title of third party :	In this case, the third party will not acquire a good title, even if he is working in good faith.	In this case, if the third party is working in good faith, it will acquire a better title, before the contract is avoided.
5. Compensation :	In this case, no compensation will be allowed due to non-performance of the contract. *For example*, Mr. A agrees to sell his scooter to Mr. B on 25 Jan., but unfortunately on 24 Jan. the scooter catches fire and turn into ashes. In this case, Mr. B cannot file any suit against	In this case, compensation can be claimed by the aggrieved party.

Basis	Void Contract	Voidable Contract
	Mr. A on the ground that he did not meet his promise on 25 Jan.	
6. Restitution :	If the contract becomes void, the party who has received any benefit under the contract is bound to return it. In the above example, if B has given Rs. 10,000 to A for the scooter as consideration on 23rd Jan, then it becomes the responsibility of A to restore the amount to B, as soon as the scooter caught fire.	In this case, any party who has received any benefit must restore it to the aggrieved party when the contract is declared void.

OFFER/PROPOSAL

☞ Meaning [Sec. 2(a)]:

To form an agreement, there must be at least two elements — one offer and the other acceptance. Thus offer is the foundation of any agreement.

"When one person signifies to another his willingness—

- to do or to abstain from doing anything,
- with a view to obtaining the assent of that other to such act or abstinence, he is said to make a proposal."

—— *Sec. 2(a)*

The person who makes an offer is called '**Offeror**' or '**Promisor**' and the person to whom the offer is made is called the '**Offeree**' or '**Promisee**'.

For example: Mr. A says to Mr. B, "Will you purchase my car for Rs. 1,00,000?" In this case, Mr. A is making an offer to Mr. B. Here A is the offeror and B is the offeree.

TYPES OF OFFER

Kinds of Offer
1. Specific Offer
2. General Offer
3. Cross Offer
4. Counter Offer
5. Standing Offer
6. Expressed and Implied Offer

1. Specific Offer: A specific offer is one which is made to a specific person. It can be accepted only by that person to whom it is made.

For example: Mr. A says to Mr. B, "Will you purchase my car for Rs. 1,00,000?" This is a specific offer made by A to B and only B can accept it.

2. General Offer: A general offer is one, which is made throughout the world and anybody can accept it. ***For example***,

(a) The police advertised in a newspaper that a reward of Rs. 10,000 would be given to the person who would give information about "*Daku Gover Singh*." This is a general offer and any person can accept it.

(b) Company advertised that a reward of Rs. 100 would be given to any person who would suffer from influenza after using the medicine (Smoke balls) made by the company according to the printed directions.

One lady, Mrs. Carlill, purchased and used the medicine according to the printed directions of the company but suffered from influenza. She filed a suit to recover the reward of Rs. 100. The court held that there was a contract as she had accepted a general offer by using the medicine in the prescribed manner and as such she was entitled to recover the reward from the company.

—*Carlill* v *Carbilic Smoke Ball Co.* 1893

3. Cross Offer: When two parties make similar offers to each other without knowing the offer made by the other, the offers are called 'Cross Offer.' In such case, no contract will be created as no one has accepted the offer of others.

For example: A of Bombay offers B of Calcutta, "will you purchase my car for Rs. 1,00,000 by writing a letter?" At the same time, B offers A, "Will you sell your car to me for Rs. 80,000?" Neither A nor B has knowledge of the other's offer. The offers of A and B are called cross offers.

It is to be noted that A's offer will not be assumed to be the acceptance of B's offer. In the same way, B's offer will not be assumed to be the acceptance of A's offer. Therefore, there is no contract.

4. Counter Offer: When the offeree offers to accept the offer of offeror subject to some modifications or conditions, the offer of offeree is called Counter Offer.

For Example: Mr. A says to Mr. B, "will you purchase my car for Rs. 1,00,000?" Mr. B replies, "I will purchase your car, if you sell it for Rs. 75,000." In this case, the offer of Mr. B is called is called counter offer.

5. Standing Offer/Open Offer/Continuous Offer:

For example: When we ask the newspaper vendor to supply the newspaper daily. In such case, we do not repeat our offer daily and the newspaper vendor supplies the newspaper to us daily. The offers of such types are called Standing Offer.

6. Express and Implied Offer:

- **Express offer**. *For example*, A offers B, "will you purchase my car for Rs. 1,00,000 by writing a letter?" The offer of A is an expressed offer.
- **Implied Offer**. *For example*, public telephones or weighing machines in public places offer their services for a certain amount (one rupee). The offers of these machines are called implied.

LEGAL RULES REGARDING OFFER

1. There must be Two persons: One offeror and the other offeree.

2. Offer must be Communicated: Offer must be communicated to the person to whom it is made. It is a very general rule that a person can accept an offer only when he has knowledge. If he has no knowledge, how can he accept the offer.

For Example: Mr. S offered a reward to any one who returned his lost dog. Mr. F brought the dog to S without hearing the offer. Held, that F was not entitled to the reward, as the offer was not communicated.

—*Fitch* v *Snedaker,* 1868

3. Offer must be made with a view to obtaining the assent of other party: Offer must be made with an intention to obtaining the assent of the other party. In this respect, Sec. 2(a) clearly lays down, "When one person signifies to another his willingness to do or to abstain from doing anything, with a view to obtaining the assent of that other to such act or abstinence, he is said to make a proposal."

***For example*:** Mr. A says to Mr. B, "I want to sell my cycle for Rs. 1,000." This is not an offer because the statement is not made with an intention to obtaining the assent of B.

4. An offer must be distinguished from a mere Declaration of Intention: For a valid offer, it is also very necessary that it must be distinguished from a mere declaration of intention. Mere declaration of intention does not amount to offer. That is why an advertisement for sale in a Newspaper is not an offer for sale.

For Example: A advertised to sell certain furniture by auction. B reached A's house to purchase the furniture. However, A changed his mind not to sell the furniture. It was held that B cannot compel A to sell the furniture or even to recover the damages, such as conveyance charges, etc. —*Harris* v *Nickerson*

5. An offer must be distinguished from an invitation to offer: It is very necessary for a valid offer that it must be distinguished from an invitation to offer. Generally, it is seen that shopkeepers generally display their goods in show-cases with a price. In such case, the shopkeeper is not making an offer, but he is inviting the public to make an offer which he may or may not accept. Thus the shopkeeper may not be compelled to sell his goods displayed in show-cases.

6. Offer should not contain a term, the non-acceptance of which may be assumed to amount to acceptance: Thus a man cannot say that if acceptance is not communicated up to a certain time, the offer would be considered as accepted.

For example: A offers B to sell his car for Rs. 20,000 saying, "If you do not reply by Sunday next, I shall assume, you have accepted the offer."

In this case, no contract will be created even if the acceptor does not reply by next Sunday.

7. Offer may be Expressed or Implied; General or Specific.

8. Other Essentials of a Valid Contract: For Example—

(i) Offer must give rise to legal obligation. *For Example*: Balfour v/s Balfour (1919) case.

(ii) Terms of offer must be definite and certain.

For Example: A has two cycles, one red and the other green. He agrees to sell one of his cycles to B. In this case, it is not clear that which cycle is he ready to sell. Hence, there is no valid offer.

ACCEPTANCE

☞ Meaning of Acceptance [Sec. 2(b)]:

As we know that to form an agreement, there must be at least two elements— one offer and the other acceptance. Acceptance is the second element, which is essential to make any offer a contract.

"When the person, *to whom the proposal is made*, signifies his assent thereto, the proposal is said to be accepted. A proposal, when accepted, becomes a promise."

—— Sec. 2(b)

LEGAL RULES REGARDING ACCEPTANCE

1. There must be two persons: One offeror and the other offeree.

2. Who will accept? Acceptance must be made by the person to whom the offer is made. In case of specific offer, the acceptance must be made by the person to whom the offer is made. While in case of general offer, it may be accepted by anyone. ***For example***: *Carlill* v *Carbilic Smoke Ball Co.* (1893) case.

3. Acceptance must be for an offer communicated: At first, there must be communication of an offer, and then it can be accepted. If the offer is not communicated, it cannot be accepted. ***For Example:*** *Fitch* v *Snedaker*, 1868 case.

4. Communication of Acceptance is necessary:

For example: Mr. P was appointed the Principal of a school. One of the members of the college privately informed P that he had been appointed principal. But no official communication was sent by the School to P in this respect. Later, the management of the school decided not to appoint P, as the principal. P filed a suit against the school for cancellation of his appointment.

Held, he cannot do so as there is no communication of acceptance and therefore, there is no contract —*Powell* v *Lee* (1980)

5. Acceptance must be absolute and unqualified: All the terms of an offer must be accepted. If all the terms of offer are not accepted, it will not be a valid acceptance. It will be called 'counter offer'.

For example: Mr. A says to Mrs. B, "Will you purchase my car for Rs. 1,00,000?" Mrs. B replies, "I will purchase your car, if you sell it for Rs. 75,000." In this case, the acceptance is not valid as all terms of the offer is not accepted.

6. Acceptance must be made in the mode prescribed: Where the mode of acceptance is prescribed by the offeror, it must be accepted in that prescribed mode. Otherwise, the offeror may revoke the offer.

For example: Mr. A says to Mrs. B, "will you purchase my car for Rs. 1,00,000? Reply by telegram." Mrs. B accepts the offer, but replies by post. In this case, Mr. A may refuse to sell his car to B on the ground that the offer is not prescribed in the mode prescribed.

7. Acceptance may be Express or Implied.

- **Express Acceptance**. *For example*, if Mr. A of Agra offers to sell his car for Rs. 1,50,000 to Mr. B of Delhi by writing a letter and Mr. B accepts the offer by writing a letter. In this example, the acceptance is express.
- **Implied Acceptance**. *For example*, when we enter a bus without saying anything, then we impliedly accept the services of Bus.

8. Silence can never be Acceptance: As we have already seen that an offer should not contain any term, the non-acceptance of which may be assumed to amount to acceptance. In other words, we can say that silence can never amount to acceptance. *Thus*, a man cannot say that if acceptance is not communicated up to a certain time, the offer would be considered as accepted.

For example: A offers B to sell his car for Rs. 20,000 saying, "If you do not reply by Sunday next, I shall assume, you have accepted the offer."

In this case, no contract will be created even if the acceptor does not reply by next Sunday.

9. Offer must be accepted in the time specified.

For example: A offers B to sell his car for Rs. 20,000, saying to reply by Sunday next. In this case, if A want to accept the offer, he should reply by Sunday next, otherwise A may reject the acceptance of B. Thus if B accepts the offer on Monday next, A may refuse to sell his car.

10. Other Essentials of a Valid Contract: For Example—

(i) Acceptance must give rise to legal obligation. *For Example*: the *Balfour* v/s *Balfour* (1919) case.

(ii) Terms of acceptance must be definite and certain.

Comment on:

"Acceptance is lighted match, while Offer is a train of gun powder."

This quotation is given by ***Sir William Anson***. In this quotation, Prof. William has compared the acceptance with light of match and offer with a train of gun powder. He makes so comparison due to the following reasons:

1. As soon as the lighted match is brought in contact with the train of gunpowder, an explosion takes place. In the same way, when Acceptance is brought in contact with offer, a contract takes place and offer loses its entity.
2. A train may be removed before the match is applied to the gun powder. In the same way, an offer may be revoked before it is accepted by the offeree.

Thus, we see that there is nothing wrong when Prof. William says, "Acceptance is lighted match, while Offer is a train of gun powder."

RULES REGARDING COMMUNICATION [Sec. 4]

– Communication of Offer:

Communication of offer is completed as soon as it comes to the knowledge of OFFEREE.

For example: Mr. A of Agra offers to Mr. B of Bombay to sell his car for Rs. 1,00,000 by writing a letter on 1-Jan. B receives the letter on 10-Jan. In this case, the offer is assumed to be communicated on 10-Jan, not on 1-Jan.

– Communication of Acceptance:

1. As against the Proposer : *As against the proposer*, communication of an acceptance is completed, when it is put in a course of transmission so as to be put out of the power of the acceptor.

For example, Mr. A of Agra offers to Mr. B of Bombay to sell his car for Rs. 1,00,000 by writing a letter on 1-Jan. Mr. B accepts the offer and posts a letter of acceptance on 10-Jan. A receives the letter of acceptance on 15-Jan. Then in this case, the communication of acceptance as against A is completed on 10-Jan.

2. As against the Acceptor : *As against the acceptor*, communication of offer is completed as soon as it comes to the knowledge of the proposer. Thus, in the above example, the communication of acceptance as against the acceptor is completed on 15-Jan.

– Communication of Revocation:

1. As against the person who makes the revocation : The communication of a revocation is completed, when it is put into a course of transmission to the person to whom it is made, so as to be out of the power of the person, who makes it.

For example, suppose Mr. A revokes his proposal by telegram. The revocation is complete as against A, when the telegram is dispatched.

2. As against the person to whom the revocation is made : The communication of a revocation is completed, when it comes to his knowledge.

For example, in the above case, the revocation is completed as against Mr. B when he receives the telegram.

REVOCATION OF OFFER & ACCEPTANCE [Secs. 5 & 6]

Revocation of Offer: An offer may be revoked at any time before the communication of acceptance is completed as against the offeror, but not afterwards. ***For example:***

Revocation of Acceptance: Any acceptance may be revoked at any time before the communication of acceptance is completed as against the acceptor, but not afterwards. In the above example, B may revoke his acceptance, before the letter is received by A.

How An Offer Is Revoked [Sec. 6]:

As per Sec. 6, an offer is revoked in the following situations-

1. Revocation by Notice: An offer can be revoked by giving a notice of revocation at any time before the communication of acceptance is completed as against the proposer, but not afterwards.

For example: A offers B to sell his house on 1st Jan by sending a letter. B receives the letter on 5th Jan and posts a letter of acceptance on 10th Jan. A at once changes his mind and decides not to sell his house to B, but he informs B about the revocation of offer on 11th Jan. In this case, A cannot revoke the offer, as B has already sent a letter of acceptance before the letter revocation.

2. Revocation by Lapse of Time: If the offer cannot be accepted within the time prescribed by the offeror, it will automatically be revoked.

3. Revocation by the death of Proposer: If the fact of death of the proposer comes to the knowledge of the acceptor before acceptance, the offer is revoked.

4. Revocation by the insanity of Proposer: If the fact of insanity of the proposer comes to the knowledge of the acceptor before acceptance, the offer is revoked.

5. Revocation by Counter Offer.

6. Revocation by not accepting the offer in the mode prescribed.

7. Revocation by failure of the acceptor to fulfill a condition precedent to acceptance: As we know that all the conditions of an offer must be satisfied by the acceptor, and if the acceptor fails to fulfill a condition precedent to acceptance, it will be revoked.

For Example: A applies for 100 shares of a company on the condition that he should be appointed Secretary of the company. The company allots him shares, but does not appoint him secretary. In this case, the offer lapses, as the company does not fulfill the condition precedent to acceptance, i.e. it does not appoint A as Secretary of the company.

CONSIDERATION

Meaning: Generally, a person makes a promise with the intention that he would get something in return. This something in return is called 'CONSIDERATION'.

"When, at the desire of the promisor, the promisee or any other person-

- **has done or abstained from doing, or**
- **does or abstains from doing, or**
- **promises to do or to abstain from doing something,**

then, such act or abstinence or promise is called a consideration for the promise."

—— Sec. 2(d)

Suppose, A sells his house to B, for Rs. 10,000. B's promise to pay the Rs. 10,000 is a consideration for A's promise to sell the house, and A's promise to sell the house is consideration for B's promise to pay Rs. 10,000.

LEGAL RULES REGARDING CONSIDERATION

1. Consideration must move at the desire of Promisor: It is a fundamental rule that the action or forbearance must be done at the desire of the promisor. If it is not done at the desire of the promisor or done at the desire of a third party, then it will not be a valid consideration.

For Example: X polished Y's car without obtaining any permission of Y. In this case, Y is not liable to pay anything to X, as the action of polishing was not done at the desire of X.

2. Consideration may move from the promisee or any other person on his behalf.

– Chinnaya V. Ramaya (1818)

Facts of : Case	A father, by a gift deed, made over certain property to his daughter, with the direction that the daughter should pay an annuity to the father's brother. On the same day, the daughter entered into an agreement with her uncle and agreed to pay the annuity. *Later*, the daughter declined to fulfill her promise on the ground that no consideration was paid by the father's brother to her.
Decision of : Case	In this case, the honourable court held that the consideration was paid by the father on behalf of her uncle. So the uncle was entitled to recover the annuity.

3. Consideration may be Past, Present or Future: The words 'Has done', 'Does' or 'Promises to do' which are used in Sec. 2(d) indicate that the consideration may be past, present or future.

(a) Past Consideration: If a person has already done something for another, and then comes a promise from the other, the consideration is said to be past consideration.

For example, A found B's dog and returned to B. After a weak, B announced to give Rs. 100 to A, as reward for the services rendered by him. In this case, B is paying Rs. 100 for past consideration.

Past consideration is not consideration in England.

(b) Present /Executed Consideration : When consideration is given simultaneously with promise, it is called present consideration.

(c) Future Consideration : When the consideration is to move at some future date, it is called future or executory consideration.

Example, A promises B to deliver his car at a future date. B also promises to pay on delivery.

4. Consideration must be real not illusory: By reality of consideration, we mean that it should have some value in the eye of law.

For Example: A promised to give Rs. 1000 to a doctor (over and above his fees), who performs a successful operation of his son. The consideration of Rs. 1000 is illusory, as it was the duty of the doctor to do his best. Therefore in this case, A is not legally bound to pay the money.

5. Consideration need not be adequate: In the Indian Contract Act, 1872, it is clearly said that consideration is something in return and this something in return is not necessary to be adequate.

For example: A agrees to sell his house to B for Rs. 1000. The house could be sold for about Rs. 100000. Later on, A cannot refuse to sell his house to B on the ground that the consideration is not adequate.

However, if B had received A's consent by unfair means, i.e. at the knife point etc., then A can refuse to sell the house to A as the consent of A is not free.

6. Consideration must not be illegal, impossible, Uncertain, Ambiguous, Fraudulent, Immoral or Opposed to Public Policy:

(a) Illegal Consideration	:	Illegal consideration refers to do an act, prohibited by law. *For example*, A tells B, "I will give you Rs. 1,00,000, if you murder C." In this case, consideration is illegal.
(b) Impossible Consideration	:	Impossible consideration refers to do an act, whose performance is impossible. *For example*, Mr. A agrees to give Rs. 1,000 to Mr. B provided B flies in the sky like a bird. This is an example of impossible consideration.
(c) Uncertain Consideration	:	Uncertain consideration makes a contract void. *For example*, A tells B, "Will you purchase my car for something." B accepts A's offer. In this case, the agreement between A and B is void, as the consideration is not certain.
(d) Immoral consideration	:	If a consideration is immoral or opposed to public policy, then it will not be enforceable by Law.

Stranger to Consideration and Stranger to Contract

☞ **Stranger to Consideration:**

As we know, a consideration may be moved either by the promisee himself or by any other person on his behalf. When it is moved by a third party on behalf of the promisee, the third party is called 'stranger to consideration.' *For example*, *Chinnaya* v *Ramaya* (1818) case.

☞ **Stranger to Contract or the Doctrine of Privity of Contract:**

- The person who is not a party to a contract is called stranger to the contract. *For example*, A was in debt of B for Rs. 1,000. B asks A to give the money to C. In this case, C is stranger to the contract.
- As we know, only parties to a contract may sue and be sued on that contract. Therefore, a stranger to a contract cannot file a suit against promisee, even if the contract was not made in his favour. This rule is called "***Doctrine of Privity of Contract***." In the above example, C can not file a suit against A if he refuses to pay the amount (Rs. 1,000).

– Exceptions to the 'Doctrine of Privity of Contract':

When can a Stranger to Contract Sue to enforce the contract?

1. Beneficiary of a trust
2. Family settlements for females
3. Assignment of a contract
4. Estoppel or Acknowledgement
5. Contract entered through Agent
6. Covenants running with land

1. Beneficiary of a Trust: A trust is always created for the benefit of some person, called beneficiary. The beneficiary can file a suit to enforce his right, even if he is not a party to contract.

For example: A transfers his property to his neighbour in trust in favour of his son. In this case, if after A's death, the neighbour refuses to give the benefit of the trust, the son can file a suit against the neighbour, although he is a stranger to the contract. —*M.K. Rapai* v *John*, (1965).

2. Family Settlements for Females: Generally in the HUF, some provision is made for females for their marriage or feeding at time of partition of family. In such cases, the female members have right to enforce the contract, even if they are not a party to contract.

For example: Mr. X divides his all the property between his three sons on the condition that they will give Rs. 1,000 p.m. to their old mother. In this case, the old mother can file a suit against her sons if they refused to pay the amount, although she is not a party to the contract.

3. Assignment of a contract: Where a contract is assigned in favour of someone, the assignee can enforce the contract, even if he is not a party to the contract.

For example: Mr. A assigned his insurance policy in favour of his son. The son can enforce the contract, although he is not a party to the contract.

4. Estoppel or Acknowledgement: Where a party by his conduct admits a liability, that party is deemed to be an agent of a third party and a binding obligation is thereby incurred by him towards the third party.

For example: A receives some money from P to be paid over to Q. A admits of this receipt to Q and therefore, Q can recover the amount from A, who shall be regarded as the agent of Q.

5. Contracts entered through Agent: The principal can enforce the contracts entered into by his duly authorized agent.

6. Covenants running with land: The purchaser of immovable property who has noticed that the owner of the land is bound by certain conditions or covenants created by an agreement affecting the land, shall be bound by such conditions, even though he is not a party to the original agreement containing those conditions or covenants.

<u>'No Consideration, No Contract'—Exceptions</u> [Sec. 25]

In our Indian Contract Act, 1872, consideration is made one of the essential elements to form a contract. It is a general rule, "*No Consideration, No contract*." Therefore, an agreement without consideration is void.

Exception to the Rule: No Consideration, No Contract
1. Love and affection
2. Compensation for voluntary services
3. Written promise to pay time-barred debt
4. Gift, etc. actually made
5. Agency
6. Contract under Seal
7. Contract of bailment
8. Contract of guarantee

However, the law recognises certain exceptions—

1. Love and Affection: An agreement, without consideration, will be enforceable, if the agreement –

- is in writing and registered under the law for the time being in force for the registration of documents, and
- is made on account of natural love and affection.

For example: A father promises in written and registered to pay his son Rs. 1,000 p.m. in love and affection. *Later on*, the father cannot refuse to pay the amount on the ground that he is not getting consideration.

2. Compensation for Voluntary Services: A promise to compensate, wholly or in part, a person who has voluntarily done something for the promisor, is enforceable by law without consideration.

For example: A found B's purse and returns it to him. B promised to pay a reward of Rs. 100 to A. B cannot refuse to pay on the ground that there was no consideration.

3. Written Promise to Pay time-barred debt: A promise made in written to pay a time-barred debt* is enforceable even without consideration.

For example: A owes B Rs. 2000 but the debt is time-barred as per the Limitation Act. If A promises in written to pay the sum to B, then there will be a valid contract.

4. Gift actually made.

For example: On the birthday of Mr. A, Mr. B gives him a golden chain as a birthday gift. In this case, B cannot demand back the chain on the ground that there was no consideration.

5. Agency: No consideration is needed to create agency.

For example: Mr. A agrees to become the agent of Mr. B for nothing. If A enters into a contract on behalf of B, then B cannot refuse to accept the contract on the ground that he is not giving any consideration to A.

6. Contract under Seal

7. Contract of Bailment

8. Contract of Guarantee

---

* **Time Barred Debt:** Where the contract is not performed within the fixed time or where the time is not fixed, within the reasonable time, the aggrieved party should take legal action within three years as laid down in The Limitation Act, 1963. After the expiry of this period, the aggrieved party cannot take any legal action against the party not performing the contract and the contract is called time barred.

CAPACITY TO CONTRACT [Sec. 11]

Parties Unable to Enter into a Contract

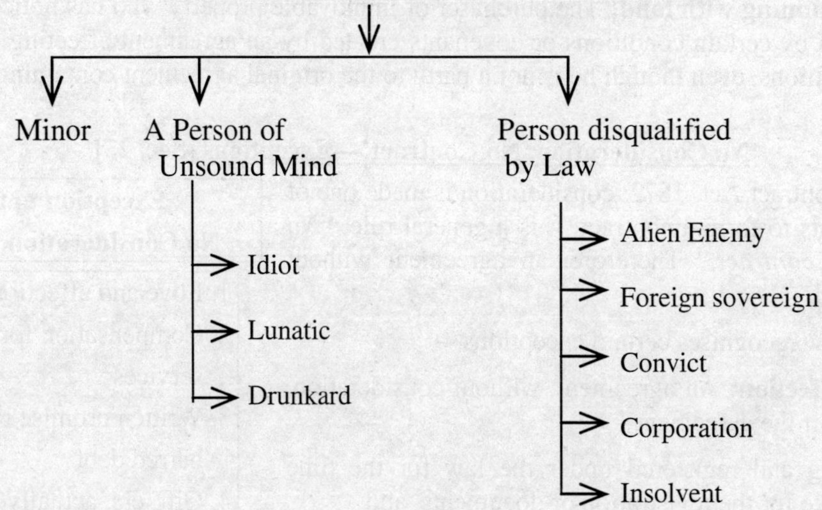

MINOR

– Who is minor?

"A minor is a person who has not completed the age of 18 years." **—— *Indian Majority Act, 1875***

– Position Of Minor In Indian Law:

"The Judges are their (i.e., minor) counsels, the Jury are their Servants and Law is their Guardian."

—— *Prof. Salmon*

1. An agreement with a minor, in which the minor is promisor, is *void-ab-initio*:

For Example: Mr. D, a minor, mortgaged his house for Rs. 20000 to a money-lender, but the mortgagee, i.e. the money-lender, paid him a sum of Rs. 8000. Subsequently, the minor sued for setting aside the mortgage. Held that the contract was void, as Mr. D was minor and therefore he is not liable to pay anything to the lender. —*Mohori Bibi* v *Dharmodas Ghose* (1930)

2. A minor can be Promisee (i.e. beneficiary) in a contract.

For Example: Mr. A, who is a major, accepts a bill of exchange in favour of Mr. B, who is a minor, then Mr. B can enforce the contract.

3. Ratification Not Possible: Since contract with a minor is void *ab-initio*, so such agreement cannot be ratified by him, even after he attains majority.

For Example: A minor borrowed Rs. 500 and executed a promissory note. After attaining majority, he issued another promissory note in settlement of the first note. The second promissory note is void for lack of consideration. —*Rama Swamy* v *Chettiar* (1906)

Exception: However, where services were rendered to the minor at his request during his minority and the same are continued at his request after majority, he can be held liable to pay for the services rendered both during his minority and majority.

4. A minor can always plead minority or infancy: That is why, even if he has, by misrepresenting his age, induced the other party to contract with him, he cannot be sued for fraud.

For Example: *In the Mohory Bibi* v *Dharmodas Ghose case*, actually the minor has misrepresented his age and therefore the other party paid him Rs. 8000. But the court did not stop him from denying that he is a minor and therefore not liable to pay the amount.

However it is to be noted that the law has given minors protection, but does not permit them to cheat others. Therefore in such cases, the court can direct the minor to restore the goods to the aggrieved party.

For Example: A minor misrepresents himself as a major and agrees to sell his house. He received Rs. 10000 as an advance. Out of this amount, he took delivery of a car for Rs. 6000 and spent the balance on a pleasure trip. The buyer of the house filed a suit for conveyance of property or refund of the amount. The court may order the minor to restore the car, if the car is with him. But the minor is not bound to sell the house or refund Rs. 10000. —*Leslie Ld* v *Sheill* (1914)

5. Liability of Minor in torts: Sometimes a minor, who cannot be made liable in a contract, can be made liable in tort. The test is whether the act done by him was done in the performance of the contract though wrongfully, or whether it was something never related to the contract.

For Example: A minor hires a horse from B expressly for riding, not for jumping. He jumps on the horse from a long distance and kills it. What is the liability of A to B?

Here the horse was hired for riding and used for jumping, there is a tort — wholly independent of the contract. Therefore, A is liable for damage caused by the death of B's horse. —*Burbard* v *Hagis,* (1863)

6. Minor's Liability for Necessaries: As per Sec 68, minor's estate is liable for the price of the necessaries, supplied to him or to any other person lawfully dependent upon him. He will not be personally liable for the same, only his estate will be liable. Therefore, if a minor has no personal property then no recovery is possible.

For Example: Mr. A supplies ration goods to a minor, then A can recover the amount through the minor's estate.

***Meaning of Necessaries*:** It is to be noted the word necessaries is not limited only to food, clothes and house rest, but it also includes the price of the goods and services, which are rendered to him and are according to his standard.

For Example: A minor entered into an agreement with a well-known billiards player to learn the game and play matches with him. The player spent time and money in arranging world tour for the minor. The minor later refused to pay the sum spent on him. The court held that the agreement was for necessaries because it was for the education of the minor and therefore the minor's estate was liable to pay.

—*Robers* v *Grey* (1913)

For Example: A minor purchased 11 fancy coats. At that time he had sufficient clothes. Therefore, the court held that the coats were not necessaries of life and the minor was not liable to pay for them.

—*Nash* v *Inman* (1908)

7. A minor cannot be declared insolvent.

8. A minor can be an agent, but he cannot be Principal.

9. A minor cannot be a partner: It is a very fundamental rule that to become a partner, a contract is necessary, which is not possible for a minor. Therefore, a minor cannot become a partner, but he can be admitted for the benefits of partnership with the consent of all partners.

10. A minor cannot be a member of a company.

11. No liability of Guardians for the acts of a minor: The Guardian of a minor is not liable for the acts of the minor. But where a minor is acting as an agent of the guardian, the guardian can be held liable for the acts of a minor.

12. Liability of minor for the acts of a guardian: A guardian may enter into an agreement on behalf of a minor and it will be valid and binding on him, provided-

(a) The Guardian is authorised to do so,

(b) The agreement must be for the actual benefit of the minor,

13. Specific performance of a minor's contract: Again, since a minor's contract is absolutely void, there is no question of specific performance of such contract.

A MAN OF UNSOUND MIND

"A person is said to be of sound mind for the purpose of making a contract, if at the time when he makes it, he is capable of—

(i) understanding the contract, and

(ii) forming a rational judgement as to its effect on his interests."

— ***Sec. 12***

Thus, to decide whether a person is of sound mind or not, we have to see two things:

1. capacity to understand the contract,
2. Ability to form rational judgment as to its effect on a person's interests.

Therefore, a person who cannot understand a contract and form a rational judgment as to its effect on his interests is a person of unsound mind.

Sec. 12 also lays down that -

"A person who is usually of unsound mind, but occasionally of sound mind can make a contract when he is of sound mind. Similarly, a person who is usually of sound mind, but occasionally of unsound mind, may not make a contract when he is of unsound mind."

For Example: A patient in a lunatic asylum, who is at intervals of sound mind, may contract during those intervals.

Examples of Unsoundness of Mind

1. Idiot: An idiot is a person who is permanently of unsound mind. Such a person has no lucid interval.

2. Lunatic: In this case, the unsoundness is not permanent. Such person has some interval of sound mind.

3. Drunkards: A drunkard is a person who is under the influence of drink or some drug. When he is drunk, he cannot understand a contract, and therefore cannot enter into a contract.

PERSONS DISQUALIFIED BY LAW

1. Alien Enemy : An alien is a person who is the citizen of a foreign country. So, an alien enemy is a person, whose country is at war with India.

It is to be noted that the word Alien Enemy includes even an Indian citizen or a citizen of a third country, living in the country whose government is at war with the government of India.

As per the Indian Contract Act, 1872, a contract with an alien friend† is valid, but when an war breaks out, such a contract should be suspended or put to an end. If the contract cannot be postponed, it may be suspended. But if the contract cannot be suspended, it will be dissolved.

2. Foreign Sovereign, State, Ambassador or Representative : Foreign sovereign, state, ambassador and representatives have been given honourable status and therefore, enjoy some special privileges.

They can enter into contracts and enforce those contracts in our courts, but an Indian citizen has to obtain a prior permission of the Central Government in order to sue them in our law courts. Our law however provides that an ex-king can be sued against in our courts without any such permission.

3. Convict : A convicted person, during the period of imprisonment, cannot enter into contracts. After the imprisonment is over, he becomes capable of entering into contracts. *Sometimes*, he is granted a ticket of leave. During this period of leave also he can enter into a contract.

† An alien friend cannot be employed as master or any other Principal Officer of a ship. He is also prohibited to acquire property or ownership in an Indian ship.

4. Corporations : A corporation is an artificial person created by law, having a legal existence separate from its members. It comes into existence by a special Act of legislature, or by registration under the Companies Act, 1956.

The contractual capacity of corporations is limited by the statute governing it. *For example*, in the case of a company, formed under the Companies Act, 1956, its contractual capacity is limited by its memorandum of Association and the provisions of the Companies Act.

It is also to be noted that corporations cannot enter into contracts of personal nature. For example, it cannot enter into a contract of marriage.

5. Insolvent : When a person is declared insolvent, his property vests in an officer appointed by the court and he is deprived of power to deal in that property.

Therefore, he cannot enter into contracts, unless he has been discharged by the court. After he is discharged by the court, he also suffers some disqualification.

FREE CONSENT

Free consent is an essential element of a valid contract. If the consent of the parties is not free, then the contract will be voidable at the option of the parties whose consent is not free. Now the questions arise, "*What is meant by Consent?*" and "*What is Free Consent*?"

– What is Consent [Sec. 13]:

"Two or more persons are said to consent when they agree upon the same thing in the same sense." (consensus-ad-idem)

For example: Mr. A has two cars — one black and one other red. He agrees to sell one of his cars to Mr. B. if he is thinking to sell the Black Car and B is thinking to buy the Red Car, then A and B do not agree on the same thing in the same sense and therefore there is no contract between both.

– What is Free Consent? [Sec. 14]:

Parties to a contract may agree upon the same thing in the same sense. But that is not enough. Their consent must be free. Sec. 14, therefore, defines free consent as follows:

"Consent is said to be free, when it is not caused by-

1. **Coercion,**
2. **Undue Influence,**
3. **Fraud,**
4. **Misrepresentation,**
5. **Mistake."**

COERCION [Sec.15]

Coercion simply means forcing a person to enter into contract by adopting unfair means. Sec. 15 defines coercion as follows:

"Coercion is-

(i) Committing (or threatening to commit) of any act forbidden by the Indian Penal Code, or

(ii) unlawful detaining (or threatening to detain) any property to the prejudice of any person;

WHATEVER with the intention of causing any person to enter into an agreement."

For example: A at the knife-point asks B to sell his scooter for Rs. 50. B accepts the offer due to fear. Here A obtains B's consent by coercion and therefore, later on, B can refuse to sell the scooter on the ground that his consent was not free.

– Essential Elements of Coercion:

1. Mode Of Coercion: Sec. 15 lays down two modes for exercising of coercion-

(*i*) *By Committing or Threatening to commit any act forbidden by IPC.*

(*ii*) *By Unlawful detaining or threatening to detain any Property.*

2. The act of coercion must be done with the object of inducing the other person to enter into an agreement.

For Example: A and B were returning to India from England by a ship. When the ship was passing through the Suez Canal, A threatened B to throw him into the Canal, if he did not sign a promissory note for Rs. 1000. B sighed and gave the promissory note to A. B on reaching India refused to pay the amount of the promissory note. In this case, A cannot succeed in recovering the amount of the promissory note, as B accepted it under coercion.

3. Coercion may be applied against any person, not necessarily against the other party to the contract:

For Example: A threatens B to shoot him, if his father does not sell his car to him. The father accepts his offer. In this case, coercion is applied against B, but the acceptance of the contract is made by his father.

– Whether Threat to Commit Suicide Amounts to Coercion?

Sec. 306 of the Indian Penal Code punishes abetment of suicide. Again Sec. 309 punishes an attempt to commit suicide. Thus we see that although suicide in no crime, yet its attempt and abetment is prohibited by the Indian Penal Code. Therefore it will be well to say that a threat to commit suicide amounts to coercion, as prohibited by the Indian Penal Code.

– Leading Case: Chikham Amiraju V. Seshamma

In this case, a person threatened his wife and his son to commit suicide, if they did not execute a release deed in favour of his bother in respect of certain properties. The wife and son executed the release deed under the threat. Held that the deed was executed under a threat of suicide and therefore, amounts to coercion and voidable.

– Consequence of Coercion: The contract will be violable at the option of the party, whose consent is not free.

UNDUE INFLUENCE [SEC.16]

"A contract is said to be induced by 'undue influence', where the relation subsisting between the parties are such that one of the parties -

(i) is in a position to dominate the will of the other and

(ii) uses that position to obtain an unfair advantage over the other."

——Sec. 16

☞ When a person can dominate the will of Other Person? Sec. 16(2):

(i) Where he holds a *real or apparent authority* over the other, e.g., as between master and servant, or

(ii) Where he stands in *fiduciary relation* to the other. This implies a relationship of mutual trust and confidence. For example –

(a) Guru and Chela,

(b) Doctor and Patient,

(c) Solicitor and client,

(d) Parent and Child,

(e) Trustee and Beneficiary

(f) Fiancé and fiancée

(g) Lender and borrower etc.

Cases, where no fiduciary relation is presumed
(a) Creditor and debtor
(b) Landlord and tenant
In these cases, undue influence should be proved.

(iii) Where he makes a contact with a person whose mental capacity is (temporarily or permanently) affected by reasons of age, illness, or mental or bodily distress.

– Consider the following examples:

(a) An old man of 85 years is induced by his neighbour to pay an unreasonable sum for helping him during his illness. The neighbour has employed undue influence in this case.

(b) A applies to a banker for a loan at a time when there is stringency in the money market. The banker declines to make the loan except at an unusually high rate of interest. A accepts the loan on these terms. This is a transaction in the ordinary course of business, and the contract is not induced by undue influence.

(c) A spiritual guru induced his chela to donate all his property to the ashram and said that in return of it, he will certainly get salvation. The chela did the same. Held, that this is a case of undue influence so it becomes void. —*Manu Singh* v *Umadutt Pandey*

– Consequence of Undue Influence: When an agreement is accepted under undue influence, it will be violable at the option of the party whose consent is not free.

✍ Burden of Proof

Where a person who is in a position to dominate the will of another, enters into a contract with him, the burden of proving that such contract was not induced by undue influence, shall be upon the person in a position to dominate the will of the other.

FRAUD [SEC. 17]

As per Sec. 17–

"Fraud" means and includes any of the following acts committed by a party to a contract, with intent to deceive another party thereto—

(a) The suggestion that a fact is true when it is not true by a person who does not believe it be true.

For Example: A knows that his watch is made in India, but to sell it, he tells to B that it is made in Japan. In this case, A is guilty of Fraud.

(b) The active concealment of a fact by a person, having knowledge or belief of the fact.

For Example: Mr. A sells his horse to Mr. B. The horse is blind and A knows this fact very well. When B asks, "Is the horse blind?" he clearly says that it is not blind. In this case, A is guilty of Fraud.

(c) A promise made without any intention to perform it.

(d) Any other act fitted to deceive.

For Example: A agrees to double B's gold by magic and runs away with his gold. It is fraud.

(e) Any such act or omission as the law specifically declares to be fraudulent.

– **Whether Silence Amounts To Fraud:**

Explanation to Sec. 17 makes it clear that mere silence, without any duty to speak, does not amount to fraud. When we analyse this section in detail, we find the following result:

1. Mere silence is not fraud: Because a person is not bound to disclose the defects of his goods.

For example,

(a) A lady buys synthetic pearls at a high price thinking that they are natural pearls. The seller does not correct her mistake. This is not a fraud.

(b) Negotiations for settlement of a suit were going on between X and Y. Before the final agreement was arrived at, the solicitor of X learnt that the suit is going against X; Y was unaware of this fact.

Neither X nor his solicitor communicated this fact to Y. In ignorance of it, Y agreed to make Out of Court settlement. The court held that mere silence as regards a material fact, which the other party is not bound to disclose to the other, is not a ground for fraud. —*Turner* v *Green* (1895)

2. Silence is fraud, if there is duty to speak: Duty to speak exists where –

(i) the parties stand in fiduciary relationship, *i.e.* father and son, guardian and ward, etc. or

(ii) the contract requires utmost good faith.

For Example: In the example (a) above, if B is A's daughter, then the relation between the parties would make it A's duty to tell if the horse is blind.

3. Silence is fraud if silence is equivalent to speech:

For Example: If B says to A, "if you do not deny it, I shall assume that the horse is sound." A says nothing. Here, A's silence is equivalent to speech.

– Effect of Fraud (Sec. 19):

1. The contract shall be voidable at the option of the aggrieved party.

   For Example: A frauds B by saying that his factory is producing 1000 sugar bags per day. B examines the accounts of factory, which shows that the factory is producing 800 sugar bags per day. After this, B buys A's factory. The contract is not avoidable on account of A's misrepresentation.

2. The aggrieved party may accept the contract, and claim the difference.
3. He can sue for damages.

MISREPRESENTATION [SEC.18]

In simple words, misrepresentation is a wrong statement made innocently, i.e., without any intention to deceive others.

As per Sec. 18, misrepresentation may be made by any of following manner:

1. By Positive Statement: When a person makes a positive statement without any reasonable ground, i.e., believing it to be true though it is not true, he makes a misrepresentation.

For Example: A says B that his car runs 20 km. per litre. He believes the statement to be true although the car actually runs at 15 km. per litre. In this case, A is making misrepresentation.

2. By Breach of Duty: If a person commits, without an intention to deceive, a breach of duty, which gives him some advantage, then he is making misrepresentation.

For Example: While taking a life insurance policy, A states his age as 23 years believing it to be true. Actually, he is 25 years old. Thus L.I.C. charges a lower premium. A is guilty of misrepresentation.

3. When a person induces another person, innocently, to make a mistake regarding the subject matter of an agreement, he is making a misrepresentation.

– Effect of Misrepresentation (Sec. 19): Same as fraud, but no right to claim damages.

Valid Contract

1. In case of misrepresentation, the contract shall not be Voidable, if the aggrieved party has *means to discover the truth with ordinary deligence* and has failed to discover it. However, this rule will not apply in case of fraud (other than fraudulent silence).
2. Where a party to a contract commits fraud/misrepresentation, but the other party is *not misled by such fraud/ misrepresentation*, the contract shall not be voidable.

⇒⇒⇒

MISTAKE [SECS. 20-22]

(Mistake means an erroneous belief about something)

1. Mistake of Indian Law (Sec. 21)

- Not voidable, merely on the ground of mistake of Indian law
- However, a mistake as to foreign law is treated as a mistake of fact.

For Example: A and B enter into a contract on the erroneous belief that a particular debt is barred by the Law of Limitation. This contract is not voidable.

2. Mistake of Fact

(i) A Bilateral Mistake (Sec. 20) as to any fact essential to Agreement

Void-*ab-initio*

– *Examples:* Mistake as to –

1. Existence of subject matter
2. Identity of subject matter
3. Quality of subject matter
4. Quantity of subject matter
5. Title to subject matter
6. Price of subject matter
7. Possibility of performance:
   (a) Physical impossibility, or
   (b) Legal Impossibility.

(ii) A Unilateral Mistake (Sec. 22)

General Rule	Voidable	Void-*ab-initio*
A Contract is ***not voidable*** merely because one party is under a mistake as to a matter of fact.	A Contract is voidable, if unilateral mistake is brought about by the other party's fraud or misrepresentation.	Refer to Case (a) and (b) below

Case– (a) <u>Mistake as to the identity of the person contracted with</u>:

For Example: In May 1938, a lady, known as Ann Robinson, was convicted of permitting disorderly conduct in her cafe. In July of the same year, she assumed another name, Ann Potter, and took a lease of Sowler's premises.

Held, the lease was void *ab-initio* because of Sowler's mistaken belief that Ann Potter was not Ann-Robinson. —*Sowler* v *Potter,* (1949)

In this regard, the following points have to be noted:

— In this case the contract will become void only when the identify of the contracting party is important.

— Generally, the seller is prepared to enter into a contact with anyone, who enters the shop. In such a case, the identity of the purchaser is immaterial. So, a mistake as to the purchaser's identity will not make the contract void.

— If D induces P to enter into a contract with him by falsely representing that he is a rich man, the contract is not void for mistake, but at the most voidable for fraud.

Case– (b) Mistake as to the nature of contract:

Where in signing a document, the mind of the signer does not go with the signature, there is a mistake which would vitiate the contract.

For Example: M, an old man of poor sight, endorsed a bill of exchange thinking that it was a guarantee. Held, there was no contract on the ground that the mind of the signer did not accompany the signature.

—*Foster* v *Mackinnon*, (1869)

DISTINCTION BETWEEN COERCION & UNDUE INFLUENCE

Basis	Coercion	Undue Influence
1. Section	Sec. 15.	Sec. 16.
2. Meaning	Coercion is - committing (or threatening to commit) of any act, forbidden by the Indian Penal Code, or - Unlawful detaining (or threatening to detain) any property to the prejudice of any person whatever; with the intention of causing any person to enter into an agreement.	A contract is said to be induced by 'undue influence' where the relation subsisting between the parties are such that one of the parties— (a) is in a position to dominate the will of the other, and (b) uses that position to obtain an unfair advantage over the other.
3. Nature of Act	It involves an illegal act.	It does not include doing an illegal act.
4. Nature of Threat	It is a physical threat.	It is a mental threat.
5. Penalty	In this case, the contract becomes voidable, as well the party may be punished.	In this case, no party is punished, but the agreement becomes voidable at the option of the aggrieved.
6. Relationship	No special relationship between the parties is required for coercion.	For undue influence, special relationship (such as teacher and student,m etc.) between the parties is necessary.
7. Parties	Coercion may be exercised against the third party.	Undue Influence cannot be exercised against third party.
8. Burden of Proof	In this case, the burden of proof lies on the aggrieved party.	In this case, the burden of proof lies on the party who is in a position to dominate the will of another party.
9. Mode of Obtaining	In this case, one party binds the other party.	In this case, one party induces the other party.

DISTINCTION BETWEEN FRAUD & MISREPRESENTATION

Basis	Fraud	Misrepresentation
1. Section	Sec. 17.	Sec. 18.
2. Meaning	Fraud means a wrong statement made with an intention to cheat others.	Misrepresentation means a wrong statement made innocently, i.e., without any intention to cheat others.
3. Nature	It is made on purpose.	It is made in innocence.
4. Intention	In case of fraud, the intention of a party is to cheat others.	In this case, there is no such intention.
5. Right to avoid contract	In this case, the contract can be avoided even if the aggrieved party had proper means to discover the truth.	In this case, the contract cannot be avoided if the aggrieved party had proper means to discover the truth.
6. Recovery of Damages	In case of fraud, the aggrieved may recover the damages.	In this case, the aggrieved may not recover the damages.

LAWFUL OBJECT & CONSIDERATION

☞ *When Consideration and Object are Unlawful* (*Sec. 23*)?

1. If the object is forbidden by law.

For Examples: (1) A and B agreed to deal in stolen goods. It is forbidden by law and therefore void.

(2) A committed B's murder in the presence of C. Mr. A promises to pay Rs. 500 to C, if C does not inform the police about the murder. This agreement is illegal. Besides, C will be liable for concealment of B's murder under the Indian Penal Code.

2. If the Object would defeat the provisions of any law.

For Example: (1) A was licensed under an Excise Act to run a liquor shop. The Act forbade the creation of a partnership to run the shop. A took B into partnership. Held, the agreement is void.

(2) A debtor agrees not to raise the plea of the Law of Limitation. Held, the agreement is void, as it would defeat the object of the law of limitation.

3. If the object is fraudulent.

For Example: A, B & C enter into an agreement to distribute the stolen money. The agreement is void as it is fraudulent and thereby unlawful.

4. If the object involves injury to the person or the property of another person.

For Example: A promises to pay Rs. 5,000 to B, if B sets fire to C's house. It involves damage to the property of C, hence it is also unlawful and void.

5. If the objects is immoral or opposed to public policy.

☞ *Effect of Unlawful Object & Consideration*

1. An illegal agreement is *void-ab-initio*, i.e. not enforceable in law.

2. Collateral transactions to illegal transactions are also *void-ab-initio*.

For Example: A borrows Rs. 20,000 from B to buy a revolver to shoot C. Since the object of the transaction is illegal, B cannot recover his Rs. 20,000, if he has given the loan knowing that A is taking the loan to purchase a revolver to shoot C.

3. Where the agreement is illegal, the law will not help any of the parties. The reason is that both the parties are equally guilty and the law does not help a guilty person. The law wants to discourage both the parties. Consider the above example.

4. Where the illegality is the result of coercion and fraud of the other party, the Court can compel the guilty to return the money or property, obtained by way of coercion/fraud.

5. Agreement partly legal and partly illegal (Sec. 24):

(i) If the legal promise can be separated from the illegal one, the legal promise can be enforced. In such a case the illegal part will be *void-ab-initio*.

(ii) Where the legal promise cannot be separated from the illegal one, the whole of it would be *void-ab-initio*.

(iii) Where there is a single consideration for one or more unlawful objects, the agreement is *void-ab-initio*.

For Example: A promises to manage B's factory, where genuine and bogus motor parts are manufactured. B agrees to pay A a salary of Rs. 10,000 per month. The whole agreement is void, as partly it is legal and illegal and the legal part cannot be separated from the illegal one.

6. Reciprocal promises, legal and illegal (Sec. 57): Where persons reciprocally promise, firstly to do certain things, which are legal, and secondly to do certain other things, which are illegal, the first set of promises is a contract, but the second is a void agreement.

For Example: A and B agree that A shall sell a house to B for Rs. 10,000, but that if B uses it as a gambling house, he shall pay A Rs. 50,000 for it.

The first set of promises, i.e., to sell the house and to pay Rs. 10,000 is a contract. But, the second set of promises, i.e., B may use the house as a gambling house and pay Rs. 50,000 is a void agreement.

7. Alternative Promise, legal and Illegal (Sec. 58): In the case of an alternative promise, one branch of which is legal and the other illegal, the legal branch alone can be enforced.

For Example: A agrees to deliver rice or smuggled opium to B for Rs. 1,000. This is a valid contract to deliver rice and void agreement as to the delivery of opium.

AGREEMENT OPPOSED TO PUBLIC POLICY

☞ What is Public Policy?

Public policy is that principle of law, which states that no one shall lawfully do an act, which has a mischievous tendency to cheat public or which is against the public good or welfare.

Every Government tries to maximise the welfare of its citizens. Therefore, it makes some policies to prohibit anything, which is against the welfare or interest of society. For example, trading with enemy, agreement restraining people from carrying on lawful trade, etc. are injurious to society.

It is not possible to give an exact definition of the term 'Public Policy'. It is an elastic term.

☞ Agreements declared against Public Policy by the Courts:

1. Agreements for Trading with an Enemy.

2. Agreements Interfering with Administration of Justice: The Interfere with administration of justice may be of 3 types:

(a) Agreements stifling prosecution: Stifling implies abuse of law. It is based on the noble doctrine that if a person has committed a crime, he must be prosecuted and punished.

For Example: A promises to drop prosecution, which he has instituted against B for robbery, and B promises to restore the stolen property, the agreement is unlawful.

(b) Maintenance and Champerty: Maintenance implies financing of suits by third parties, who have no legal interest in the suit. Further financing may be for prosecution or defence. For example, Mr. A offers to pay Mr. B Rs. 10,000, if B will sue C. A's motive is only to annoy C. Such agreement between A and B is known as Maintenance agreement.

On the other hand, Champerty implies an agreement, whereby one party is to assist another to bring an action for recovering money or property and is to share the proceeds of the action. *For example*, A agrees to pay the expenses if B sues C and B agrees to give A one- half of any proceeds received by B as a result of the said suit. Such an agreement is known as Champerty.

Under the English Law, both of these agreements are void. But in our Law, such agreement shall be valid, if the object of the contract is just to assist the other party in making a reasonable claim.

(c) Agreements, which interfere with Administration of Justice: Such agreements are unlawful.

For Example: (1) A agrees to pay a bribe of Rs. 1,00,000 to a judge. It is unlawful and hence void.

(2) A agrees to pay fee to a holy man to pray for the success of his suit. Such agreement is not interference with the administration of justice. Hence, it is valid and binding.

—*Balasundara Mudaliar* v *Mohd. Usman* (1929) Mad.

3. Traffic in Public Offices: It implies transfer of public office for some consideration or inducing public officers to act for consideration in cash or kind. Such agreements are void.

For Example: (1) A agrees with B to procure a job in UPSC for a consideration of Rs. 1,00,000. It is void.

(2) A agrees to transfer to B his post in a Government office for Rs. 5,000, it is void.

4. Agreements creating interest opposed to Duty: Such agreements are also likely to increase corruption and inefficiency among the officials. Hence, such agreements are void.

For Example: A agrees to pay Rs. 5,000 to a municipal officer not to report unauthorised construction to the municipal authorities. The agreement is void.

5. Agreements restraining personal freedom: Such agreements are void, as personal freedom has been guaranteed by our Constitution (under Article-21).

For Example: An agreement by a borrower to do manual work for the creditor so long as the debt was not paid in full is void.

6. Agreements interfering with Parental Rights and Duties: Guardianship rights cannot be allowed to be sold away. However, a child validly adopted by a Hindu under the Adoption and Maintenance Act, 1956, cannot be taken back.

For Example: A father agreed to transfer the guardianship of his two minor sons permanently. Later on, he filed a suit to recover their custody. The court allowed the father to get back his sons.

—*Giddu Narayanish* v *Mrs. Annie Besant* (1915) Mad.

7. Agreement in the restraint of Marriage: Any agreement in the restraint of marriage of any person, other than a minor, is void. This is because the law regards marriage as the right of every individual.

An agreement in the restraint of the marriage of a minor is not void, as it is considered to be in the interest of the minor.

For Example: P promised to marry L and none else and to pay L a sum of Rs. 20,000, if he married someone else. P married X. Held, L could not recover the sum agreed as the agreement was in the restraint of marriage. —*Lowe* v *Peers* (1768)

8. Agreement of Marriage Brokage or Brokerage: Every one has a liberty to marry according to his free choice. This free choice should not be disturbed by engaging paid brokers to procure matches. Such agreements shall be void.

9. Agreement to vary the period of Limitation: An agreement to vary the period of limitation will be void, as it would defeat the object of the Law of Limitation.

10. Agreement in the restraint of Trade: See next Topic.

VOID AGREEMENT

An essential element of a valid contract is that it must not have been expressly declared void by law. A void agreement is not enforceable in a court of law. The following agreements have been expressly declared void:

1. Agreement by an incompetent person, *i.e.* minor, lunatics, etc (Sec. 11).
2. Agreements made under a mutual mistake of fact (Sec. 20).
3. Agreements made for unlawful consideration or object (Sec. 23).
4. Agreements made for partly unlawful consideration or object (Sec. 24).
5. Agreements made without consideration (Sec. 25).
6. Agreements in restraint of marriage (Sec. 26).
7. Agreements in restraint of trade (Sec. 27).
8. Agreements in restraint of legal proceedings (Sec. 28).
9. Agreements in the meaning of which is uncertain (Sec. 29).
10. Agreements by way of wager (Sec. 30).
11. Agreement contingent upon impossible events (Sec36).
12. Agreements to do impossible acts (Sec. 56).
13. In case of reciprocal promises to do things legal and also other things illegal, the second set of the reciprocal promises is void agreement (Sec. 57).

-Agreement in restraint of Trade (Sec. 27):

As per section 27, any agreement in the restraints of a lawful trade, profession or business is void. This is because public policy requires that every man shall be at liberty to work for himself. He shall not be at liberty to deprive himself of his labour, skill or talent, by any contract.

Exceptions to the above Rule

(*1*) *Sale of Goodwill:* A seller of goodwill of a business may be restrained from carrying on—

(i) a similar business

(ii) within specified local limits

(iii) so long as the buyer or his assignee carries on a like business

(iv) provided it is regarded as reasonable by the court.

(*2*) *Partnership contracts:* The Partnership Act also provides certain exceptions to the above rule. In the following cases, an agreement in restraint of trade will be valid:—

(a) A partner may agree not to carry on any other business than that of the firm so long as he is a partner.

(b) An outgoing partner may agree not to carry on a similar business to that of the firm within a specified period, or specified local limits.

(c) Partners may agree that none of them, on ceasing to be a partner, shall carry on a similar business to that of the firm within a specified period or specified local limits.

(d) Any partner may agree with the buyer of goodwill not to carry on a similar business to that of the firm within a specified period or specified local limits.

(*3*) *Service Agreements:* Sometimes under the service agreement, an employee is prevented from accepting—

(i) any other engagement during his employment,

(ii) a similar engagement after the termination of his services.

The first type of the restriction is valid, but the second restriction is void.

For Example: (1) Doctors are debarred from private practice during the term of their employment.

(2) A, a tailor, employed L, as assistant, under a contract that L, on the termination of his employment, will not carry on business as a tailor within 16 kms. of A's establishment.

Held, the agreement was void.

No doubt a master is not entitled to restrain his servant after the termination of employment, but he is entitled to reasonable protection against exploitation of trade secrets or enticing away of his customers by the previous employee.

For Example: A was engaged in glass bottle manufacturing. He employed a Works Manager to whom certain secrets of correct mixture of gas and air in the boiler were told on the condition that he will not engage in glass bottle manufacturing for five years in the United Kingdom.

Held, the restraint was reasonable and as such A was entitled to protection.

—*Forster & Sons Ltd.* v *Suggett* (1918)

(*4*) *Trade Combinations:* Trade combinations are valid, if they are not in the nature of a monopoly.

For Example: An agreement between certain ice manufacturers fixed the minimum price for sale of ice. It was also agreed in what proportion, they will manufacture the ice and receive the profits. As per terms of the agreement, some of the ice manufactures were restrained from selling at Poona and some others at Steamers.

The court held that the agreement was not hit by Section 27, as the whole object was to regulate business and not to restrain it. —*Eraser & Co.* v *Bombay Ice Mfg. Co.* (1905) Bom.

- Agreement in restraint of Legal Proceedings (Sec. 28):

If there is any agreement, which prevents the parties absolutely from enforcing their rights by usual legal proceeding, then such agreement shall be void.

However, an agreement to refer a dispute (present or future) between the parties to arbitration is perfectly valid.

- Wagering Agreements (Sec. 30):

The law has not defined a wagering agreement, but has declared it *void ab initio*. A wager is an agreement to pay money or money's worth upon the happening or non-happening of an uncertain event.

For Example: If A and B enter into an agreement that if it rains within one hour, A shall pay B Rs. 1000, otherwise Mr. B shall pay Rs. 1,000. It is a wagering agreement.

Essentials of a Wagering Agreement

1. There should be a promise to pay money or money's worth.
2. The promise must be dependent upon the happening or non-happening of an event.
3. The event on which the promise is dependent must be uncertain.

   The event may be uncertain as it has to happen in future or the event has already happened but its result is not known to either party.
4. There must be mutual chance of gain or loss.
5. Neither party should have control over the events, otherwise it will not be a wager. For example, in the 'Sholay' picture, you might have noticed that the coin which 'Amitabh Bachchan' used to toss had 'head' on both the sides of the coin. Consequently, he always won. He did not have a chance to lose.
6. Neither party should have any other interest in the happening of the event except that he will lose or win.

Kinds of Wagering Agreements

1. Lotteries: A lottery is a game of chance. So, the agreement to buy a lottery ticket is a wagering agreement. Even if the lottery is authorised by the Government it is a wagering agreement. The only effect of such authorisation is that the person conducting the lottery will not be punished.

Sec. 294A of Indian Penal Code

Anyone who keeps any office or place for the purpose of drawing a lottery (other than a State Lottery or a lottery authorised by the State Government) shall be punished with upto 6 months imprisonment and/or fine.

2. Crossword competition: A crossword puzzle in which prizes depend upon the correspondence of the competitor's solution with a previously prepared solution kept with the editor of a newspaper is a lottery and, therefore, a wagering transaction.

3. Prize competition in excess of Rs. 1,000: Strictly speaking, prize competitions in games of skills are not wagering in nature. However, the Prize Competition Act, 1955 has declared prize competitions in games of Skill in excess of Rs. 1,000 as void.

4. Horse Race Prize below Rs. 500: A contribution of a sum of Rs. 500 or more as a prize to the winner of a horse race is not void, but below Rs. 500 is void.

5. Gambling.

***Effect of Wagering Agreement* (Sec. 30)**

In Maharashtra and Gujarat, wagering agreements have been declared illegal. Consequently, transactions collateral to wagering agreements in Maharashtra and Gujarat, are also void.

But in rest of India, wagering agreements have been expressly declared *void-ab-initio*. In these areas, collateral transactions to wagering agreements are not *void-ab-initio*.

For Example: (1) An agent is allowed to recover his commission from the principal, even if the agreement entered into on behalf of the principal was a wagering agreement.

(2) Money lent for the purpose of gambling or repaying a gambling debt can be recovered, even though lent with the knowledge of its purpose.

Agreements which are not Wagering Agreements

1. A contribution of a sum of Rs. 500 or more as a prize to the winner of a horse race is a valid agreement, not a wager agreement.
2. Stock exchange transactions in which there is an intention to give and take delivery of shares is not a wagering agreement.

3. Contributions to chit fund are not wager. Contributions made by the members are refunded by draw of lots.
4. Prize competitions which are games of skills are valid, provided the amount of prize does not exceed Rs. 1,000.
5. ***Contracts of Insurance:*** A contract of insurance is a contract by which an insurer in consideration of premium agrees to bear the loss of property or life of another person, (i.e. insured).

For Example: An insurance company promises to pay B Rs. 1,00,000, if his (B) house is destroyed by a fire within a year on payment of a premium of Rs. 5,000.

☞ Restitution (Sec. 64 and 65):

Restitution implies to return. When a contract becomes void, it is fair that the party, who has received any benefit under it, must restore it to the other party and if restoration is not possible it must compensate the other party.

This rule is based on the noble principle of justice and equity. The law does not allow any person to become rich at the case of another.

The rules relating to the restitution are as under:

1. **When an agreement is discovered to be *void-ab-initio* (Section 65):** In this case, a party which has received any benefit under such an agreement must return it to the other party or compensate him.

   For Example: A agrees to sell his car to B. B has paid an advance of Rs. 1,000 to A. Unknown to both the parties, the car had already been destroyed by fire before the date of agreement. The agreement is void, but A must return the Rs. 1,000 paid by B.
2. **When a contract becomes subsequently void (Sec. 65):** In this case also, a party which has received any benefit should restore it to the other party from whom the benefit was received.

   For Example: Suppose in the above contract, if the car had been destroyed by fire after the agreement to sell but before the sale, the contract becomes impossible and hence void. A must return Rs. 1,000 paid by B.
3. **When the contract is Voidable (Sec. 64):** Where a voidable contract is avoided, then the party avoiding the contract shall restore any benefit received by it to the person from whom it was received.

Exceptions to the above Rules

Sec. 65 does not apply in the following cases:

(i) An agreement with an incapable person. *For example*, in the case of a minor, a person of unsound mind etc. (Refer to the case, *Mohiri Bibi* v *Dharamodas Ghosh*:).

(ii) Illegal agreements. ***For Example:*** Mr. A pays Rs. 50,000 to Mr. B for the murder of Mr. C, the money cannot be recovered.

☑☑☑

MULTIPLE CHOICE QUESTIONS

☞ Definitions & Types of Contract

1. The Law of Contract in India is contained in—
(A) Indian Contract Act, 1862
(B) Indian Contract Act, 1982
(C) Indian Contract Act, 1872
(D) Indian Contract Act, 1972

2. An agreement enforceable by Law is known as—
(A) Agreement
(B) Contract
(C) Promise
(D) Offer

3. Every promise and every set of promises forming consideration for each other is called—
(A) Agreement
(B) Contract
(C) Promise
(D) Offer

4. The leading case "Balfor v. Balfor" is related to–
(A) Intention to create legal relation
(B) Possibility of performance
(C) Lawful Object
(D) Legal formality

5. A contract, which ceases to be enforceable by law, becomes______, when it ceases to be enforceable by law—

(A) Contract

(B) Void contract

(C) Void-ab-initio Contract

(D) Valid Contact

6. Which of the following is not an essential on a valid contract?

(A) Valid offer and valid acceptance

(B) Intention to create legal relation.

(C) Free consent

(D) Mistake

7. Indian mercantile Law is based on—

(A) Australian Law

(B) American law

(C) Russian Law

(D) English Law

8. An agreement created by words spoken or written is called—

(A) Void agreement

(B) Voidable agreement

(C) Express agreement

(D) Implied agreement

9. Voidable agreement is an agreement which is–

(A) Enforceable by law

(B) Not enforceable by law

(C) Enforceable at the option of one of the parties

(D) Forbidden by law

10. A contract created by law is called—

(A) Express contract

(B) Implied contract

(C) Quasi-contract

(D) E-commerce contract

11. A agrees to sell his car to B at a price, which B may be able to pay. This agreement is—

(A) void

(B) valid

(C) voidable

(D) contingent

12. A contract was entered before 1st September, 1872 is governed by the Indian Contract Act, 1872.

(A) Yes, if the contract was entered in Indian soil.

(B) Yes, if there was performance of the contract on or after 1st September 1872.

(C) No, as the act does not apply retrospectively.

(D) No, as there was no performance on or after 1st September 1872.

13. An agreement which is enforceable by law at the option of one or more of the parties thereon, but not at the option of the other or others is a valid contract—

(A) True

(B) False

14. Which of the following statements is true?

(A) An agreement is an unaccepted proposal.

(B) An agreement enforceable by law is a contract.

(C) An agreement can only consist of an offer.

(D) An agreement can only consist of an acceptance.

15. A voidable contract is one which—

(A) can be enforced at the option of an aggrieved party.

(B) can be enforced at the option of both the parties.

(C) cannot be enforced in a court of law.

(D) courts prohibit.

16. Valid Contract—

(A) In case of this collateral agreements are void.

(B) Not enforceable in a court of law.

(C) An agreement enforceable by law at the option of one or more of the parties thereon but not at the option of the other or others.

(D) Enforceable at the option of both the parties.

17. If the terms of a contract are expressly agreed upon (whether by words spoken or written) at the time of formation of the contract, the contract is said to be an—

(A) Express contracts

(B) Implied contracts

(C) Quasi contracts

(D) None of the above

18. Which of the statements is incorrect?

(A) All illegal agreements are void, but all void agreements are not necessary illegal.

(B) A voidable contract is not voidable at the option of the aggrieved party.

(C) Contracts that are immoral or opposed to public policy are illegal in nature.

(D) All of the above

19. The following are the essential elements which need to co-exist in order to make a valid contract–

(A) Lawful consideration.

(B) Lawful agreement.

(C) Free consent.

(D) All of the above.

20. The Indian Contract Act, 1872 came into operation on and from—

(A) 1st October, 1872

(B) 1st July, 1872

(C) 15th August, 1872

(D) 1st September, 1872

21. An Agreement is a—

(A) Set of reciprocal promises

(B) Acceptance of a proposal

(C) Contract

(D) Promise

22. Which of the following is true—

(A) All agreements are contracts

(B) All contracts are agreements

(C) All promises are agreements

(D) A set of promises is contract

23. Agreement the meaning of which is uncertain is—

(A) Valid.

(B) Void.

(C) Voidable.

(D) Illegal.

24. Implied contract, even if not in writing or expressed in words, is perfectly valid, if other conditions are satisfied—

(A) True, as an implied contract has the same effect as an express contract

(B) False, as the Contract Act recognises only express contracts.

(C) Such contracts are voidable at the option of the party, whose consent is implied.

(D) Both (A) and (C)

25. Which of the following statements is true?

(A) An agreement enforceable by law is a contract.

(B) An agreement is an accepted proposal.

(C) Both (A) and (B)

(D) None of these

26. A_________agreement is one, which is enforceable at the option of one party.

(A) Voidable

(B) Void

(C) Valid

(D) Illegal

27. R, an optical surgeon, employs S as the assistant for a term of three years and S agrees not to practise as a surgeon during this period. This contract is—

(A) Valid.

(B) Void.

(C) Illegal.

(D) Voidable.

28. Implied contract, even if not writing or express words, is perfectly______, if other conditions are satisfied.

(A) Void

(B) Valid

(C) voidable

(D) Illegal

29. Contracts classified on the basis of formation are of the following types—

(A) Express contracts

(B) Implied contracts

(C) Quasi contracts

(D) All of the above

30. Implied contract, even if not in writing or express words, is perfectly valid, if other conditions are satisfied.

(A) True, as an implied contract has the same effect as an express contract

(B) False, as the Contract Act recognizes only express contracts.

(C) Partly True

(D) None of the above

31. Valid Contracts —

(A) are made by free consent

(B) are those where the parties to the contract are competent to enter into an agreement

(C) have lawful consideration and lawful object

(D) all of the above.

32. Illegal agreements are —

(A) not enforceable by law

(B) forbidden under law

(C) either (A) or (B)

(D) both (A) and (B)

33. __________ is good in substance but suffers from some technical defect.

(A) Valid Contract

(B) Illegal Contract

(C) Voidable Contract

(D) Unenforceable Contract

34. A contract which is valid initially however, ceases to be enforceable subsequently —

(A) becomes void when it ceases to be enforceable

(B) remains valid

(C) becomes voidable when it ceases to be enforceable

(D) becomes void since inception.

35. Agreements which do not create legal obligations can also be considered as contracts

(A) True

(B) Partly True

(C) False

(D) None of the above

36. A invites B for his son's wedding. B accepts the invitation. In this case, there is an agreement but no contract, since —

(A) there is no consideration.

(B) there is no intention to create legal relationship.

(C) there is no written document.

(D) there is no formal acceptance of the offer.

37. *Jus-in-personam* means–

(A) A right against or in respect of a thing.

(B) A right against or in respect of a person.

(C) Both (A) and (B)

(D) None of the above.

38. An agent authorised by a power of attorney to operate a business, but not to borrow money asked for a loan on a representation that he is authorised to borrow and produced the power of attorney for the perusal of the lender. But the lender did not read it and advanced a loan. Is the principal bound by the loan?

(A) Yes

(B) No

39. Arun's estate is sold for arrears of revenue. As per the Act, the defaulter is prohibited from purchasing it. Bhat agrees with Arun to purchase the estate and convey it back to Arun for the price which Bhat has paid. The agreement is —

(A) legal

(B) valid

(C) voidable

(D) void

☞ Offer and Acceptance

40. Quotation of price is a—

(A) Offer

(B) Invitation to Offer

(C) Cross offer

(D) None of these

41. When offer is accepted, it is called—

(A) Agreement

(B) Contract

(C) Promise

(D) Offer

42. When offer is accepted and there is consideration, then it is called—

(A) Agreement

(B) Contract

(C) Promise

(D) Offer

43. Offer comes to an end by—

(A) Acceptance

(B) Communication

(C) Revocation

(D) Infinity

44. Offer can be accepted by—

(A) Offeror

(B) Promisor

(C) Offeree

(D) Acceptor

45. A Tender will be irrevocable, where—

(A) Tenderer has, for some consideration, promised not to withdraw.

(B) There is a statutory prohibition against withdrawal.

(C) Either (A) or (B)

(D) Neither (A) nor (B)

46. Death or insanity of the proposer—

(A) Operates as revocation of the proposal, irrespective of whether the acceptor has the knowledge of the same prior to his acceptance.

(B) Operates as revocation, only if the acceptor knows about it before acceptance.

(C) Operates on court order only.

(D) Does not operate on court order

47. X's brother runs away from the house. Y, who is an employee of X, offers to search for the brother and goes out for the purpose. In the absence of Y, X offers a reward of Rs. 100 to any one, who can either find out the brother or give clues enabling X to find his brother. Later on, Mr. Y, without having any knowledge about reward, found the X's brother and brought him back. Whether Y can claim the reward?

(A) Yes

(B) No

48. A, by a letter dated 22 December, 2008, offers to sell his house to B for Rs. 50 lakh. The letter reaches B on 27th December, 2008, who posts his acceptance on 28th December, 2008 which reaches A on 30th December, 2008. Here, the communication of offer is completed on—

(A) 25th December, 2008
(B) 27th December, 2008
(C) 28th December, 2008
(D) 30th December, 2008

49. In *Q. 48* above, the communication of acceptance is complete against A on 28th December, 2008, and against B on–
(A) 25th December, 2008
(B) 27th December, 2008
(C) 28th December, 2008
(D) 30th December, 2008

50. A, by a letter, offers to sell his car to B for Rs. 1,00,000. Without knowing A's offer, B, by a letter, offers to buy the same car from A for Rs. 1,00,000. Here—
(A) A binding contract comes into existence as B's letter is equivalent to implied acceptance of A's offer
(B) No binding contract comes into existence as B's letter is merely a cross offer.
(C) A voidable contract is entered into.
(D) None of these

51. Which of the following is false?
An acceptance—
(A) Must be communicated.
(B) Must be absolute and unconditional.
(C) Must be accepted by a person having authority to accept.
(D) May be presumed from silence of offeree.

52. Which of the following is false?
An offer to be valid must–
(A) intend to create legal relations.
(B) have certain and unambiguous terms.
(C) contain a term that non-acceptance would amount to acceptance.
(D) be communicated to the person to whom it is made.

53. B has posted his letter of acceptance on a particular day and two days thereafter sends a telegram revoking his acceptance. But the telegram reaches A after the letter. Will the acceptance be deemed to have been revoked ?
(A) Yes
(B) No

54. An offer may lapse by–
(A) Revocation
(B) Counter Offer
(C) Rejection of Offer by Offeree
(D) All of these

55. Cross Offers means—
(A) Exchanging identical offers by two parties in ignorance.
(B) Offer made to the public in general.
(C) Offer allowed to remain open for acceptance over a period of time.
(D) Offer made to a definite person.

56. Which one of the offer is a valid offer?
(A) A garment store gave the following advertisement in a newspaper—"Special sale for tomorrow only. Men's night suits reduced from Rs. 200 to Rs. 100."
(B) P says to Q, "I will sell you a digital camera." P owns three different types of digital cameras of various prices.
(C) An auctioneer displays a refrigerator before a gathering in an auction sale.
(D) A advertises in a leading daily newspaper that he would pay Rs. 2,000 to anyone who finds and returns his lost dog.

57. Which one of the following is not a contract?
(A) A engages B for a certain work and promises to pay such remuneration as shall be fixed by C. B does the work.
(B) A and B promises to marry each other.
(C) A takes a seat in a public vehicle.
(D) A invites B to a card party. B accepts the invitation.

58. An offer made to the public in general which anyone can accept and do the desired act is—
(A) General offer
(B) Special offer
(C) Cross offer
(D) Counter offer

59. Standing offer means—
(A) After allowed to remain open
(B) After made to public in general
(C) When the offeree offers to qualified acceptance of the offer
(D) Offer made to a definite person

60. A proposal when accepted becomes—
(A) Acceptance
(B) Agreement
(C) Promise
(D) Lawful promise

61. An acceptance must be conditional.
(A) True
(B) False

62. Communication of offer and acceptance can be made only when the parties are face to face.

(A) True.

(B) False.

63. Which of the following is/are the essential elements of a valid offer?

(1) Offeror must have an intention to be bound by his offer.

(2) Offer must be made to a specific person and not to public at large.

(3) Must be definite.

(4) Offer can be vague.

(A) 1 & 3

(B) 2 & 3

(C) 3 & 4

(D) 1 & 4

64. An offer, *accepted without knowledge*, does not confer any legal rights on the acceptor.

(A) True, as the offer cannot be accepted without its knowledge.

(B) False, as there is no such legal provision/ decision in this regard.

(C) Such contracts are Voidable at the option of the party, whose consent is implied.

(D) Both (A) and (C)

65. A general offer made to the public at large is valid, and binding contract is made with a person, who having the knowledge of the offer–

(A) comes forwards and acts accordingly

(B) acts accordingly, and his act is ratified by the offeror

(C) Acts accordingly, and his act is not ratified by the offeror

(D) None of these

66. On the acceptance of an offer by an offeree,

(A) Only the acceptor becomes bound by accepting the offer.

(B) Only the offeror becomes bound as his terms are accepted.

(C) Both the acceptor and offeree becomes bound by the contract.

(D) None of these.

67. A, by a letter dated 15th March, offers to sell his car to B, who posts his acceptance on 20th March. *Here*—

(A) A can revoke his offer before he receives the letter of acceptance

(B) A cannot revoke his offer as he becomes bound by the acceptance on 20th March

(C) A can revoke the offer at any time

(D) None of the above

68. In *Q.* 67 above—

(A) B can revoke his acceptance at any time till his letter reaches A.

(B) B cannot revoke his acceptance as he becomes bound by posting his acceptance letter.

(C) B can revoke the acceptance at any time.

(D) None of the above

69. Standing Offer means—

(A) Offer allowed to remain open for acceptance over a period of time.

(B) Offer made to the public in general.

(C) When the offeree offers to qualified acceptance of the offer.

(D) Offer made to a definite person.

70. When the offeree offers to qualified acceptance of the offer subject to modifications and variations, he is said to have made a—

(A) Standing, Open

(B) Counter Offer

(C) Cross Offers

(D) Special Offer

71. X of Agra sends a letter to Y of Delhi offering to sell his Car for Rs. 4,00,000. This letter is posted on 1st January and reaches Y on 6th January. Y sends his acceptance by post on 10th January, but X receives this letter of acceptance on 14th January. When is the communication of the offer complete?

(A) 1st January

(B) 6th January

(C) 7th January

(D) 10th January

72. In *Q. 71* above, when is the communication of the acceptance complete as against acceptor?

(A) 6th January

(B) 10th January

(C) 11th January

(D) 14th January

73. In *Q. 71* above, If X sends a telegram on 7th January revoking his offer, and his telegram reaches Y before the letter of acceptance is posted. Is revocation of offer valid?

(A) It is Valid

(B) It is invalid

(C) It is uncertain

(D) None of the above

74. In *Q. 71* above, If Y sends a telegram on 13th January revoking his acceptance, and his telegram reaches X before the letter of the acceptance is received by Y. Is revocation of acceptance valid?

(A) It is valid
(B) It is invalid
(C) It is uncertain
(D) None of the above

75. The person making the proposal is called —
(A) Offeror
(B) Offeree
(C) Participator
(D) Principal

76. When the offers made by two persons to each other containing similar terms of bargain cross each other in post, they are known as—
(A) Cross Offers
(B) Implied Offers
(C) Direct Offers
(D) Express Offers

77. When an Offer is made to a definite person, it is known as—
(A) General Offer
(B) Cross Offers
(C) Counter Offer
(D) Special Offer

78. A writes to B, "Will you buy my car for Rs. 4.5 Lakhs? Reply by next Sunday." B communicates his acceptance on Monday next. In such case—
(A) A is not bound to B's delayed acceptance
(B) A is bound to B's acceptance
(C) B has to make a Counter Offer
(D) There is no offer at all.

79. In cases of acceptance on phone, the contract is made at the place—
(A) where the acceptance is communicated
(B) where the offer was made
(C) from where the acceptance is made
(D) all of the above.

80. If the offeror prescribes the mode and manner of acceptance, the acceptance —
(A) Should be in the manner and mode prescribed
(B) need not be in the manner and mode prescribed
(C) can be in any reasonable manner and mode
(D) all of the above.

81. S knew that on account of his criticism of plays in the past, he would not be allowed entry at a theatre. The Managing Director of the theatre, gave instructions that a ticket should not be sold to S. S, however, obtained a ticket through one of his friends. On being refused admission to the theatre, he sued for damages for breach of contract.
(A) S is entitled to damages.
(B) S is entitled to enter the theatre.
(C) There is a valid contract between the theatre Company and S.
(D) There is no contract between the theatre Company and S.

82. Communication of a proposal is complete when it comes to the knowledge of the person to whom it is made.
(A) True
(B) Partly true
(C) False
(D) None of the above.

83. No contract can arise, if—
(A) the offer is not made to an ascertained person
(B) the acceptance is made by an unascertained person
(C) the offer is made to an ascertained person
(D) the acceptance is made by an ascertained person

84. M agreed on Monday to sell his property N by a written agreement which stated "that this offer to be left open until Saturday 10 a.m." In the meantime on Wednesday, M enters into a contract to sell the property to O. N, who was sitting in the next room, hears about the deal between M and O. On Friday, N accepts the offer and deliveres to M the letter of acceptance. Is N's acceptance valid?
(A) No, since offer is revoked by M
(B) Yes, since overhearing by N does not amount to a valid revocation by M
(C) No, since O has a clean title to the property
(D) Cannot decide based on the above facts.

85. U sends a letter to Y proposing to sell his land. Y sends his acceptance by post. U can revoke the offer at any time before or at the moment when Y posts his letter of acceptance, but not afterwards.
(A) True
(B) Partly true
(C) False
(D) None of the above.

86. Communication of offer and acceptance can be made only when the parties are face to face
(A) True
(B) Partly True
(C) False
(D) None of the above

87. Which of the following is an Offer?
(A) Mere quotation of terms by a trader

(B) Quotation of the lowest price in answer to an enquiry

(C) Advertisement for sale or auction of goods

(D) Bids in an auction sale.

88. Where a letter of acceptance sent by post is lost in transit there is

(A) no contract as the acceptance has not come to the knowledge of the offeror

(B) is no contract as the acceptance has not been communicated to the offeror

(C) a contract as the letter of acceptance is put in the course of transmission

(D) all of the above.

89. A general offer made to the public at large is valid, and binding contract is made with a person, who having the knowledge of the Offer—

(A) comes forward acts accordingly.

(B) acts accordingly, and his act is ratified by the Offeror.

(C) Neither (A) nor (B)

(D) Both (A) and (B)

90. On the acceptance of an offer by an offeree—

(A) Only the acceptor becomes bound by accepting the offer.

(B) Only the offeror becomes bound as his terms are accepted.

(C) Both the acceptor and offeror become bound by the contract.

(D) None of the above

91. Which of the following is an invitation to offer?

(A) A tender to supply goods at a certain time

(B) A request for a loan

(C) Bids in an auction sale

(D) A catalogue of goods for sale

92. Silence constitutes a valid acceptance, only if—

(A) Offeree has, by his previous conduct, indicated that silence amounts to his acceptance.

(B) Offer contains a term that Offeree's silence will constitute acceptance.

(C) Both (A) and (B)

(D) Either (A) or (B)

93. Which of the following conditions is not necessary for a valid offer?

(A) Intention to obtain consent of the offeree

(B) Communication to the person to whom it is made

(C) Intention to create legal obligation

(D) Expressed in written form.

94. In a self-service departmental store, a valid contract is concluded by an offer and its acceptance, when—

(A) Customers enter the Departmental Store

(B) Customers pick up the articles

(C) Customers take the articles to the cashier's desk

(D) Cashier accepts the payment from the Customers

95. M offers to sell his house to N for Rs. 36 Lakhs and states in his letter that the offer would be considered as accepted if acceptance is not communicated within a certain time. Here, the letter of M would —

(A) Amount to a proposal

(B) Not amount to a proposal

(C) Amount to a promise

(D) Amount to acceptance

96. Which of the following results in an offer?

(A) a declaration of intention

(B) an invitation to offer

(C) an advertisement offering reward to anyone who finds the lost dog of the advertiser

(D) an offer made in a joke

97. Performance of conditions of an offer for the acceptance of any consideration for a reciprocal promise which may be offered with a proposal, is a/an—

(A) acceptance of the offer.

(B) rejection of the offer.

(C) counter-offer.

(D) revocation of the offer.

98. In case, where a proposal and its acceptance are not made by words and are inferred from the conduct of the parties. They are known as—

(A) Implied offers

(B) Expressed offers

(C) Specific offers

(D) General offers

99. L offered to take a house on lease for a period of three years at Rs. 1 Lakh p.a. if the house was "put through repairs and rooms were handsomely decorated". Here, there is no offer since—

(A) there is no legal obligation

(B) there is no communication of offer

(C) the terms of offer is too vague

(D) the offer is conditional

100. A, by a letter dated 15th March, offers to sell his car to B, who posts his acceptance on 20th March. Here—

(A) B can revoke his acceptance at any time till his letter reaches A

(B) B cannot revoke his acceptance as he becomes bound by positing his acceptance letter

(C) Neither (A) nor (B)

(D) We cannot decide without further information

101. A by a letter, offers to sell his ipod to B for Rs. 20,000. Without knowing A's offer, B, by a letter, offers to buy the same ipod from A for Rs. 20,000. Here—

(A) a binding contract comes into existence B's letter is equivalent to acceptance of A's offer

(B) no binding contract comes into existence as B's letter is merely a cross offer

(C) no binding contract comes into existence as consideration is insufficient

(D) the Indian Contract Act is silent on such issues

102. When a person signifies to another his willingness to do or to abstain from doing anything, with a view to obtaining the assent of that other to such act or abstinence, he is said to—

(A) enter into a contract

(B) make a proposal

(C) accept an offer

(D) create legal obligation

103. S sent his servant L, to trace his missing nephew. Later, S offered a reward for anyone who traced his nephew. L, ignorant of the announcement, traced the boy. *Subsequently*, he claimed the reward, when he came to know of it.

(A) L is entitled to the reward

(B) L was not entitled to the reward

(C) S has to find his nephew himself

(D) No reward can be given for tracing missing persons

104. M offers to sell his car for Rs. 3.8 lakhs to N. N says he would buy it for Rs. 3.5 lakhs. This is a case of —

(A) Counter offer

(B) Implied offer

(C) Direct offer

(D) Express offer

105. A company announced a reward of £ 100 to anyone who contacted influenza after using its smoke balls for a certain period. Mrs. C used the smoke balls but contacted influenza. She claimed the reward but the company rejected her claim stating that she did not communicate her acceptance to the Company. Here—

(A) Acceptance is not communicated and reward cannot be claimed

(B) Offer is not communicated and reward cannot be claimed

(C) Acceptance need not be communicated and reward can be claimed

(D) There is no claim since reward cannot be given for contacting diseases

106. Yaatra Travels operates buses from Delhi to Agra. The bus standing at its Bay in the bus terminus is with a view to taking the passengers. There is _____ to take passengers.

(A) Implied offer

(B) Express offer

(C) Internal offer

(D) External offer

107. An acceptance in ignorance of an offer is also a valid acceptance.

(A) True

(B) Partly True

(C) False

(D) None of the above.

108. A change in law or circumstance rendering the original offer unlawful or impossible, will lead to termination of the offer.

(A) True

(B) Partly true

(C) False

(D) None of the above

109. Counter offer/cross offer made by the other party, does not terminate the original offer.

(A) True

(B) Partly true

(C) False

(D) None of the above

110. A launderer had given to his customer a receipt for clothes received for washing. Special conditions for this were printed on the reverse of the receipt. The Customer claimed that he could not understand the conditions. Is the Customer's claim valid?

(A) Yes, the customer had not understood the special conditions

(B) Yes, there is no consensus *ad idem*

(C) No, the customer is deemed to have understood the special conditions

(D) No, the receipt is invalid in law.

111. Death of offeree before acceptance terminates the offer.

(A) True

(B) Partly True

(C) False

(D) None of the above

112. Which of the following constitute invalid acceptance?

(A) Mental acceptance without communicating to the Proposer

(B) Failure to answer/respond to the proposer

(C) Silence on the part of the offeree

(D) All of the above

113. Revocation of offer need not be communicated to the Offeree.

(A) True

(B) Partly true

(C) False

(D) None of the above

114. B sent a draft agreement relating to supply of coal and coke to the manager of a railway company for his acceptance. The manager wrote "approved" on the same and put the draft in his table drawer, intending to send it to the company' solicitors for a formal contract to be drawn up. Overright the draft agreement remained in the drawer. The transaction is—

(A) a valid contract

(B) not an agreement as the acceptance was never communicated to the proposer

(C) a voidable contract

(D) a void contract

115. Where special terms are communicated by way of conditions on the reverse of a train ticket, receipt, etc., acceptance of the document (e.g. ticket or receipt) without protest tantamounts to a tacit acceptance of conditions.

(A) True

(B) Partly True

(C) False

(D) None of the above

116. A sends a letter to B, offering to sell his old carriage. He asks B to reply by telegram. In such case, B shall reply

(A) in any mode

(B) only by telegram

(C) in any mode other than telegram

(D) in any reasonable mode

117. Under section 2(c) of the Indian Contact Act, promisee is the person—

(A) who makes the proposal

(B) who accepts the proposal

(C) who makes the promise

(D) to whom proposal is made

118. Who said "Acceptance is to a proposal is what a lighted match-stick is to a train of gun-powder"?

(A) Anson

(B) Baumol

(C) Salmond

(D) Drucker

119. A passenger deposited a bag in the cloakroom at a railway station. The Acknowledgement Receipt given to him carried, on the face of it, the words "see back". One condition limited the liability of the Railways for any package to Rs. 100. The bag was lost, and the passenger claimed Rs. 2,400 being its value, pleading that he had not read the conditions. Can the passenger win the case?

(A) Yes, the Railway company cannot take undue advantage

(B) Yes, damages are payable for loss of property

(C) No, a suit for value below Rs. 5,000 is not permissible in law

(D) No, the passenger had constructive notice of conditions whether he read them or not

120. A passenger was travelling with luggage from Dublin to Whitehaven on a ticket, on the back of which there was a term that exempted the shipping company from liability for loss of luggage. He never looked at the back of the ticket and there was nothing on the face of it to draw his attention to the terms on its back. He lost his luggage and sued for damages. Can the passenger win the case?

(A) Yes, the Shipping company cannot take undue advantage.

(B) Yes, the Passenger is not bound by something which was not communicated to him

(C) No, a suit for loss of luggage is not permissible in law.

(D) No, the passenger had constructive notice of conditions whether he read them or not

121. An acceptance on telephone should be—

(A) heard by the Offeror

(B) audible to the Offeror

(C) understood by the Offeror

(D) all of the above

122. In which of the following situation, the acceptor is not bound by the special conditions?

(A) Conditions limiting or defining his rights are not brought to the acceptor's notice

(B) The Document does not give reasonable notice on its face that it contains certain special conditions

(C) Conditions are contained in a document that is delivered after the contract is complete

(D) All of the above.

123. F offers to sell his house to G for Rs. 20 lakhs. G replies that he would buy the house provided his solicitor approves of F's title to the house. The offer did not contain any mention as to title. The acceptance is—

(A) Qualified, hence invalid

(B) Conditional, hence invalid

(C) valid

(D) Both (A) and (B)

124. When the offeree gives acceptance on different terms, it is treated as a counter offer and it is up to the original offeror to accept the same or not.

(A) True

(B) Partly true

(C) False

(D) None of the above

125. According to the Indian Contract Act, 1872, a promise is —

(A) A communication of intention to do something

(B) A proposal which has been accepted

(C) A gentleman's word to do something

(D) A statement on oath

126. A proposal can be revoked by —

(A) Communication of notice of revocation by the Offeror

(B) Failure of acceptor to fulfill a condition precedent

(C) Insanity or death of an offeror to the knowledge of the acceptor

(D) All of the above

127. F offered by a letter to buy his nephew N's horse for Rs. 25,000, saying: "*If I hear no more about it, I shall consider the horse is mine at Rs. 25,000.*" The Nephew did not reply, but he told an auctioneer who was selling his horses not to sell that particular horse as he had sold it to his uncle. By mistake, the auctioneer sold it. F sued the auctioneer for conversion. In this case—

(A) F can recover the amount from the Auctioneer

(B) There is no agreement between F and N, as the acceptance was not communicated to F.

(C) F can claim the horse back from the successful bidder at the auction

(D) F can claim damages from N.

128. General offers open to the world at large can be accepted by—

(A) Any person in the world

(B) Any person within the country

(C) Any person who complies with the conditions of the offer

(D) Any person who reads the advertisement

129. In order to convert a proposal into a promise, the acceptance must be—

(A) absolute

(B) unqualified

(C) express/Implied

(D) all of the above

130. In cases of general offer, for a valid contract, the acceptor—

(A) Must have the knowledge of the offer before acceptance by performance

(B) need not have the knowledge of the offer

(C) may acquire the knowledge of the offer after the performance of the condition amounting to acceptance.

(D) should not accept at all

131. In cases of general offer to the public at large, notifying the acceptance to the Proposer is necessary

(A) True

(B) Partly true

(C) False

(D) None of the above

132. A specific Offer can be accepted by—

(A) any person

(B) any friend of offeror

(C) only the person to whom it is made

(D) any friend of offeree

133. An acceptance containing additions, limitation or other modifications shall amount to—

(A) rejection of the offer

(B) a counter offer

(C) a valid acceptance

(D) both (A) and (B)

134. Express offers and acceptance may be proved by the agreement between the parties but implied offers can be proved only by—

(A) Words

(B) Conduct

(C) Circumstantial evidence

(D) *Prima facie* evidence

135. Acceptance cannot be implied merely from the silence of the offeree, even if it is expressly stated in the offer itself. In such cases, mere silence cannot constitute acceptance.

(A) True
(B) Partly true
(C) False
(D) None of the above

136. S offered a reward to anyone who returns his lost dog. F brought the dog to S without having heard of the offer. F is not entitled to the reward, since—

(A) Acceptance cannot precede the Offer
(B) Offer was not made to an ascertained person
(C) S has to find the dog himself
(D) No reward can be given for return of a lost dog

137. Performance of conditions of an offer for the acceptance of any consideration for a reciprocal promise which may be offered with a proposal, is a/an—

(A) acceptance of the offer
(B) rejection of the offer
(C) counter-offer
(D) revocation of the offer.

138. An Offer may be revoked at any time before the communication of its acceptance is complete, as against the _________, but not afterwards.

(A) Offeree
(B) Proposer
(C) Acceptor
(D) Third party

139. A General offer can be accepted by —

(A) sending a communication of acceptance
(B) tendering himself to comply the conditions of offer
(C) complying with the conditions of an offer
(D) making a counter-offer

140. M offers to sell his car for Rs. 3.8 Lakhs to N. N says, he would buy it for Rs. 3.5 Lakhs. The counter-offer by N for Rs. 3.5 lakh—

(A) cannot be accepted by M
(B) may be accepted by M
(C) is irrational
(D) is illegal

141. T send to S by post an offer to sell his cycle. S sends his acceptance *via* Post. S could revoke his acceptance up to any time before or at the moment, when—

(A) S posts his letter of acceptance
(B) T receives the letter of acceptance
(C) T reads the letter of acceptance
(D) Earliest of the above

142. It has been said that "Acceptance is to a proposal what a lighted match-stick is to ...."

(A) A matchbox
(B) a train of gun-powder
(C) a cigarette
(D) a cotton storage yard

143. A sends a letter to B, offering to sell his house property. He asks B to reply by telegram. If B accepts by registered letter, and A does not insist acceptance by telegram within a reasonable time, the contract is—

(A) invalid
(B) valid
(C) voidable
(D) unenforceable

144. An acceptance is not according to the mode prescribed but the Offeror decides to keep quiet. In such a case there is—

(A) a contract
(B) no contract
(C) a voidable contract
(D) an unenforceable contract

145. Acceptance should be given within the time specified by the Offeror.

(A) True
(B) Partly true
(C) False
(D) None of the above

146. Acceptance should be given within—

(A) the time specified by the offeror
(B) a reasonable time
(C) such time as the offer lapses
(D) all of the above

147. When there is a counter-offer, the original offeror may accept the terms of the counter-offer made by the Offeree and form a valid contract.

(A) True
(B) Partly true
(C) False
(D) None of the above

148. A Tradesman receives an order from a customer and executes the order by sending goods. Sending of goods by the Tradesman consequent to the customer's order constitutes—

(A) acceptance by conduct
(B) invalid acceptance
(C) counter-offer for supply of goods
(D) rejection of the original offer

149. Acceptance may be signified either—

(A) in writing

(B) by word of mouth

(C) by performance of some act

(D) all of the above

150. If a person performs some act intended by the Proposer as consideration for the promise offered by him, the performance of such act constitutes—

(A) an invalid acceptance.

(B) a valid acceptance.

(C) rejection of the offer.

(D) a counter-offer.

151. Acceptance should be communicated to the offeror, before—

(A) the offer lapses

(B) the offer terminates

(C) the offer is revoked by the offeror

(D) All of the above

152. Where a letter of acceptance sent by post is lost in transit there is—

(A) no contract as the acceptance has not come to the knowledge of the Offeror.

(B) is no contact as the acceptance has not been communicated to the Offeror.

(C) a contract as the letter of acceptance is put in the course of transmission.

(D) all of the above

153. Even if the letter is lost in transit, acceptance is still valid provided that the Acceptor has—

(A) properly addressed it to the Offeror

(B) affixed correct value of postage stamps

(C) infacted post it at the Post Office

(D) all of the above

154. Communication of acceptance is complete as against the Proposer—

(A) only when it comes to the knowledge of the Proposer

(B) only when the acceptance is communicated to the Proposer

(C) only when it is put in the course of transmission to him so as to be out of power of the Acceptor

(D) None of the above

155. An acceptance can be revoked after its acceptance comes to the knowledge of the Promisee.

(A) True

(B) Partly True

(C) False

(D) None of the above

156. H, in response to G's offer, sends a letter of acceptance by post. As regards G, communication is complete, when —

(A) G makes the offer.

(B) H decides to accept the offer.

(C) The letter is posted by H.

(D) G receives the letter.

157. An acceptance can be revoked at any time before such acceptance comes to the knowledge of the—

(A) Proposer

(B) Acceptor

(C) Third Party

(D) Court.

158. A letter of acceptance sufficiently stamped and duly addressed is put into course of transmission. Here, there is—

(A) a contract voidable at the option of Acceptor.

(B) a contract voidable at the option of the Offeror.

(C) no contract at all.

(D) a valid contract.

159. An acceptance can be revoked at any time before such acceptance —

(A) is understood by the Proposer.

(B) comes to the knowledge of the Acceptor.

(C) comes to the knowledge of the Proposer.

(D) is understood by the Acceptor.

160. When no mode is prescribed by the Offeror for the acceptance of his offer, such acceptance shall be made—

(A) as decided by the Court.

(B) as desired by the Offeree.

(C) in some usual and reasonable manner.

(D) any of the above

161. B owes A Rs. 20,000. A desires B to pay the amount to A's account with SBI banker. B, who also banks with SBI, orders the amount to be transferred from the account to A's credit and this is done by SBI. Afterwards, and before A knows of the transfer, SBI fails. Who shall bear the loss?

(A) A

(B) B

(C) A and B equally

(D) None of the above

162. A agrees to pay Rs. 15 lakh to B, if he (B) procures an employment for A in the Income Tax Department. This agreement is—

(A) void
(B) valid
(C) voidable
(D) contingent.

163. A agrees to pay Rs. 15,00,000 to B, if he kills C. The agreement is—
(A) void
(B) valid
(C) voidable
(D) contingent.

164. A agrees to sell to B, 200 tons of oil. A deals only in coconut oil. The agreement is—
(A) valid.
(B) void due to uncertainty of meaning.
(C) illegal.
(D) opposed to public policy.

165. Z agrees with Y to sell all his grain in his granary at Ropar for Rs. 50,000. The agreement is—
(A) valid.
(B) void due to uncertainty of meaning.
(C) illegal.
(D) opposed to public policy.

166. F agrees to sell his produce to G, provided H shall come, inspect and fix the price. The agreement is —
(A) valid.
(B) void due to uncertainty of meaning.
(C) illegal.
(D) unenforceable.

167. A clause in a Tender authorising the party inviting tenders to terminate the contract at any time for future supplies —
(A) destroys the very basis of the contracts and the clause is void.
(B) Makes the entire contract void.
(C) Makes the contract voidable.
(D) does not destroy the basis of the contract and the clause is valid.

168. Persons entering into contracts on special terms are deemed to have impliedly accepted those terms only if such special terms are—
(A) reasonably communicated to them.
(B) non-restrictive in nature.
(C) legal.
(D) enforceable.

169. A transport carrier accepted goods for transport without any conditions. Subsequently, he issued a circular to the owners of goods limiting his liability for goods. Is this circular binding on the owners of goods?
(A) No, these were not communicated prior to the date of contract for transport
(B) No, a carrier cannot restrict/limit his own liability
(C) Yes, a reasonable notice to the Acceptor is sufficient
(D) Yes, a carrier can restrict/limit his own liability

170. A writes to B, 'I am willing to sell my car as it is today for Rs. 40,000.' B replies, 'I can buy it for Rs. 35,000'. A keeps quiet. Subsequently, B writes, 'I will buy the car at Rs. 40,000'. Is it binding promise?
(A) Yes
(B) No

171. 'X agrees to sell to Y 100 tons of oil'. If X, who is a dealer in coconut oil only, decides to sell @ Rs. 10,000 per ton.' Decide, whether it is—
(A) Valid contract.
(B) Void contract.
(C) Voidable contract.
(D) Uncertain contract.

172. In ***Q. 171*** above, If X is a dealer in coconut oil and price is not fixed—
(A) Valid contract
(B) Void agreement
(C) Voidable contract
(D) Uncertain contract

173. In ***Q. 171*** above, If X is a dealer in coconut oil and price is to be fixed by Z—
(A) Valid contract
(B) Void contract
(C) Voidable contract
(D) Uncertain contract

174. In ***Q. 171*** above, If X who, is a dealer in coconut oil agrees to sell at Rs. 10,000 per ton or at Rs. 1,000 per ton—
(A) Valid contract
(B) Void agreement
(C) Voidable contract
(D) Uncertain contract

175. In ***Q. 171*** above, If X is a dealer in coconut oil and mustered oil–
(A) Valid contract
(B) Void agreement
(C) Voidable contract
(D) Uncertain contract

☞ Consideration

176. Which of the following statement is false? Consideration—

(A) Must move at the desire of the promisor.

(B) May move from any person.

(C) Must be illusory.

(D) Must be of some value.

177. Which of the following statement is true?

(A) There can be a stranger to a contract.

(B) There can be a stranger to a consideration.

(C) There can be a stranger to a contract and consideration.

(D) None of the above.

178. A and B make contract grounded on the erroneous belief that a particular debt is barred by the Indian Law of Limitation. The contract is—

(A) Valid.

(B) Void.

(C) Illegal.

(D) Voidable.

179. Consideration in simple term means—

(A) Anything in return.

(B) Something in return.

(C) Everything in return.

(D) Nothing in return.

180. As a general rule, an agreement made without consideration is—

(A) void.

(B) voidable.

(C) valid.

(D) unlawful.

181. Which of the following statement is true?

(A) Consideration must result in a benefit to both parties.

(B) Past consideration is no consideration in India.

(C) Consideration must be adequate.

(D) Consideration must be something, which a promisor is not already bound to do.

182. Which is/are the exception(s) to the general rule–*No consideration, No contract.*

(A) Natural love and affection

(B) Compensation for past voluntary services

(C) Written Promise to pay a time barred debt

(D) All of the above

183. Which of the following is not an exception to the rule—*'No consideration, No contract'.*

(A) Compensation for involuntary services.

(B) Love & Affection.

(C) Contract of Agency.

(D) Gift.

184. An agreement made without consideration is valid u/s 25 of the Indian Contract Act, 1872 if—

(A) The agreement is expressed in writing.

(B) The agreement is made on account of natural love and affection or the parties to the agreement stand in a near relation to each other.

(C) The document is registered under the law for the time being in force for registration of such document.

(D) All of the above

185. Which of the following is not correct?

(A) Consideration must be at the desire of the promisor.

(B) Consideration may be past, present or future.

(C) Consideration need not be adequate, but should be real and supported by free consent.

(D) Consideration should be always monetary.

186. Which one of the following is a legal requirement regarding consideration—

(A) Consideration should move at the desire of the promise.

(B) Consideration may move from promisee or any other person.

(C) Consideration may be past, present or future.

(D) All of the above

187. Exceptions to the statement "*No consideration no contract*" are the following–

(A) No consideration is required to create an agency as also in the case of completed gifts.

(B) A promise made without consideration is valid if it is a promise, made in writing and signed by the person to be charged therewith, or by his agent generally or specially authorized in that behalf, to pay wholly or in part a debt, which is barred by the Law of Limitation.

(C) A promise made without any consideration is valid if it is a promise to compensate wholly or in part a person who has already voluntarily done something for the promisor or something which the promisor was legally compellable to do.

(D) All of the above

188. H sued her father-in-law K to recover Rs. 15,000 being arrears of allowance called Pin money payable to her by K under an agreement between K and H's father, consideration being H's marriage to K's son D. Both H and D were minors at the time of marriage. Which of the following statements is correct?

(A) Agreement is in restraint of marital duties and hence void.

(B) The agreement is void since H and D were minors.

(C) No suit can lie in a Court in respect of Pin Money due.

(D) The promise can be made enforceable by H.

189. A owes C Rs. 10,000, but the debt is barred by the Limitation Act. A signs a written promise to pay C Rs. 5,000 on account of the debt. Choose the best alternative—

(A) A promise to pay a time barred debt is not enforceable.

(B) It is not a valid contract.

(C) It is a voidable contract.

(D) A promise to pay full amount of Rs. 10,000 is a valid contract.

190. Which of the following statement is true?

(A) If there is no consideration, there is no contract.

(B) Past consideration is no consideration in India

(C) Consideration must result in a benefit to both the parties.

(D) Consideration must be adequate

191. Past consideration is no consideration in India.

(A) True

(B) False

192. Consideration must be adequate.

(A) True

(B) False

193. Consideration must move at the desire of the promisor.

(A) True

(B) False

194. There can be a stranger to a consideration, but not a stranger to a contract.

(A) True

(B) False

195. A finds B's purse, and gives it back to him. B promises to give A Rs. 50. This is a/an—

(A) Agreement.

(B) Contract.

(C) Acceptance.

(D) Offer.

196. A invited B and his family to dine with him on a particular night. The latter accepted the former's invitation. On the scheduled date, B drove with his family from *Raja Mandi* to the residence of A in *Loha Mandi* (at a distance of 2 km.) and found that A has not made any arrangement for dinner. Whether B can file suit against A for the same?

(A) Yes

(B) No

197. Is a promisor normally bound by his promise, unless some consideration is offered by the promisee ?

(A) Yes

(B) No

198. Can consideration be offered by a person other than the promisee ?

(A) Yes

(B) No

199. Where the consideration has moved from the promisee, but not at the request of the promisor, can the promisor enforce the promise ?

(A) Yes

(B) No

200. Is past consideration valid in India?

(A) Yes

(B) No

201. Can a stranger to a contract normally sue thereon?

(A) Yes

(B) No

202. Marriage Settlement, Partition and other Family Arrangements can be enforced by a beneficiary who is not a party to the contract, only if such agreement is—

(A) registered.

(B) reduced to writing.

(C) either (A) or (B)

(D) both (A) and (B)

203. R's son was missing. N, who was a distant relation of R made a search for the missing son, found him and brought him back. R then promised N that he would compensate him for the services rendered. Later R refuses to keep his promise. Could N enforce it in the court?

(A) Yes

(B) No

(C) May be 'Yes' or may be 'No'

(D) None of the above

204. A promised to pay a subscription of Rs. 5,000 to *the Prime National Relief Fund*. He later changed his mind. Could the amount be recovered from A ?

(A) Yes

(B) No

205. Can a contract which is made by a deed (i.e., a contract under seal) be valid, even if it is made without consideration ?

(A) Yes

(B) No

206. At the time of marriage between A and B, A's father promised to B's parents that he will pay Rs. 5,000 per month to B after her marriage with his son. On his failure to pay the amount B wants to sue A's father for the amount promised by him at the time of her marriage with A.

Which of the following statement(s) is correct?

(A) B cannot sue A's father as the contract is void for lack of consideration.

(B) B cannot sue A's father under the doctrine of privity of contracts.

(C) B can sue A's father for breach of contract.

(D) B cannot sue A's father as the contracts made at the time of marriage are not enforceable by law.

207. Two brothers, on partition of family joint properties, agreed to invest in equal shares for their mother's maintenance. There was no separate agreement with the mother. In such case, the mother–

(A) cannot enforce the contract.

(B) can sue for setting aside the partition.

(C) is entitled to require her sons to make the investment.

(D) is entitled to the entire property.

208. A gives to B Rs. 300 to be given to C. B informs C that he is holding the money for him. But, afterwards B refuses to pay the money. C sues B for the money. B contends that C cannot sue as he was not a party to the contract. Will the contention of B be upheld?

(A) Yes

(B) No

209. Which of the following is void contract?

(A) Agreement with unlawful consideration

(B) Agreement with inadequate consideration, if inadequacy is not supported by free consent

(C) Agreement the meaning of which is certain

(D) Agreement in respect of legal proceedings

210. All agreements made without consideration are void—

(A) True, as there is no exception to this rule.

(B) False, as there are certain exceptions also.

(C) None of these

(D) Either (A) or (B)

211. If the consideration to an agreement is furnished by a stranger and not by the Promisee himself, the agreement will be void–

(A) True, as the consideration must be furnished by the promisee

(B) False, as the law requires that there must be some consideration, who furnished it is immaterial.

(C) There is no consideration in the contract.

(D) None of these

212. A person, who is not a party to the contract, can enforce the contract on the same principle that consideration furnished by a stranger is valid.

(A) True, as the rule is that a stranger to a contract can sue.

(B) True, as the stranger to consideration can enforce the contract.

(C) False, as the rule is that a stranger to a contract cannot sue.

(D) None of these.

213. A person who is not a party to the contract can enforce the contract on the same principle that consideration furnished by a stranger is valid.

(A) True, as the rule is that a stranger to a contract can sue

(B) False, as the rule is that a stranger to a contract cannot sue

(C) The Indian Contract Act is silent on such issues

(D) None of the above

214. A buyer may make some payment in advance to the seller as a guarantee for performance of contract. This money is known as—

(1) Earnest money

(2) Security deposit

(3) Fixed deposit

(4) Deposit

(A) 1 & 2

(B) 1 & 3

(C) 2 & 4

(D) 3 & 4

215. Which of the following statement is false?

(A) Generally a stranger to a contract cannot sue.

(B) A verbal promise to pay a time barred debt is valid.

(C) Completed gift need no consideration.

(D) No consideration is necessary to create an agency.

216. The Doctrine of Privity of Contract states that-

(A) A contract cannot confer any right on one who is not a party to the contract, even though the very object of the contract may have been to benefit him.

(B) A contract can confer right on one who is not a party to the contract, if the contract benefits him.

(C) A contract always confers right on one who is not a party to the contract.

(D) A contract can confer rights on strangers.

217. Consideration may be—

(A) Past

(B) Present

(C) Future

(D) All of the above.

218. What is legal terminology for the doing or not doing of something, which the promisor desires to be done or not done?

(A) Desires.

(B) Wishes.

(C) Consideration.

(D) Promise.

219. ______ consideration is not consideration in England.

(A) Past

(B) Present

(C) Future

(D) Past and Present

220. Which of the following is/are false?

(1) Consideration must be real.

(2) Consideration can be inadequate.

(3) A promise to do something which one is already bound to do by law, will be treated as good consideration.

(4) Consideration must be adequate.

(A) 1 & 2

(B) 2 & 3

(C) 3 & 4

(D) 1 & 4

221. Consideration may also be offered by a person other than the promisee—

(A) True

(B) Partly True

(C) False

(D) None of the above

222. Consideration must be —

(A) Inadequate

(B) Adequate

(C) Either (A) or (B)

(D) Neither (A) nor (B)

223. What does the maxim "*Ex Nudo pacto non oritur actio*", mean ?

(A) An agreement without consideration is void.

(B) An agreement without consideration is valid.

(C) An agreement with consideration is void.

(D) An agreement with consideration cannot be enforced.

224. Where the consideration has moved from the Promisee but not at the request of the Promisor, can the Promisor enforce the promise?

(A) Yes

(B) No

(C) Partly Yes

(D) We cannot conclude with this information.

225. Consideration and object of an agreement is unlawful, if it —

(A) is fraudulent.

(B) is vague.

(C) is inadequate.

(D) all of the above

226. D constructed a market at the instance of District Collector. Occupants of shops promised to pay D a commission on articles sold through their shops. Money was not spent by D at the request of the shop occupants, but at instance of a third person viz. the Collector. Which of the following statements is correct?

(A) Shop Occupants have to pay the commission to D.

(B) D can claim commission or damages from shop occupants.

(C) D can claim reimbursement from the Collector.

(D) There is no contract since Consideration has not moved at the desire of the Promisor.

227. If a person promises to contribute to charity and on this faith, the promisee undertakes a liability to the extent not exceeding the promised subscription, the contract shall be valid.

(A) True

(B) Partly true

(C) False

(D) None of the above

228. A and B makes a contract on erroneous belief that a particular debt is time-barred by Indian Law of Limitation. The contact is —

(A) Void.

(B) Voidable.

(C) Valid.

(D) Illegal.

229. An Executory Consideration is —

(A) Consideration promised by executive of a Company.

(B) Consideration which consists simply of a mutual exchange of promise each being a consideration for the other.

(C) Consideration which should be executed before the Registrar.

(D) Consideration which should be executed before the Court.

230. K engages M, an artist, to paint a portrait of his uncle and promises to pay M Rs. 10,000 for the work. Later, K refuses to pay stating that consideration must move from his uncle. Which of the following statements is correct?

(A) K is bound to pay M.

(B) K is not bound to pay M.

(C) Uncle is bound to pay M.

(D) M cannot claim anything from K or his uncle.

231. M promised to pay N for his services at his (M) sole discretion found to be fair and reasonable. However, N dissatisfied with payment made by M wanted to sue him. N's suit will be —

(A) valid.

(B) invalid.

(C) restricted only to payment of remuneration and not damages.

(D) restricted only to damages and not remuneration.

232. Provision of marriage expenses of female members of a Joint Hindu Family, entitles the female member to sue for such expenses on a partition between male members.

(A) True

(B) Partly true

(C) False

(D) None of the above

233. Which of the following statement is false?

(A) Generally a Stranger to a contract cannot sue.

(B) A verbal promise to pay a time barred debt is valid.

(C) Completed gifts need no consideration.

(D) No consideration is necessary to create an agency.

234. If the consideration to an agreement is furnished by a stranger and not by the Promisee himself, the agreement will be void.

(A) True, as the consideration must be furnished by the Promisee.

(B) False, as the law requires that there must be some consideration, who furnished it is immaterial .

(C) Neither (A) nor (B)

(D) The Indian Contract Act is silent on such issues.

235. Inadequacy of consideration is relevant in determining the question of —

(A) Capacity of parties.

(B) Possibility of performance.

(C) Legality of object.

(D) Free Consent.

236. An essential feature of consideration is that—

(A) It must be encashable.

(B) It must be given by the Promisee alone.

(C) It must be at the desire or request of the Promisor.

(D) It must be guaranteed.

237. Adequacy of consideration is to be seen from the view point of—

(A) Court.

(B) Promisee.

(C) Promisor.

(D) Beneficiary.

238. An Agreement made on account of natural love and affection, but without consideration is valid, if it is—

(A) expressed in writing.

(B) registered under law for the time being in force for registration of documents.

(C) made between parties standing in a near relation to each other.

(D) all of the above

239. When no consideration is paid by the Buyer for the goods received from the Seller, it is called—

(A) Sale.

(B) Barter.

(C) Gift.

(D) Bailment.

240. Past consideration means—

(A) The price received in the past without making even a proposal of any sort.

(B) The price which is more than what the promisor expected.

(C) The price or service rendered at the desire or request of the Promisor in the past followed by a subsequent promise.

(D) All of these

241. X invites Y (a famous Film Actor) to his daughter's engagement and dinner party. Y accepts the invitation and promises to attend. X made special arrangement for Y at the party but he did not turn up. X enraged with Y's behaviour, wanted to sue for loss incurred in making special arrangements.

(A) X has no remedy against Y.

(B) X has to conduct the engagement party again and invite Y.

(C) X can sue Y for not honouring his words.

(D) X has to invite Y again, to perform the promise.

242. L promises to give Rs. 5,000 per month pocket money to his son M. If L does not give the pocket money—

(A) M can sue his father.

(B) M has no remedy against L.

(C) M can accept a lower pocket money also.

(D) M has to give Rs. 5,000 to his father.

243. A invites B for coffee in a restaurant and B accepts the invitation. On the appointed date, A is present there but B does not turn up. In this case —

(A) A has no remedy against B.

(B) A has to make another invitation to B.

(C) A can sue B for not honouring his words.

(D) A has to invite B again, to perform the promise.

244. Consideration need not necessarily be provided by the promise, it may flow from a third party also. Such a person is called—

(A) Stranger to Contract.

(B) Stranger to Consideration.

(C) Stranger to the Court.

(D) Absolute Stranger.

245. An agreement not supported by consideration is called —

(A) *Nudum Pactum*

(B) *Consensus ad idem*

(C) *Ab initio*

(D) *Ignorantia juris non excusat*

246. M engages N as his employee and promises to pay N a "reasonable" salary for services rendered. Here, the consideration is—

(A) illusory .

(B) unlawful.

(C) uncertain.

(D) valid.

247. Which of the following is good and valid consideration?

(A) Forbearance to sue

(B) Compounding with Creditors

(C) Compromise of Disputed Claims

(D) All of the above

248. The assignee of a contract cannot enforce the promise, since there is no consideration flowing from him to the Promisor.

(A) True

(B) Partly True

(C) False

(D) None of the above

249. Consideration—

(A) must move from the Promisee.

(B) may move from the Promisee or any other person.

(C) must move from the third party.

(D) may move from the promisor.

250. An act or abstinence or promise u/s 2(d) of Indian Contract Act, is called—

(A) Reciprocal Promise.

(B) Counter-Offer.

(C) Consideration for the promise.

(D) Quasi-Contract.

251. An essential feature of consideration is that—

(A) It must be encashable.

(B) It must be given by the Promisee alone.

(C) It must be at the desire or request of the Promisor.

(D) It must be guaranteed.

252. A consideration is—

(A) Doing or abstaining from doing something at the desire of the Promisor.

(B) A reason for making a proposal.

(C) Regard for the condition of other party.

(D) Compensation for breach of contract.

253. An Executory Consideration—

(A) is an outstanding liability on both the parties.

(B) consists of a promise in future.

(C) is a promise for a promise.

(D) all of the above

254. As long as there is a consideration for a promise, it is immaterial who has furnished it.

(A) True

(B) Partly True

(C) False

(D) None of the above

255. "Consideration" means a reasonable equivalent or other valuable benefit passed on—

(A) By the Promisor to the Beneficiary.

(B) By the Promisee to the Promisor.

(C) By the Promisor to the Promisee.

(D) By the Promisee to the Beneficiary.

256. Consideration must move at the desire of the Promisor. If it is done at the instance of a third party or without the desire of the Promisor, it is—

(A) Consideration.

(B) Not consideration.

(C) Offer.

(D) Promise.

257. Section ___ of the Indian Contract Act mentions three exceptions when an agreement, even though without consideration, is enforceable.

(A) Sec. 23

(B) Sec. 24

(C) Sec. 25

(D) Sec. 26

258. Where a witness who has received summons to appear at a trial, a promise to pay him anything beyond his expenses is—

(A) void since consideration is illusory.

(B) valid.

(C) unlawful.

(D) in restraint of legal proceedings.

259. Consideration must be something which the Promisor—

(A) is already bound to do.

(B) is not already bound to do.

(C) may voluntarily do.

(D) must not do.

260. An executed consideration—

(A) can be positive or negative.

(B) liability is outstanding on one side only.

(C) is an act or actual forbearance against, future promise.

(D) all of the above

261. If P renders some service to D at D's desire and after a month D promises to compensate P for the service rendered to him, it is a —

(A) Present Consideration.

(B) Past Consideration.

(C) Future consideration.

(D) Not a consideration at all

262. The expression "Privity of Contract" means—

(A) A contract is contract between the parties only.

(B) A contract is a private document.

(C) Only private documents can be contracts.

(D) The contracts may be expressed in some usual and reasonable manner.

263. A promise to pay, wholly or in part, a debt which is barred by law of limitation can be enforced if—

(A) it is in writing.

(B) is signed by the debtor or his authorised agent.

(C) either (A) or (B)

(D) both (A) and (B)

264. An elder brother, on account of natural love and affection, promised to pay the debts of his younger brother. Agreement was put to writing and registered. There was no consideration in the above. The agreement is—

(A) Void.

(B) Valid.

(C) Illegal.

(D) Unenforceable.

265. Mere nearness of relation does not necessarily imply natural love and affection for making contracts without consideration valid.

(A) True

(B) Partly True

(C) False

(D) None of the above

266. A husband, by a registered agreement promised to pay his earnings to his wife. There was no monetary consideration flowing from the wife to the husband.

(A) Void

(B) Illegal

(C) Valid

(D) Unenforceable

267. M, by a Gift deed transferred certain property to her daughter, with a direction that daughter should pay an annuity to M's brother, as had been done by M. On the same day, the daughter executed a deed in writing in favour of M's brother, agreeing to pay annuity. Afterwards, she declined to fulfil her promise saying that no consideration had moved from her uncle. Which of the following statements is correct?

(A) The daughter is bound to pay annuity.

(B) There is valid consideration in this contract.

(C) M's Brother is a third party to the contract and cannot sue.

(D) The daughter is not bound to pay annuity.

268. A Hindu husband by a registered documents, after referring to quarrels and disagreements between himself and his wife, promised to pay his wife a sum of money for her maintenance and separate residence. The above contact is—

(A) Void.

(B) Illegal.

(C) Valid.

(D) Voidable.

269. Consideration is not necessary to effect a valid Gratuitous Bailment of goods.

(A) True

(B) Partly True

(C) False

(D) None of the above

270. A for natural love and affection, promises to give his son B Rs. 1,000. A puts his promise to B into writing and registers it. This is a —

(A) Contract.

(B) Agreement.

(C) Promise.

(D) Offer.

271. Agreement without consideration is valid, when made—

(A) out of love and affection due to near relationship.

(B) to pay a time barred debt.

(C) to compensate a person who has already done something voluntarily.

(D) all of the above

272. A owes B Rs. 10,000 but the debt is barred by Limitation Act. A signs a written promise to pay B Rs. 8,000 on account of this debt. The contract is —

(A) Void.

(B) Illegal.

(C) Valid.

(D) Unenforceable.

273. Consideration is not valid if it is —

(A) physically impossible.

(B) legally not permissible.

(C) uncertain.

(D) all of the above

274. Contract without consideration made on account of natural love and affection is—

(A) valid.

(B) void.

(C) voidable.

(D) unenforceable.

275. A person verbally promised the Secretary of the Mosque Committee to subscribe Rs. 500 for rebuilding of a mosque. Later, he declined to pay the said amount. The agreement is void due to —

(A) Lack of consideration.

(B) Lack of *consensus ad idem.*

(C) Lack of capacity to contract.

(D) Lack of object.

276. Inadequacy of consideration does not render a contract invalid.

(A) True

(B) Partly True

(C) False

(D) None of the above

277. A promises to pay an existing debt punctually if, B, the Creditor, gives him a discount. Is this consideration valid?

(A) Yes, it is genuine consideration

(B) No, Promisor is already bound to pay punctually

(C) No, inadequate consideration

(D) Yes, enforceable consideration

278. Past consideration is valid in—

(A) England only.

(B) India only.

(C) neither in England nor in India.

(D) both in England and India.

279. A promise made without consideration is valid, if —

(A) it is a promise to compensate wholly or in part, a person who has already voluntarily done something for the Promisor.

(B) something which the Promisor was legally compellable to do.

(C) either (A) or (B)

(D) Neither (A) nor (B)

280. Beneficiary, in whose favour a Trust of other interest in some immovable property has been created can enforce it only if he is a party to the Contract.

(A) True

(B) Partly True

(C) False

(D) None of the above

281. Inadequacy of consideration may be taken into account by the Court to determine whether the consent of Promisor was freely given.

(A) True

(B) Partly true

(C) False

(D) None of the above

282. Under the Indian Contract Act, a third person—

(A) who is the beneficiary under the contract can sue.

(B) from whom the consideration has proceeded can sue.

(C) cannot sue even if the consideration has proceeded from him.

(D) cannot sue at all for want of privity of contract.

283. Under the Indian Contract Act, a stranger—

(A) to the contract cannot sue.

(B) to the contract can sue.

(C) but beneficiary under the contract can sue.

(D) can apply to the Court for specific performance.

284. Only those persons, who are parties to a contract, can sue and be sued upon the contract. This rule is called the doctrine of —

(A) Promisory Estoppel.

(B) Right of Privilege Suit.

(C) Privity of Contract.

(D) Right *in rem*

285. In India, a person who is a stranger to the consideration—

(A) Can sue based on the contract.

(B) Cannot sue based on the contract.

(C) Can sue depending on the conditions.

(D) Can sue if permitted by the Court.

286. A person who is not a party to a contact —

(A) cannot sue.

(B) can sue.

(C) can sue only in well recognized cases.

(D) can sue the Government.

287. A person who is not a party to a contract but has some interest in the consideration of that contract—

(A) cannot enforce that contract.

(B) can enforce that contract.

(C) can enforce that contract subject to certain exceptions.

(D) can wait for the parties to perform the contract.

288. Inadequacy of consideration does not make the contract —

(A) void.

(B) voidable.

(C) valid.

(D) neither void nor voidable.

289. The Beneficiary of a Trust or other interest in specific immovable property, can enforce it even if he is not a party named in the Trust Deed.

(A) True

(B) Partly true

(C) False

(D) None of the above

290. In which of the following situations, a Stranger to Contract can file a valid suit?

(A) Beneficiary of a Trust or other interest in specific immovable property.

(B) Marriage Settlement, Partition and other Family Arrangements, in written form.

(C) Acknowledgement of liability, or by past performance thereof.

(D) All of the above

291. Two brothers, on partition of family joint properties, agreed to invest in equal shares for their mother's maintenance. There was no separate agreement with the mother. In such case, the mother—

(A) cannot enforce the contract.

(B) can sue for setting aside the partition.

(C) is entitled to require her sons to make the investment.

(D) is entitled to the entire property.

292. The purchaser of immovable property who has noticed that the owner of the land is bound by certain conditions or covenants created by an agreement affecting the land, shall be bound by such conditions, even though he is not a party to the original agreement containing those conditions or covenants.

(A) True

(B) Partly true

(C) False

(D) None of the above

293. In which of the following situations, a Stranger to Contract can file a valid suit?

(A) Assignment of a Contract

(B) Contracts entered into through an Agent

(C) Covenants running with land

(D) All of the above

294. A who is indebted to B, sells his property to C. C promises to pay off the debt to B. When C fails to pay; B has no right to sue C, because—

(A) The object is unlawful.

(B) There is no consideration between B and C.

(C) B is a Stranger to Contract between A and C.

(D) The consideration is inadequate.

295. Generally, Third Parties cannot enforce the rights of the Promisee of the contract.

(A) True

(B) Partly true

(C) False

(D) None of the above

☞ Capacity to contract

296. Identify the incorrect sentence from the following—

(A) A Minor can be a beneficiary

(B) A Minor can be admitted to the benefits of a Partnership

(C) A Minor cannot plead minority

(D) A Minor can be held liable in tort.

297. Which of the following person, has capacity to contract?

(A) Minor

(B) A person of unsound Mind

(C) Major

(D) A person specifically disqualified by Law

298. Where the guardians are appointed by court, a person becomes major on attaining the age of–

(A) 18 years

(B) 19 years

(C) 20 years

(D) 21 years

299. For the purposes of entering into a contract, a minor is a person, who has not completed the age of—

(A) 16 years

(B) 18 years

(C) 20 years

(D) 21 years

300. Which of the following persons do not fall under the category of persons of unsound mind?

(A) Idiot

(B) Lunatics

(C) Drunken persons

(D) Alien

301. A minor's liability for 'necessaries' supplied to him arises after he attains majority age.

(A) True

(B) False

302. *Ordinarily*, a minor's agreement, in which he is promisor, is—

(A) Void-ab-initio

(B) Voidable.

(C) Valid.

(D) Unlawful.

303. Which of the following statement is true?

(A) A contract with a minor is voidable at the option of the minor.

(B) An agreement with a minor can be ratified after he attains majority.

(C) A person who is usually of an unsound mind cannot enter into contract even when he is of a sound mind.

(D) A person who is usually of a sound mind cannot enter into contract when he is of unsound mind.

304. A contract with the minor, which is beneficial for him, is—

(A) void-*ab-initio*.

(B) voidable.

(C) valid.

(D) illegal.

305. The following persons can enter into contracts as per the provisions of the Indian Contract Act, 1872—

(A) Alien Enemy

(B) Foreign Sovereigns or representatives of a foreign state

(C) Insolvents and convicts

(D) None of the above

306. Agreement entered into by a minor is—

(A) Void as against the minor.

(B) Illegal.

(C) Unlawful.

(D) Unenforceable by the minor.

307. Which of the following is not correct?

(A) Minor can always plead minority.

(B) Minor is liable for necessaries supplied to him.

(C) Minor is a person who has not completed 18 years of age.

(D) Minor can be a beneficiary.

308. As per section 11 of the Indian Contract Act, 1872, every person is competent to contract provided he—

(A) Is of the age of majority according to the law to which he is subject.

(B) Is of sound mind.

(C) Is not disqualified from contracting by any law to which he is subject.

(D) All of the above.

309. Which of the following statements is not true about minor's position in a firm?

(A) He cannot become a partner in an existing firm.

(B) He can become a partner in an existing firm.

(C) He can be admitted only to the benefits of any existing firm a major.

(D) He can become partner on becoming a major.

310. An agreement is not said to be a contract when it is entered into by—

(A) Minor.

(B) a person of unsound mind.

(C) foreign enemy.

(D) all of these

311. M, a minor aged 17, broke his right arm in a cricket match. He engaged a physician to set it. Does the physician have a valid claim for his services. Choose the best alternative.

(A) The physician cannot claim for his services due to contract with a minor which is void.

(B) The physician has a valid claim for his services which are included in the "necessaries".

(C) The physician has no claim for one minor's "necessaries" and the minor will be personally liable.

(D) The physician can claim for his services from the minor's parents.

312. Can a person who is usually of unsound, but occasionally of sound mind, make a contract?

(A) Yes, he can always make a contract.

(B) Yes, but only when he is of sound mind.

(C) No, he cannot make a contract.

(D) None of these

313. A contract with a minor is voidable at the option of the minor.

(A) True

(B) False

314. Can a minor, though incompetent to contract, receive a benefit arising thereunder ?

(A) Yes

(B) No

315. A, a minor, lent Rs. 100 to B at the market rate of interest on the basis of a promissory note. A year thereafter, when he had attained majority, he filed a suit against B for the recovery of the amount thereon. B contended that since A was a minor at the time of agreement, so the agreement was void and so not enforceable by law. Therefore, B is not liable to return the money. Will the contention of Mr. B be upheld?

(A) Yes

(B) No

316. A grocer supplied monthly rations for five months to B, who was aged 17 years and 5 months. B having failed to pay the bills for the supplies, the grocer decided to sue his estate for the realisation of his dues. Would he succeed ?

(A) Yes

(B) No, as B is minor

(C) No, as there is absence of free consent.

(D) Both (B) and (C)

317. Who among the following is not disqualified by law to enter into a contract?

(1) A major person.

(2) A lunatic.

(3) An Insolvent person.

(4) Diplomatic staff of foreign states.

(A) 1 & 2

(B) 2 & 3

(C) 3 & 4

(D) 1 & 4

318. Which of the following is/are not competent to enter into a contract?

(1) A person of the age of majority

(2) A minor

(3) A person who is not capable of understanding the contract at the time of its making.

(4) A lunatic during lucid intervals (period of soundness)

(A) 1 & 2

(B) 2 & 3

(C) 3 & 4

(D) 1 & 4

319. Can a minor be held personally liable for the 'necessaries' supplied to him?

(A) Yes, u/s 68 minor is personally liable.

(B) Yes, u/s 68, a minor's guardians are personally liable.

(C) No, u/s 68, only the minor's property is liable.

(D) Both (B) and (C)

320. Which of the following persons are not competent to contract?

(A) Minors

(B) Persons of unsound mind

(C) Persons disqualified by law

(D) All of these

321. Ankit, aged 17 years, falsely representing himself to be of 22 years, enters into an agreement to sell his property to Praveen and receives from him a sum of Rs. 10,00,000 in advance. Out of this sum, Ankit buys an imported car worth Rs. 5,50,000 and spends the rest on a pleasure trip to France. After Ankit attained majority, Praveen sues him for the conveyance of the property or, in the alternative, for the refund of Rs. 10,00,000 and damages. The agreement between Ankit and Praveen is–

(A) Void-*ab-initio*, as it is a contract with a minor.

(B) Voidable, at the option of Praveen.

(C) Would be valid, if Ankit ratifies the agreement on attainting the age of majority.

(D) Valid as Ankit has sold his own property for personal use.

322. Which of these is a not a "necessary" for a minor?

(A) Lending money to a Minor for defending a suit on his behalf in which his property is in jeopardy.

(B) Lending money to a Minor for defending him in a necessary prosecution.

(C) Lending money to a minor for paying his creditors in respect of horse racing and betting debts.

(D) Lending money to a minor for saving his property from sale in execution of a decree.

323. A minor's agreement is void. This was held in the case of—

(A) Mohiri Bibee Vs. Dharmadas Ghosh

(B) Nihal Chand Vs. Jan Mohamed Khan

(C) Suraj Narain Vs. Sukhu Aheer

(D) Chinnaiya Vs. Ramaiya.

324. K gave a loan to the guardian of a minor to enable him to celebrate the minor's marriage in contravention of the Child Marriage Restraint Act. The agreement is—

(A) valid

(B) valid, if ratified by the minor

(C) not enforceable

(D) voidable

325. A supplies B, a lunatic, with necessaries suitable to his condition in life. A is—

(A) Not entitled to be reimbursed from B's property.

(B) Entitled to be reimbursed from B's property.

(C) Personally liable.

(D) Jointly and Severally liable.

326. Minors entering into contracts of apprenticeship, or for training or instruction in a special art, education, etc. are permissible, since—

(A) all contacts by a Minor are valid.

(B) such contracts generate benefits to the Minor

(C) such contracts are outside the purview of the Indian Contract Act.

(D) all of the above

327. Claim for necessaries supplied to a person incompetent to contract, from the property of such person is enshrined in ______ of the Indian Contract Act, 1872.

(A) Section 68

(B) Section 69

(C) Section 70

(D) Section 71

328. A is a minor, B approaches A for a loan on the basis of a mortgage of the house owned by B. Hence, A advances the money and B executed a mortgage in favour of A, a minor. In these circumstances —

(A) The mortgage is not enforceable by A, because he is a minor.

(B) The mortgage is enforceable but only when he attains majority.

(C) The mortgage is enforceable by A even though he is a Minor.

(D) There is no mortgage at all.

329. If a person, incapable of entering into a contract, or anyone whom he is legally bound to support, is supplied by another person, with necessaries suited to his condition in life, the person who has furnished such supplies is entitled to be reimbursed from the property of such incapable person.

(A) True

(B) Partly True

(C) False

(D) None of the above

330. Agreement entered into with a Minor is an example of —

(A) Valid agreement.

(B) Voidable agreement.

(C) Void agreement.

(D) Illegal agreement.

331. Two persons have the capacity to contract—

(A) If both are not of unsound mind.

(B) If none is disqualified from contracting by any law to which he is subject.

(C) If both have attained the age of majority.

(D) All of the above

332. An agreement made with an alien enemy is—

(A) unlawful on the ground of public policy.

(B) unlawful because it becomes difficult to be performed.

(C) valid.

(D) voidable.

333. A person is disqualified to enter into a Contract, if he is—

(A) An alien enemy.

(B) An insolvent.

(C) A convict undergoing imprisonment.

(D) All of the above

334. Foreign sovereigns, their diplomatic staff and representatives of Foreign States have special privilege that they cannot be sued upon by others without the special permission of the Central Government. Contracts with such privileged persons are—

(A) voidable at the option of either party.

(B) valid.

(C) void.

(D) illegal.

335. An insolvent person is incapacitated to contract. Only the official receiver can enter into contracts on behalf of the Insolvent.

(A) True

(B) Partly true

(C) False

(D) None of the above

336. A person who is not an a Indian citizen is an alien. Contracts with an alien friend, subject to certain restrictions are—

(A) Void

(B) Unenforceable

(C) Valid

(D) Invalid

337. A convict undergoing imprisonment can enter into contracts only when his term is complete.

(A) True

(B) Partly true

(C) False

(D) None of the above

338. A Minor can be an agent and bind his Principal/ parents or guardian acting in the capacity of Principal.

(A) True

(B) Partly true

(C) False

(D) None of the above

339. Capacity to contract has been defined in—

(A) Section 10

(B) Section 11

(C) Section 12

(D) Section 25

340. On attaining the age of majority, a minor's agreement—

(A) is void.

(B) cannot be ratified.

(C) becomes void.

(D) becomes valid.

341. X supports Y's infant son. Y promises to pay X's expenses. The contract is—

(A) Void.

(B) Illegal.

(C) Valid.

(D) Unenforceable.

342. Which of the following statements are correct? A minor cannot—

(A) become a Partner.

(B) be liable even in case of fraudulent representation of age.

(C) ask for specific performance of a contract.

(D) all of the above

343. Where a Minor has received any benefit under a contract, he—

(A) can be asked to refund the same.

(B) cannot be asked to refund the same.

(C) has to refund the benefit after attaining majority.

(D) can ask for similar benefits after attaining majority.

344. A Minor cannot even enter into contracts of apprenticeship, service, education or instruction that are beneficial to him.

(A) True

(B) Partly True

(C) False

(D) None of the above

345. A minor speculated in the stock exchange and became liable to Stock Brokers for Rs. 1 Lakh. subsequent to attaining majority, he gave two bills of exchange for Rs. 45,000 each in satisfaction of the original debt.

(A) Minor is liable for Rs. 1 lakh.

(B) Minor is liable for Rs. 90,000.

(C) Minor is liable for Rs. 10,000.

(D) Minor is not liable for any amount.

346. M, a minor makes a promissory note in favour of D. On attaining majority, M makes out a fresh promissory note (P/N) in lieu of the old one. In this case—

(A) The original P/N is invalid but the fresh P/N is valid.

(B) The original P/N is valid but the fresh P/N is invalid.

(C) Both the original and the fresh P/N are valid.

(D) Both the original and the fresh P/N are invalid.

347. S, a minor, entered into a contract for borrowing a sum of Rs. 20,000 out of which the lender paid him a sum of Rs. 8,000. D executed a mortgage of property in favour of the lender. The mortgage is—

(A) valid to the extent of Rs. 8,000 only.

(B) valid to the extent of Rs. 20,000.

(C) totally invalid.

(D) valid on attaining majority.

348. Parents or guardian shall ______ for breach of contract by minor.

(A) be held liable

(B) not be held liable

(C) be imprisoned

(D) not be questioned

349. Any money advanced to a minor under a mortgage during his minority cannot be recovered.

(A) True

(B) Partly true

(C) False

(D) None of the above

350. A Minor's liability '*for necessaries*' supplied to him–

(A) Arises after he attains majority age.

(B) Is against only minor's property.

(C) Does not arise at all.

(D) Arises if minor gives a promise for it.

351. A Corporation cannot enter into Contracts that are—

(A) *ultra vires* (beyond powers of) its Memorandum of Association.

(B) strictly of a personal nature as it is only an artificial person.

(C) either (A) or (B)

(D) neither (A) nor (B)

352. Where the agent has acted within his capacity and in the name of Principal, the Principal can sue any third party with whom the agent has contracted, even if there is no direct contract between the Principal and such Third Party.

(A) True

(B) Partly True

(C) False

(D) None of the above

☞ Free Consent

353. By consent, we mean—

(A) Both parties must agree on the same thing in the same sense.

(B) Consent must not be influenced by coercion, fraud, mistake, misrepresentation, undue influence.

(C) Lawful consideration.

(D) Lawful Object.

354. A applies to a banker for a loan at a time when there is stringency in the money market. The banker declines to make the loan, except at an unusually high rate of interest. A accepts the loan on these terms. Is the contract induced by undue influence?

(A) Yes

(B) No

355. Which of the following statements are correct?

(A) In the case of fraud, the person making the representation believes it to be true.

(B) In the case of misrepresentation, the maker does not believe it to be true.

(C) Fraud does not afford a ground for bringing an action in tort for damages; whereas misrepresentation does.

(D) In the case of misrepresentation, the fact the plaintiff had means of discovering the truth by exercising ordinary diligence can be a good defence against the repudiation of the contract, but such defence cannot be set up in the case of fraud.

356. The threat to commit suicide amounts to—

(A) Coercion.

(B) Undue Influence.

(C) Misrepresentation.

(D) Fraud.

357. When the consent of a party is not free, the contract is—

(A) Void.

(B) Voidable.

(C) Valid.

(D) Illegal.

358. When the consent of a party is obtained by coercion, undue influence, fraud or misrepresentation, the contract is—

(A) void

(B) voidable

(C) valid

(D) illegal

359. Which of the following elements does not affect the free consent of the parties?

(A) Coercion

(B) Fraud

(C) Incompetence

(D) Undue influence

360. A advanced money to his son B during his minority. Upon B's coming of age of majority, A obtains by use of his parental influence, a bond from B, for a greater amount than the sum due in respect of the advance. Can A enforce the loan ?

(A) Yes, because all essentials of a valid contract are satisfied.

(B) Yes, because minor can ratify the agreement made by him during the age of minority.

(C) No, because minor cannot ratify the agreement made by him during the age of minority.

(D) Both (A) and (B)

361. A, enfeebled by disease or age, is induced by B, his attendant, to agree to pay B an unreasonable sum for his professional services. Can B enforce the agreement ?

(A) Yes, due to the presence of consideration

(B) No, due to coercion

(C) No, due to undue influence

(D) None of the above

362. Which of the following statement is true?

(A) A threat to commit suicide does not amount to coercion.

(B) Undue influence involves use of physical pressure.

(C) Ignorance of law is no excuse.

(D) Silence always amounts to fraud.

363. A, intending to deceive B, falsely represents that 750 tons of sugar is produced per annum at the factory of A and thereby induces B to buy the factory. The contract is avoidable at the option of—

(A) B

(B) A

(C) Congruence of A & B

(D) Either party cannot avoid the contract

364. Moral pressure is involved in the case of—

(A) Coercion.

(B) Undue Influence.

(C) Misrepresentation.

(D) Fraud.

365. A wrong representation when made without any intention to deceive the other party amounts to—

(A) Coercion.

(B) Undue influence.

(C) Misrepresentation.

(D) Fraud.

366. A agrees to sell his car worth Rs. 1,00,000 to B for Rs. 20,000 only, and A's consent was obtained by coercion. Here, the agreement is—

(A) void.

(B) valid.

(C) voidable.

(D) unlawful.

367. Where one party is in a position to dominate the will of another and uses his superior position to obtain the consent of a weaker party, the consent is said to be obtained by

(A) coercion

(B) undue influence

(C) fraud

(D) misrepresentation

368. Which of the following acts does not fall under the categories of fraud?

(A) Intentional false statement of facts

(B) Active concealment of facts

(C) Innocent false statement

(D) Promise made without intention to perform

369. Consent is not said to be free, when it is caused by—

(A) Coercion.

(B) Undue Influence.

(C) Fraud.

(D) All of these

370. An agreement made with free consent to which the consideration is lawful, but inadequate, is—

(A) void.

(B) valid.

(C) voidable.

(D) unlawful.

371. Where the consent of a party is obtained by misrepresentation, the contract is—

(A) valid.

(B) void.

(C) voidable.

(D) illegal.

372. As per Sec. 20, the contract is void on account of bilateral mistake of fact. But as per section 22, if there is a mistake of only one party, then the contract is—

(A) void.

(B) valid.

(C) voidable.

(D) illegal.

373. A sells to B a horse which A knows to be unsound. B is A's daughter. Choose the best alternative—

(A) The relation between A and B would make it A's duty to tell B if the horse is unsound.

(B) If A is silent, silence will not be equivalent to speech.

(C) Here it is not duty of A to tell the horse's defect.

(D) A is not bound to tell the defect as the rule of *caveat emptor* applies.

374. A mistake as to a law not in force in India has the same effect as–

(A) mistake of fact.

(B) mistake of Indian law.

(C) fraud.

(D) misrepresentation.

375. A person, who has been induced to enter into a contract by misrepresentation, has the following remedies–

(A) Affirm the contract and insist on the misrepresentation being made good, if possible.

(B) Rescind the contract.

(C) Rely upon the misrepresentation as a defense to an action on the contract.

(D) All of the above

376. According to Sec. 14 of the Indian Contract Act, 1872, consent is said to be free when it is not caused by—

(A) Misrepresentation.

(B) Undue Influence.

(C) Coercion.

(D) All of the above

377. The distinction between fraud and misrepresentation are the following—

(A) Misrepresentation is innocent, whereas fraud is deliberate or willful.

(B) In misrepresentation, the person making the suggestion believes it to be true. While in case of a fraud, he does not believe it to be true.

(C) In misrepresentation, there can be no suit for damages, whereas in fraud there can be a suit for damages.

(D) All of the above

378. Coercion involves–

(A) Physical Force or Threat.

(B) Mental Pressure.

(C) Both (A) and (B)

(D) None of the Above

379. Misrepresentation means and includes–

(A) The positive assertion, in a manner not warranted by the information of the person making it, of that which is not true, though he believes it to be true.

(B) Any breach of duty, which, without an intention to deceive, gains an advantage to the person committing it, or any one claiming under him, by misleading another to his prejudice or to the prejudice of any one claiming under him.

(C) Causing, however innocently, a party to an agreement to make a mistake as to the substance of the thing which is the subject of the agreement.

(D) All of the above

380. A had offered B, a price of Rs. 10,00,000 for B's flat. But B was not ready to sell the flat at all. A says to B that "I shall kill you if you don't agree to sell me your house for Rs. 10,00,000". B thereafter did all that was the desire of A in order to save his life. What is immediate answer?

(A) A can enforce the contract.

(B) B can enforce the contract.

(C) A has applied coercion.

(D) The contract is unenforceable.

381. Which of the following is not correct–

(A) Coercion involves physical force.

(B) Undue influence involves physical force.

(C) Coercion need not be directed at the promisor.

(D) Undue influence is always exercised between the parties to the contract.

382. Which of the following agreements is void?

(A) Agreement made under the unilateral mistake of fact.

(B) Agreements made under the bilateral mistake of fact.

(C) Agreement made under the influence of fraud.

(D) Contingent agreement.

383. 'A', a man enfeebled by disease is induced by B's influence over him as his medical attendant, to agree to pay 'B' an unreasonable sum for his services. It is the case of—

(A) Undue Influence.

(B) Coercion.

(C) Fraud.

(D) Mistake.

384. Which of example is not the case of Undue influence, where one party is in a position to influence the will of other party?

(A) Agreement between one trader with other trader

(B) Doctor and patient

(C) Father with his son

(D) Employer and his employee

385. Where a party to a contract perpetrates fraud or misrepresentation, but the other party is not, in fact, misled by such fraud or misrepresentation, the contract cannot be avoided by the later.

(A) True.

(B) False.

(C) Partly yes

(D) None of the above.

386. Which of the following is a requirement for misrepresentation to exist?

(1) Misrepresentation should relate to a material fact.

(2) the person making a misrepresentation should believe it to be true

(3) It must be made with an intention to deceive the other party

(4) The person making a misrepresentation should not believe it to be true

(A) 1 & 2

(B) 2 & 3

(C) 3 & 4

(D) 1 & 4

387. A and B are friends. B treats A, during A's illness. B does not accept payment from A for the treatment and A promises B's son X to pay him Rs. 1,000. A, being in poor circumstances, is unable to pay. X sues A for the money. Can X recover?"

(A) Yes

(B) No

388. A by misrepresentation, leads B erroneously to believe that 50,000 units of a product are made annually at A's factory. B examines the accounts of the factory, which shows that only 10,000 units have been made. *After this*, B buys the factory. Can the contract be avoided on the ground of misrepresentation/fraud ?

(A) Yes

(B) No

(C) Partly Yes

(D) None of above

389. A's son had forged B's name to a promissory note. B under threat of prosecuting A's son, obtains a bond from A for the amount of the forged note. B sues on bond. Will he succeed?

(A) Yes

(B) No

390. When the consent of a party is obtained by fraud, the contract is illegal.

(A) True.

(B) False.

391. Where the consent of both the parties is given by mistake, the contract is—

(A) Void-*ab-initio*.

(B) Valid.

(C) Voidable.

(D) Illegal.

392. A contract made by mistake about the Indian Law, is—

(A) void.

(B) valid.

(C) voidable.

(D) illegal.

393. A contract made by mistake about some foreign law, is—

(A) void.

(B) valid.

(C) voidable.

(D) illegal.

394. A threatens to kill B, if he does not agree to sell his scooter to him for Rs. 1,000 only. Here, B's consent is obtained by—

(A) undue influence.

(B) fraud.

(C) coercion.

(D) none of these

395. When the consent to an agreement is obtained by coercion, the agreement is voidable at the option of—

(A) Either party to the agreement.

(B) A party, whose consent was so obtained.

(C) A party, who obtained the consent.

(D) None of these

396. A contracts with B to buy a necklace, believing it is made of pearls, whereas in fact it is made of imitation pearls of no value. B knows that A is mistaken and takes no steps to correct the error. Now A wants to cancel the contract on the basis of fraud. Which of the following statement is correct?

(A) A can cancel the contract alleging fraud.

(B) A cannot cancel the contract.

(C) A can cancel the contract alleging undue influence.

(D) A can claim damages.

397. 'Threat to commit suicide' amounts to—

(1) Coercion.

(2) Offence under the Indian Penal Code.

(3) Undue Influence.

(4) Fraud.

(A) 1 & 2

(B) 2 & 3

(C) 3 & 4

(D) 1 & 4

398. Contract caused by which of the following is Voidable—

(1) Fraud.

(2) Mis-representation.

(3) Coercion.

(4) Bilateral Mistake.

(A) 1, 2, 3

(B) 2, 3, 4

(C) 1, 2, 4

(D) 1, 2, 3, 4

399. Mere expression of opinion constitutes misrepresentation. It need not relate to a material fact.

(A) True

(B) Partly true

(C) False

(D) None of the above.

400. Misrepresentation results not only from misstatement of facts, but also from suppression of material facts.

(A) True

(B) Partly True

(C) False

(D) None of the above

401. Which of the following are essential features of Misrepresentation?

(A) Representation should be of a material fact.

(B) It must be made with an intention that the other partly should act upon it.

(C) Representation must be wrong, but the person making it believed it to be true.

(D) All the above

402. Misrepresentation means—

(A) Causing advantage to the doer.

(B) Any breach of duty without an intent to deceive.

(C) Misleading another to his prejudice.

(D) Causing advantage to a person not a party to the contract.

403. Which of these are features of Misrepresentation, not treated as Fraud?

(A) Innocent and Unintentional

(B) Believes the representation to be true

(C) No intention to deceive or defraud the other party

(D) All of the above

404. The Positive assertion of such fact, which is not true, though he believes it to be true, made in a manner not warranted by the information of the person making it, constitutes —

(A) Representation.

(B) Misrepresentation.

(C) Fraud.

(D) Mistake.

405. The _______of such fact, which is not true, though he believes it to be true, made in a manner not warranted by the information of the person making it, constitutes misrepresentation.

(A) Suppression

(B) Negative Assertion

(C) Positive Assertion

(D) Fabrication

406. Causing innocently, the other party to make mistake as to the substance of the subject matter of the agreement, is covered under—

(A) Representation.

(B) Mistake.

(C) Fraud.

(D) Misrepresentation.

407. Any Breach of Duty made without an intent to deceive constitutes —

(A) Suppression of Facts.

(B) Breach of Contract.

(C) Misrepresentation.

(D) Fraud.

408. A woman, falsely misrepresenting herself to be wife of a well known Baron obtained two pearl necklaces from a Firm of jewellers on the pretext of showing them to her husband before buying. She pledged them with a broker who took them in good faith. In this case, —

(A) There was no contract between jeweller and impersonating woman.

(B) Sale made by Jeweller to the woman is valid.

(C) Pledge made by the woman to the Broker is valid.

(D) Jeweller has to bear the risk of bad debts.

409. In which of the following cases, the contract cannot be avoided on grounds of misrepresentation?

(A) Where the consent was caused by misrepresentation, if the party whose consent was so caused, had the means to discover the truth with ordinary diligence.

(B) Where a party whose consent was obtained by misrepresentation, cannot be put in a position, in which he would have been if the representations had been true.

(C) Misrepresentation which did not cause the consent of the party to the Agreement.

(D) All of the above

410. A Company's prospectus stated that it had the right to use steam power to run its tramways provided the Government authority's consent was obtained. This statement was made on the belief that the Government would grant the consent. But permission was not granted and the Company had to be wound up. In this case, the Directors are guilty of—

(A) Misrepresentation.

(B) Fraud.

(C) Undue Influence.

(D) Mistake.

411. In case of Misrepresentation, the aggrieved party can avoid the contract even if he had the means of discovering the truth with ordinary diligence.

(A) True

(B) Partly True

(C) False
(D) None of the above.

412. Except where the silence amounts to fraud, the contract is voidable even if the party defrauded had the means of discovering the truth with ordinary diligence.
(A) True
(B) Partly True
(C) False
(D) None of the above

413. A person is deemed to be in a position to dominate the will of another if—
(A) He holds a real or apparent authority over the other.
(B) He stands in a fiduciary relation to the other.
(C) He makes a contract with a person whose mental capacity is temporarily or permanently affected by reason of age, illness or mental or bodily distress.
(D) All of the above

414. P offers, to sell a painting to K which P knows is the copy of a well known masterpiece. K thinking that the painting is original decides to buy it at a very high price. Is this a valid contract?
(A) No, P is guilty of misrepresentation.
(B) No, P is guilty of fraud.
(C) Yes, K has an erroneous belief as to the value of the painting.
(D) Yes, price is not a criteria for setting aside the contract.

415. Section ______ of the Indian Contract Act deals with "Bilateral Mistake".
(A) Section 19
(B) Section 20
(C) Section 21
(D) Section 22

416. Bilateral Mistake may relate to —
(A) Subject Matter.
(B) Possibility of performance.
(C) Neither (A) nor (B).
(D) Both (A) and (B).

417. An agreement is void when there is—
(A) mistake of fact by one party.
(B) mistake of fact by both the parties.
(C) mistake of foreign law.
(D) all the above

418. A sells a painting to B saying that is an original work of Picasso. Unknown to both the parties, the original painting was stolen and its copy was placed there. The contract is void on grounds of—
(A) bilateral mistake as to the quality of the subject-matter.
(B) unilateral mistake as to the quality of the subject-matter.
(C) mistake as to law.
(D) mistake as to identity of art items.

419. Mere silence is not fraud, *unless*—
(A) the silence is deceptive.
(B) there is a change in the circumstances to be brought to the notice of other party.
(C) there is a duty to speak.
(D) all the above

420. A person to whom money has been paid, or anything delivered by mistake or under coercion, must repay or return it.
(A) True
(B) Partly True
(C) False
(D) None of the above

421. To be covered under misrepresentation, statement must be wrong, but the person making it believed it to be true.
(A) True
(B) Partly True
(C) False
(D) None of the above.

422. An act forbidden by law means—
(A) it is punishable by the Criminal Law of the land.
(B) it is prohibited by a Special legislation.
(C) either (A) or (B).
(D) neither (A) nor (B).

423. A, B & C enter into an agreement for sharing the gains acquired by fraud. This agreement is—
(A) contingent.
(B) valid.
(C) void.
(D) voidable.

424. The maxim "*Ignorantia Juris non exusat*" stands for—
(A) Law will not punish ignorant people.
(B) Law will punish illiterate people.
(C) Ignorant people can excuse law.
(D) Ignorance of law of land is no excuse.

425. The validity of contract is not affected by —
(A) Mistake of fact.
(B) Mistake of law.
(C) Misappropriation.
(D) Fraud.

426. Mistake as to law of the land will not affect the validity of the contract.

(A) True

(B) Partly true

(C) False

(D) None of the above

427. When there is a mistake as to law of the land, the contract is—

(A) Voidable.

(B) Not Voidable.

(C) Unlawful.

(D) Unenforceable.

428. A Contract where there is a mistake as to law of the land is voidable, when one party was induced by another.

(A) True

(B) Partly True

(C) False

(D) None of the above

429. Mistake as to Foreign Law is treated in the same manner as—

(A) Mistake of Indian Law.

(B) Mistake of Fact.

(C) Misrepresentation.

(D) Fraud.

430. E, an agent for a landlord G, agrees for money, without G's knowledge, to obtain a lease of land belonging to G for his friend F. The agreement between E and F is—

(A) legal.

(B) void.

(C) voidable.

(D) valid.

431. Where misrepresentation is intentional, deliberate and willful, with an intent to deceive the other party, such Misrepresentation = Fraud.

(A) True

(B) Partly True

(C) False

(D) None of the above

432. In case of payment of amount under mistake, the period of limitation starts from—

(A) date of payment under mistake.

(B) date the mistake is or could have been discovered.

(C) (A) or (B) whichever is earlier.

(D) (A) or (B) whichever is later.

433. If a disciple agrees to gift to his Spiritual Guru, his entire property in return for attainment of salvation, the agreement can be set aside on grounds of—

(A) Mistake.

(B) Undue influence.

(C) Fraud.

(D) Misrepresentation.

434. P wrote to H inquiring price of rifles suggesting that he might buy as many as 50. On receipt of information, he telegraphed, "Send three rifles". Due to telegraphic mistake, message was transmitted as "Send the rifles". H despatched 50 rifles. Though the agreement is void on account of mistake, P could be held liable to pay for three rifles on the basis of an implied contact.

(A) True

(B) Partly true

(C) False

(D) None of the above

435. To avoid a contract under the claim of "Coercion", the Indian Penal Code should be in force where the coercion is employed.

(A) True

(B) Partly true

(C) False

(D) None of the above

436. Coercion is—

(A) the committing or threatening to commit any act forbidden by IPC.

(B) the unlawful detaining or threatening to detain, any property, to the prejudice of any person whatever.

(C) either (A) or (B)

(D) neither (A) nor (B)

437. A person is deemed to be in a position to dominate the will of another by undue influence if the mental capacity is affected temporarily or permanently by reason of—

(A) age.

(B) illness.

(C) mental or bodily distress.

(D) all of the above

438. Which of these does not constitute Fraud?

(A) Suggestion as a Fact, of something which is not true, by a person who does not believe it to be true.

(B) Active concealment of a Fact by one having knowledge or belief of the fact.

(C) Innocent statement, honestly believing the same to be true.

(D) Promise made without any intention of performing it.

439. _____ is the term used in English Law to denote actual or threatened violence over the person or another including his wife, parent or child, with a view to obtain his consent to an agreement.

(A) Undue Influence
(B) Coercion
(C) Duress
(D) Misrepresentation

440. Where consent is obtained by fraud, the Defrauded party has the following remedies–
(A) He can rescind the contract within a reasonable time.
(B) He can insist on the performance of the contract upon a condition that he shall be put on the position in which he would have been if the representations made had been true.
(C) He can sue for damages.
(D) All of the above

441. Where consent is caused by Fraud or Misrepresentation, the aggrieved party can sue for damages.
(A) True
(B) Partly True
(C) False
(D) None of the above

442. Where the consent was caused by silence amounting to fraud, the contract is voidable, even if the party whose consent was so caused, had the means to discover the truth with ordinary diligence.
(A) True
(B) Partly true
(C) False
(D) None of the above

443. Mere silence as to facts, likely to affect the willingness of a person to enter into a contract is not fraud.
(A) True
(B) Partly true
(C) False
(D) None of the above

444. C wrote to W, offering to sell certain property for Rs. 50 Lakhs. The same had been already offered for Rs. 75 Lakhs which W had refused. W knowing well that the offer is a mistake for Rs. 50 Lakhs, immediately accepted it. The contract—
(A) is valid due to unilateral mistake.
(B) is unlawful due to price reduction.
(C) is not enforceable as it was offered by mistake.
(D) is not affected in any manner.

445. A being indebted to B, the money-lender of his village, contracts, a fresh loan on terms which appear to be unconscionable. Will it be presumed that the contract was induced by undue influence?
(A) Yes
(B) No
(C) Partly yes
(D) None of the above

446. The aggrieved party can rescind the contract on account of fraud. Can he also claim damages from the other party?
(A) Yes
(B) No
(C) Not possible to answer with the available information.
(D) The Indian Contract Act is silent on this issue.

447. Which of these constitute essential elements of Fraud?
(A) Representation should relate to a material fact, which exists or had existed in the past.
(B) Representation should be false, and should be made before conclusion of contract.
(C) The intention must be to induce the other party to act upon it.
(D) All of the above

448. A mere 'attempt to deceit' by one party —
(A) is not fraud unless the other party is actually deceived.
(B) is fraud whether the other party has been deceived or not.
(C) amounts to misrepresentation.
(D) amounts to undue influence.

449. In the event of fraud, the aggrieved party can set aside the contract but cannot recover damages.
(A) True
(B) Partly True
(C) False
(D) None of the above

450. Where consent is obtained by fraud, the defrauded party can insist on the performance of the contract upon a condition that he shall be put on the position in which he would have been if the representations made had been true.
(A) True
(B) Partly true
(C) False
(D) None of the above

451. In which of the following cases, the contract cannot be avoided on grounds of fraud?
(A) Where a party enters into a contract in ignorance of fraud.
(B) Where a party whose consent was obtained by fraud, cannot be put in a position, in which he would have been if the representation had been true.

(C) Where interests of third parties intervene, before the contract is avoided.

(D) All of the above

452. In which of the following cases, the contract cannot be avoided on grounds of fraud?

(A) A fraud which did not cause the consent of the party to the agreement.

(B) Where the consent was caused by silence amounting to fraud, if the party whose consent was so caused, had the means to discover the truth with ordinary diligence.

(C) Where a party enters into a contract in ignorance of fraud.

(D) All of the above

453. Where the consent was caused by silence amounting to fraud, the contract is __, if the party whose consent was so caused, had the means to discover the truth with ordinary diligence.

(A) immoral

(B) not voidable

(C) voidable

(D) opposed to public policy

454. Having regard to the circumstances of the case, if it is the duty of the person keeping silence to speak, keeping silent constitutes—

(A) Fraud.

(B) Coercion.

(C) Mistake.

(D) Undue Influence.

455. Duty to speak exists in case—

(A) where the parties stand in a fiduciary relationship.

(B) where contract is a one of *ubberima fidei* (requiring utmost good faith).

(C) Both (A) and (B)

(D) Neither (A) nor (B)

456. In which of the following relationships, there is a "duty to speak", and silence constitutes fraud?

(A) Father and Son

(B) Guardian and ward

(C) Trustee and Beneficiary

(D) All of the above

457. In a contract of insurance, keeping silent as to material facts amounts to fraud.

(A) True

(B) Partly true

(C) False

(D) None of the above

458. Where A says to B, "if you do not deny it, I shall assume that the horse is sound", If the horse is unsound and A says nothing, there is—

(A) misrepresentation.

(B) no fraud.

(C) fraud.

(D) undue influence.

459. Where consent is obtained by misrepresentation, the aggrieved party has the following remedies—

(A) He can rescind the contract within a reasonable time.

(B) He can insist on the performance of the contract upon a condition that he shall be put on the position in which he would have been if the representations made had been true.

(C) Both (A) and (B)

(D) Neither (A) nor (B)

460. Where consent is obtained by misrepresentation, the aggrieved party cannot—

(A) rescind the contract.

(B) insist on the performance of the contract upon a condition that he shall be put on the position in which he would have been if the representations made had been true.

(C) sue for damages.

(D) All of the above

461. The contract cannot be rescinded on grounds of misrepresentation—

(A) If the party takes a benefit under the contract, or in some other way affirms the contract, after coming to know of such misrepresentation.

(B) Where restoration of the original position is not possible.

(C) Where a third party has acquired rights in the subject-matter for value and in good faith.

(D) All of the above

462. Shrikrishnan, a candidate for L.L.B. Part-I exam, who was short of attendance, did not mention that fact in the admission form for the examination of Kurukshetra University. Neither the Head of Law Department nor the University authorities made proper enquiries to discover the truth. It was held by the Supreme Court that—

(A) There was fraud by the candidate.

(B) There was no fraud by the candidate.

(C) There was misrepresentation by the candidate.

(D) There was mistake on the part of the candidate.

463. A and B, being traders enter upon a contract. A has private information of a change in prices, which would affect B's willingness to proceed with the contract. Is A bound to inform B ?

(A) Yes

(B) No

464. Where a party whose consent was obtained by fraud, cannot be put in a position, in which he would have been if the representations had been true, he cannot rescind the contract.

(A) True
(B) Partly True
(C) False
(D) None of the above

465. Where interests of third parties intervene, before the contract is avoided, such contract cannot be rescinded, even if the consent of the party is caused by fraud.

(A) True
(B) Partly True
(C) False
(D) None of the above

466. Non-disclosure of the existence of liabilities of the company in the prospectus amounts to fraud and anyone who purchased shares on the faith of such prospectus can avoid the contract, since the disclosure would have changed the impression and resultant decision of the investors.

(A) True
(B) Partly true
(C) False
(D) None of the above

467. X bought shares in a company on the faith of a prospectus that contained an untrue statement as to the directorship of J. X had never heard of J and hence such statement was immaterial from his view point. X claimed damages for fraud. His claim will be dismissed on the ground that—

(A) there was no fraud at all.
(B) fraud in company prospectus is not covered by Indian Contract Act.
(C) the untrue statement had not induced him to buy the shares.
(D) all of the above

468. A, intending to deceive B, falsely represents that five hundred mounds of Indigo are made annually at A's factory and, thereby induces B to buy the factory. The contract is—

(A) Voidable.
(B) Void.
(C) Unenforceable.
(D) Illegal.

469. Which of the following statements is false?

(A) A contract is not voidable if fraud or misrepresentation does not induce the other party to enter into a contract.
(B) A party cannot complain of fraudulent silence or misrepresentation if it had the means of discovering the truth with ordinary means.
(C) In case of fraud or misrepresentation, aggrieved party can either rescind or affirm the contract.
(D) A party which affirms the contract, can also change his option afterwards if it so decides.

470. The aggrieved party can rescind the contract on account of fraud. Can he also claim damages from the other party?

(A) Yes
(B) No

471. The aggrieved party can rescind the contract on account misrepresentation. Can he also claim damages from the other party?

(A) Yes
(B) No

472. X sold his business to Y, without disclosing this to his customers. M, an old customer sent an order for goods to X by name. Y, the new owner, executed the order. Is M bound to accept the goods?

(A) Yes
(B) No

473. X sells horse to Y knowing well that the horse is vicious. X does not disclose the nature of the horse to Y. Can X be made liable to Y for the transaction?

(A) Yes, on the ground of active concealment
(B) Yes, on the ground of breachment of condition as to quality and fitness.
(C) Yes, on the ground of breachment of condition as to Merchantability.
(D) No, due to the rule of *Caveat emptor*

474. In the case of Pardanashin woman, the burden of proof lies with —

(A) the Person who enter into a contract with her.
(B) pardanashin woman herself.
(C) the Beneficiary of the contract.
(D) the Judge.

475. Which of the following statements is false?

(A) A contract is not voidable, if Fraud or Misrepresentation does not induce the other party to enter into a contract.
(B) A party cannot complain of fraudulent silence or misrepresentation if he had the means of discovering the truth with ordinary means.
(C) In case of Fraud or Misrepresentation, aggrieved party can either rescind or affirm the contract.
(D) A party who affirms the contract, can also change his option afterwards if he so decides.

☞ Lawful object, Lawful Consideration and Agreement opposed to public Policy

476. An agreement in restraint of marriage is valid in case of the following persons.

(A) Minors

(B) Educated

(C) Married

(D) None of these

477. An agreement which prevents a person from carrying a lawful business, is—

(A) Valid.

(B) Void.

(C) Voidable.

(D) Contingent.

478. An agreement to do an illegal act e.g., to share the earnings of a smuggling business, is–

(A) Valid.

(B) Void.

(C) Voidable.

(D) Contingent.

479. Where an agreement consists of two parts one legal and the other illegal, and the legal part is separable from the illegal one, such legal part is—

(A) void.

(B) valid.

(C) voidable.

(D) illegal.

480. '*An agreement is void, if it is opposed to public policy.*' Which of the following is not covered by heads of public policy?

(A) Trading with an enemy.

(B) Trafficking in public offices.

(C) Marriage brokerage contracts.

(D) Contracts to do impossible acts.

481. An agreement the object or consideration of which is unlawful, is—

(A) Void.

(B) Valid.

(C) Voidable.

(D) Contingent.

482. G paid Rs.1,00,000 to H to influence the head of a Government organisation in order to provide him some employment. On his failure to provide the job, G sued H for recovery of the amount. Which of the following is correct?

(A) The contract is valid and G can recover the amount from H.

(B) The contract is void as it is opposed to public policy and G cannot recover.

(C) G can recover the amount with interest.

(D) G can recover the amount of Rs.1,00,000 and damages.

483. A is not a minor. A agrees to B for Rs. 1,00,000 that A will never marry. Promise of A is—

(A) Binding.

(B) Not binding.

(C) Enforceable.

(D) Illegal.

484. Champerty means—

(A) An agreement to trade with the enemy owing allegiance to a government at war with India.

(B) An agreement whereby a person promises to maintain a suit, by money or otherwise, in which he has no interest.

(C) An agreement whereby a person agrees to help another in a litigation in exchange for a share of the result of the litigation.

(D) An agreement to stifle criminal prosecutions tends to be a perversion or an abuse of justice.

485. Which of the following are covered under the head-'Agreement Opposed to Public Policy'?

(1) Trading with enemy

(2) Trafficking in public offices

(3) Marriage brokerage contracts

(4) Contract to do impossible acts

(A) 1, 2, 3

(B) 2, 3, 4

(C) 1, 2, 4

(D) 1, 2, 3, 4

486. Can a promise to pay money to a witness served with a notice be enforced?

(A) Yes

(B) No

487. A agrees to marry C's daughter in consideration of dowry to be paid by C. The contract is—

(A) Valid.

(B) Voidable.

(C) Opposed to public policy

(D) Both (B) and (C)

488. A agrees with B to discover a treasure by magic. Is the agreement valid ?

(A) Yes

(B) No

489. X and Y contract to marry each other at a particular date. But prior to the scheduled time X turns lunatic. Does the contract become void?

(A) Yes

(B) No

490. The consideration or object of an agreement is considered unlawful, if it is—

(A) Forbidden by law.

(B) Fraudulent.

(C) Immoral.

(D) All of these

491. An agreement in restraint of marriage, i.e. which prevents a person from marrying, is—

(A) Valid.

(B) Voidable.

(C) Void.

(D) Contingent.

492. An agreement, which prevents a person from carrying a lawful business, is—

(A) Valid.

(B) Void.

(C) Voidable.

(D) Contingent.

493. The consideration of an agreement is considered unlawful, if it is—

(1) Forbidden by law.

(2) Fraudulent.

(3) Immoral.

(4) Very expensive.

(A) 1, 2, 3

(B) 2, 3, 4

(C) 1, 2, 4

(D) 1, 2, 3, 4

494. An agreement in restraint of legal proceedings is void. It does not cover an agreement, which–

(A) Restricts absolutely the parties from enforcing their legal rights.

(B) Cuts short the period of limitation.

(C) Discharges a party from liability or extinguishes the rights of a party.

(D) Provides for a reference to arbitration instead of a court of law.

495. A father K having two minor sons, agreed to transfer their guardianship in favour of Mrs. A and was agreed not to revoke it. Subsequently, he filed a suit for recovery of boys and a declaration that he was the rightful guardian. In this case—

(A) K has the right to revoke his authority and get back the children.

(B) K does not have the right to revoke his authority and get back the children.

(C) K's agreement is void because both his sons were Minors.

(D) K's agreement is valid but not enforceable since consideration is not given.

496. Section ___of the Indian Contract Act deals with "Completely unlawful object/consideration".

(A) Section 22

(B) Section 23

(C) Section 24

(D) Section 25

497. Section ______ of the Indian Contract Act deals with "Partially unlawful object/consideration".

(A) Section 22

(B) Section 23

(C) Section 24

(D) Section 25

498. The consideration and object of an agreement is unlawful, if it —

(A) is forbidden by law or would defeat the provisions of any law.

(B) Involves or implies injury to the person or property of another.

(C) is fraudulent.

(D) all of the above.

499. The consideration and object of an agreement is unlawful, if it —

(A) is fraudulent.

(B) involves or implies injury to the person or property of another.

(C) is regarded by court as immoral or opposed to public policy.

(D) all of the above.

500. Amar promises to drop a prosecution which he has instituted against Balu for robbery. Balu promises to restore the value of things taken. The agreement is—

(A) contingent.

(B) valid.

(C) voidable.

(D) void.

501. Amar promises to drop the prosecution which he has instituted against Balu for robbery. Balu promises to restore the value of things taken. The agreement is void on grounds of —

(A) unlawful consideration.

(B) unlawful object.

(C) both (A) and (B)

(D) neither (A) nor (B)

502. If an act is not forbidden by law but performance of the act would defeat the provisions of law, an agreement to do such an act would be —

(A) legal.

(B) void.

(C) voidable.

(D) valid.

503. Sec. 27 of the Indian Contract Act declares an agreement in restraint of trade as —
(A) Voidable.
(B) Void.
(C) Uneforceable.
(D) None

504. B is a licensed manufacturer of permitted chemicals. A promises to B to supervise B's Business and combine it with the production of some contraband items together with the permitted items. B promises to pay A, a salary of Rs. 10,000 p.m. The agreement is—
(A) void as a whole.
(B) valid as a whole.
(C) valid to the extent of permitted chemicals and void for the balance contraband items.
(D) void to the extent of permitted chemicals and valid for the balance contraband items.

505. Where there are several distinct promises made for one and the same consideration, and some of these are illegal but distinct from the legal ones—
(A) all legal promises can be enforced.
(B) all legal or illegal promises can be enforced.
(C) all legal or illegal promises cannot be enforced.
(D) all illegal promises can be enforced.

506. If the illegal part cannot be severed from a legal part of a covenant, the contract is—
(A) void in respect of illegal part only.
(B) void in respect of the legal part only.
(C) altogether void.
(D) fully valid.

507. If it is possible to sever the legal and illegal parts of a covenant, whether the illegality be due to Statute or common law, the bad part alone may be rejected and good can be enforced.
(A) True
(B) Partly true
(C) False
(D) None of the above

508. Agreements, part of the consideration or object of which is unlawful and the unlawful object, cannot be separated from the lawful objects is—
(A) legal.
(B) void.
(C) voidable.
(D) valid.

509. An agreement is void if the court considers it as—
(A) immoral.
(B) opposed to public policy.
(C) either (A) or (B)
(D) neither (A) nor (B)

510. An Agreement is void, if—
(A) any part of a single consideration for one or more objects is unlawful.
(B) any one of or any part of any one of several considerations for a single object, is unlawful.
(C) either (A) or (B)
(D) neither (A) nor (B)

511. Freedom of trade and commerce is a fundamental right protected by Article 19(*g*) of the Indian Constitution.
(A) True
(B) Partly true
(C) False
(D) None of the above.

512. Freedom of Trade and Commerce is protected by the Constitution and cannot be restrained or restricted by agreements between individuals.
(A) True
(B) Partly true
(C) False
(D) None of the above

513. In Patna, 29 out of 30 manufacturers of combs agreed with R to supply combs only to him and not to any one else. Under the agreement R was free to reject the goods if he found no market for them. The agreement is—
(A) Valid.
(B) Void.
(C) Illegal.
(D) Voidable.

514. J, an employee of a Chennai-based company, agreed not to employ himself in a similar business within a distance of 800 miles from Chennai after leaving the Company's service. The agreement is void on grounds of being—
(A) an agreement without consideration.
(B) an uncertain agreement.
(C) an agreement in restraint of trade.
(D) all of the above

515. Consideration and objects are unlawful, when it is—
(A) fraudulent.
(B) forbidden by law or defeat any provision of any law.
(C) is immoral and against the public policy.
(D) all of the above

516. Under section 28 of the Indian Contract Act, an agreement not to pursue legal remedies but to refer the dispute to the arbitrator, is—

(A) valid.

(B) void.

(C) voidable.

(D) unenforceable.

517. M and N agree that —

(i) future disputes arising between them shall be referred to arbitration only.

(ii) they shall not question the amount rewarded under such arbitration.

In this agreement —

(A) (i) is valid but (ii) is invalid

(B) (i) is invalid but (ii) is valid

(C) (i) and (ii) are valid

(D) (i) and (ii) are invalid

518. Two or more parties may agree that—

(A) any dispute which may arise between them as regards any subject(s) shall be referred to arbitration.

(B) only the amount awarded in such arbitration shall be recoverable in respect of such dispute so referred.

(C) both (A) and (B)

(D) neither (A) nor (B)

519. An agreement between two parties to refer to arbitration, any question between them that has already arisen is—

(A) valid.

(B) void.

(C) voidable.

(D) unenforceable.

520. An agreement between two parties to refer to arbitration, any question between them that has already arisen is valid—

(A) if it can be inferred by the conduct of parties.

(B) if it is in writing.

(C) either (A) or (B)

(D) neither (A) nor (B)

521. An agreement to refer the dispute to the arbitrator, is valid in respect of disputes—

(A) already arisen.

(B) which may arise in future.

(C) neither (A) nor (B)

(D) both (A) & (B)

522. The seller of goodwill of a business may agree with the Buyer to refrain from carrying on a similar business, within specified local limits, so long as the buyer or any other person deriving title to goodwill from him carries on a like business.

(A) True

(B) Partly true

(C) False

(D) None of the above

523. Where a Seller of Goodwill of a business agrees not to carry on similar business, the limits and conditions imposed have to be ________, having regard to the nature of the business.

(A) considerable

(B) understandable

(C) reasonable

(D) consistent

524. S, a seller of imitation jewellery, sells his business to B and promises, not to carry on business in imitation jewellery and real jewellery. The agreement is—

(A) valid with regard to Imitation Jewellery; and void as regards real jewellery.

(B) void with regard to imitation jewellery; and valid as regards real jewellery.

(C) wholly void.

(D) fully valid.

525. Trade Combinations and associations formed among Traders to regulate the business or to fix prices are always void.

(A) True

(B) Partly True

(C) False

(D) None of the above.

526. In case of an illegal agreement, collateral transactions also become tainted with illegality and will be treated as illegal even though they would have been lawful by themselves.

(A) True

(B) Partly true

(C) False

(D) None of the above.

527. Where in alternative promises, one part is illegal, only the legal part can be enforced.

(A) True

(B) Partly true

(C) False

(D) None of the above

528. Which of these are opposed to public policy?

(A) Restraint of marriage

(B) Restraint of personal liberty

(C) Interference with course of Justice

(D) All of the above

529. Where an illegal part cannot be severed from the legal part of an agreement, the entire transaction is —

(A) valid.

(B) enforceable.

(C) voidable.

(D) illegal.

530. In respect of reciprocal promises, the agreement as to the illegal promise is —

(A) valid.

(B) enforceable.

(C) void.

(D) voidable.

531. Where in alternative promises, one part is illegal, only the legal part can be enforced.

(A) True

(B) Partly true

(C) False

(D) None of the above

532. An agreement to murder a person is an example of—

(A) Void agreement.

(B) Illegal agreement.

(C) Either (A) or (B)

(D) both (A) and (B)

533. Trade combination agreements like opening and closing of business ventures, licensing of traders, supervision and control of dealers, etc. are —

(A) void since they are in restraint of trade.

(B) valid even if they are in restraint of trade.

(C) voidable at the option of the aggrieved party.

(D) immoral and hence void *ab initio.*

534. Can a promise to pay money to a witness served with a notice be enforced?

(A) Yes

(B) No

(C) Partly Yes

(D) none of the above

535. A contracts to act at a theatre for six months for Rs. 5 Lakhs paid in advance by B. On several occasions A is too ill to act. The contract to act becomes void on those occasions due to —

(A) initial impossibility.

(B) subsequent illegality.

(C) subsequent impossibility.

(D) destruction of subject matter.

536. Which of the following maintenance and champerty agreements will not be enforceable?

(A) gambling in litigation

(B) injuring or oppressing others, by encouraging unholy litigation

(C) both (A) and (B)

(D) neither (A) nor (B)

537. In India, Courts will refuse to enforce Champerty and Maintenance agreements only when they are found to be extortionate and unconscionable and not made with the *bona fide* object of assisting claims of person unable to carry on litigation himself.

(A) True

(B) Partly true

(C) False

(D) None of the above

538. An agreement between persons to override the jurisdiction of Courts is —

(A) contrary to public policy void.

(B) void.

(C) both (A) and (B)

(D) neither (A) nor (B)

539. An agreement to submit disputes to arbitration is—

(A) ineffective.

(B) valid.

(C) voidable.

(D) void-*ab-initio.*

540. Agreements which unduly restrict the personal freedom of persons are —

(A) void.

(B) against public policy.

(C) both (A) and (B)

(D) neither (A) nor (B)

541. Where a person agrees to maintain a suit, in which he has no interest, the proceeding is known as —

(A) Champerty.

(B) Maintenance.

(C) Stifling with Prosecution.

(D) Interference with course of justice.

542. "Maintenance" tends to encourage—

(A) purposive litigation.

(B) public interest litigation.

(C) speculative litigation.

(D) circuit of action.

543. X promises to pay Y Rs. 25,000 for bringing a suit against Z, S's sole motive being to sue Z and annoy him. This is an example of—

(A) Stifling with Prosecution.

(B) Champerty.

(C) Maintenance.

(D) Interference with course of justice.

544. An agreement whereby one party assists another in recovering money or property and, in turn share in the proceeds of the action is called —
(A) Champerty.
(B) Maintenance.
(C) Stifling with Prosecution.
(D) Interference with course of justice.

545. L agrees to pay M Rs. 50,000 for suing N and in turn seeking 60% share in the proceeds received by M in the suit. This is an example of —
(A) Stifling with Prosecution.
(B) Champerty.
(C) Maintenance.
(D) Interference with course of justice.

546. C contracts with H, a local criminal, to beat his business competitor. This is an example of—
(A) Valid Contract.
(B) Illegal Contact.
(C) Voidable contract.
(D) Unenforceable Contract.

547. If only a part of the consideration or object is unlawful, the contract is —
(A) valid to the extent the same are lawful.
(B) void to the extent the same are unlawful.
(C) valid as a whole.
(D) void as a whole.

548. If a part of the consideration or object is unlawful, the contract is—
(A) valid.
(B) void.
(C) voidable.
(D) illegal.

549. When the consideration is unlawful, the Courts —
(A) Allows an action on contract.
(B) Does not allow an action on contract.
(C) Takes it for consideration.
(D) Dismisses the consideration.

550. Agreement which involves or implies or causes injury to the person or property of another is —
(A) contingent.
(B) valid.
(C) voidable.
(D) void.

551. Illegal agreements may be punishable with —
(A) fine.
(B) imprisonment.
(C) both (A) and (B)
(D) any of the above

552. A compromise of compoundable offences is valid.
(A) True
(B) Partly true
(C) False
(D) None of the above

☞ Void Contract

553. In case of illegal agreements, the collateral agreements are–
(A) Valid.
(B) Void.
(C) Voidable.
(D) Any of these

554. All agreements in restraint of trade are void and there are no exception to this rule.
(A) True, the Indian Contract Act provides so.
(B) True, the Constitution of India provides so.
(C) False, the Indian Contract Act, and Partnership Act contains exception.
(D) None of these

555. A void agreement is one, which is—
(A) Valid, but not enforceable.
(B) Enforceable at the option of both the parties.
(C) Enforceable at the option of one party.
(D) Not enforceable in a court of law.

556. Which of the following agreements is void?
(A) Agreements made under the unilateral mistake of fact.
(B) Agreements made under the bilateral mistake of fact.
(C) Agreements, the consideration of which is unlawful.
(D) Contingent agreement.
(A) 1 & 2
(B) 2 & 3
(C) 3 & 4
(D) 1 & 4

557. Which of the following agreements are void–
(A) An agreement to share the salary of a public officer.
(B) An agreement to sell a religious office.
(C) An agreement with the objective of procuring a public post.
(D) All of the above

558. Which of the following agreements are void?
(A) An agreement to share the salary of a public officer.
(B) An agreement to sell a religious office.
(C) An agreement with the objective of procuring a public post.
(D) All of the above

559. An agreement to do an impossible Act is–

(A) Void.

(B) Voidable.

(C) Illegal.

(D) None of these

560. A sells the goodwill of his business to B and agrees with him to refrain from carrying on a similar business within specified local limits. This contract is—

(A) Valid.

(B) Void.

(C) Illegal.

(D) Voidable.

561. Which of the following agreement is/are void?

(1) Agreement in restraint of legal proceedings.

(2) Agreement to stifling prosecution.

(3) Agreement by an outgoing partner with his partners not to carry on similar business within a specified period or within specified local limits.

(4) Contingent Contracts

(A) 1 & 2

(B) 2 & 3

(C) 3 & 4

(D) 1 & 4

562. A contracts to do a certain act which is not permitted by law is void in itself.

(A) True

(B) Partly True

(C) False

(D) None of the above.

563. Which of the following agreements are valid?

(A) Agreement to enter into an agreement in future.

(B) Agreement that gives rise to social obligations.

(C) Agreement to perform an act contingent upon a certain event.

(D) Agreements entered into by incompetent parties.

564. Which of the following agreements are not void?

(A) Agreements entered into through a mutual mistake of fact between the parties.

(B) Agreements, the object or consideration of which is unlawful.

(C) Agreements, made without consideration

(D) Agreements, made for inadequate consideration

565. Which of the following agreements are void?

(A) Agreements in restraint of marriage

(B) Agreements in restraint of trade

(C) Agreement in restraint of legal proceedings

(D) All of the above

566. Which of the following agreements are valid?

(A) Uncertain agreements

(B) Wagering agreements

(C) Agreements contingent upon impossible events

(D) None of the above

567. Which of the following agreements are void?

(A) Agreements to do impossible acts

(B) Agreements to do reciprocal promises, one set of which is legal, and the other part is illegal.

(C) Both (A) or (B)

(D) Neither (A) nor (B)

568. Which one of the following is a void agreement?

(A) An agreement without consideration

(B) An agreement in restraint of marriage

(C) An agreement in restraint of trade

(D) All of the above

569. Of the following agreements, which one is not void?

(A) Agreement without consideration

(B) Agreement in restraint of marriage

(C) Wagering agreement

(D) Agreement with a handicapped person

570. In case of a void contract, there is no legal remedy for the parties to the contract. Even the Court will not permit performance of the contract even if the parties desire.

(A) True

(B) Partly True

(C) False

(D) None of the above

571. Ambiguous and Uncertain Agreements are defined in Section _____ of the Indian Contract Act, 1872.

(A) Section 26

(B) Section 27

(C) Section 28

(D) Section 29

572. In which of the following agreements, Restraint of Trade is valid?

(A) Agreement with Buyer of Goodwill

(B) Trade Combinations, to the extent they do not create monopoly or opposed to public policy.

(C) Agreements under the Partnership Act, 1932

(D) All of the above

573. A agreed to pay a certain sum, when he was able to pay. The agreement is void on grounds of —

(A) inadequacy of consideration.

(B) agreement to agree in future.

(C) uncertainty.

(D) all of the above

574. A agrees to sell to B, 1,000 tons of oil. A is a dealer in various types of oil. The agreement is—

(A) valid in all cases.

(B) void due to uncertainty of meaning.

(C) illegal.

(D) opposed to public policy.

575. Das agrees to sell his white horse to Kishan, for Rs. 5,000 or Rs. 10,000. The agreement is void on grounds of uncertainty of—

(A) subject matter.

(B) consideration.

(C) either (A) or (B)

(D) both (A) and (B)

576. If an agreement suffers from any uncertainty, it is —

(A) Voidable.

(B) Void.

(C) Unenforceable.

(D) Illegal.

577. An agreement is void, if the meaning of such agreement is —

(A) not certain.

(B) not capable of being made certain.

(C) either (A) or (B)

(D) neither (A) nor (B)

578. In order to make a contract void u/s 29, Uncertainty may relate to —

(A) Subject Matter of Contract.

(B) Terms of Contract.

(C) either (A) or (B)

(D) neither (A) nor (B)

579. L says to J "I shall sell may house; will you buy?" A says, "Yes, I shall buy". The agreement is void due to—

(A) Uncertainty of meaning.

(B) Uncertainty of price.

(C) Uncertainty of existence of subject matter.

(D) Uncertainty of quality of subject matter.

580. In case there is vagueness or uncertainty as regards the terms of contract, the Contract itself would be void and unenforceable within the meaning of section 29 of the Act.

(A) True

(B) Partly True

(C) False

(D) None of the above

581. Lalu promised to pay an extra Rs. 5,000 to Govind if the horse he purchased from Govind proved to be lucky. The promise is—

(A) valid.

(B) void.

(C) voidable.

(D) enforceable.

582. Monies paid or properties transferred under illegal agreements—

(A) can be recovered in all cases.

(B) can be recovered only if they exist *in specie*.

(C) cannot be recovered unless Court directs so.

(D) cannot be recovered at all.

583. All void agreements need not be illegal. But all illegal agreements are void.

(A) True

(B) Partly True

(C) False

(D) None of the above

584. Even legal agreements could be rendered void.

(A) True

(B) Partly True

(C) False

(D) None of the above

585. Void agreements are —

(A) not punishable.

(B) punishable.

(C) forbidden by law.

(D) unlawful.

586. Wagering Agreements —

(A) is a valid contract.

(B) is a game of chance.

(C) is a voidable contract.

(D) is a quasi-contract.

587. In a wagering agreement, each party should stand to win or lose.

(A) True

(B) Partly true

(C) False

(D) None of the above

588. If either of the parties may win but cannot lose, or both may lose and cannot win, it is—

(A) a Wagering Agreement.

(B) not a Wagering Agreement.

(C) a Voidable Agreement.

(D) a Illegal Agreement.

589. In case of Wagering Agreement, ______ should be able to control the happening or non-happening of the contingent event.

(A) Promisor

(B) Promisee

(C) either (A) or (B)

(D) neither (A) nor (B)

590. Where one party has control over the contingent event, the transaction is not a wager.

(A) True

(B) Partly true

(C) False

(D) None of the above

591. In Wagering Agreement, Neither party should have interest in the happening (or non-happening) of the event other than—

(A) his honour or prestige.

(B) the sum or stake he stands to win or lose.

(C) either (A) or (B)

(D) both (A) and (B)

592. To constitute wager, the promise should be to pay money or money's worth only.

(A) True

(B) Partly true

(C) False

(D) None of the above

593. An agreement by way of wager is—

(A) valid and enforceable by law.

(B) void.

(C) voidable.

(D) immoral.

594. A "Wagering Contract" is void under _____ of the Indian Contact Act, 1872

(A) Sec. 30

(B) Sec. 31

(C) Sec. 32

(D) Sec. 33

595. A and B bet as to whether it would rain on a particular day or not — A promising to Pay Rs. 100 to B if it rained, and B promising an equal amount to A, if it did not. This is an example of —

(A) Voidable Agreement.

(B) Unlawful Agreement.

(C) Illegal Agreement.

(D) Wagering Agreement.

596. In a Wagering Agreement, there is a promise to perform an act based on a —

(A) certain event.

(B) uncertain event.

(C) either (A) or (B)

(D) both (A) and (B)

597. In a Wagering Agreement, Uncertainty may be due to—

(A) The event is yet to take place.

(B) The event might have already happened but the Parties are not aware of its result.

(C) either (A) or (B)

(D) neither (A) nor (B)

598. Which of the following agreements in restraint of trade is valid?

(A) Partners agreeing with the buyer of Goodwill, not to use the Firm name or carry on Firm's business or solicit clients of the firm.

(B) Upon sale of Firm's Goodwill, a Partner agreeing that he will not carry on any business similar to Firm's within specified periods or local limits.

(C) both (A) and (B)

(D) neither (A) nor (B)

599. In the States of Gujarat and Maharashtra, Collateral Transactions to a Wagering Agreement are also tainted with illegality.

(A) True

(B) Partly True

(C) False

(D) None of the above

600. In India, Unauthorised Lottery is—

(A) Illegal.

(B) Void.

(C) both (A) and (B)

(D) neither (A) nor (B)

601. A, in Bangalore, bets with B and loses. A applies to C for a loan in order to pay B.C gives the loan to A to enable him to pay B. In this case —

(A) C can recover the amount of loan from A.

(B) C cannot recover the amount of loan from A.

(C) C can recover the amount from B.

(D) C can recover the amount from A or B.

602. No suit shall be brought for recovering anything—

(A) alleged to be won on any wager.

(B) entrusted to a person to abide the result of any game or other uncertain event on which any wager is made.

(C) either (A) or (B)

(D) neither (A) nor (B)

603. Where a person enters into a wagering transaction through an agent, and the agent fails to carry out the Principal's instructions—

(A) Principal can sue Agent for breach of contract of agency.

(B) Principal cannot sue Agent for breach of contract of agency.

(C) Principal can sue Agent for damagers.

(D) Principal cannot sue agent to recover the betting moneys paid.

604. In a Wagering Agreement, money deposited with a person to be paid to the party winning cannot be recovered by the winner.

(A) True

(B) Partly True

(C) False

(D) None of the above

605. Wagering Agreements have been declared illegal and hence void & illegal in—

(A) Gujarat

(B) Maharashtra

(C) both (A) and (B)

(D) neither (A) nor (B)

606. In the States of Gujarat and Maharashtra, Wagering Agreements are —

(A) Illegal.

(B) Void.

(C) Both (A) and (B)

(D) Neither (A) nor (B)

607. In the States of Gujarat and Maharashtra, Collateral Transactions to a Wagering Agreement are —

(A) Voidable.

(B) Illegal and Void.

(C) Valid and Enforceable.

(D) Contingent.

608. In places other than Gujarat and Maharashtra, Collateral Transactions to a Wagering Agreement are —

(A) Voidable.

(B) Illegal and Void.

(C) Valid and Enforceable.

(D) Contingent.

609. Both Insurance Contracts and Wagering Agreements are contracts of indemnity.

(A) True

(B) Partly true

(C) False

(D) None of the above

610. ________ is an agreement for the distribution by chance among persons purchasing tickets.

(A) Insurance

(B) Lottery

(C) gambling

(D) All of the above

611. Unauthorized Lotteries are legal.

(A) True

(B) Partly true

(C) False

(D) None of the above

612. Government Authorized Lotteries are —

(A) Void.

(B) Illegal.

(C) Voidable.

(D) Legal.

613. A Lottery, being a game of chance, is a wagering Agreement.

(A) True

(B) Partly true

(C) False

(D) None of the above

614. Transactions for sale and purchase of stocks and shares or for sale and delivery of goods, are considered as Wagering Agreements if the intention is—

(A) to give and take delivery of shares or goods.

(B) only to settle the price difference.

(C) both (A) and (B)

(D) neither (A) nor (B)

615. As per the Prize Competition Act, 1995, prize competitions in games of skill are not wagers provided the prize money does not exceed—

(A) Rs. 10

(B) Rs. 100

(C) Rs. 1,000

(D) Rs. 10,000

616. A subscription/contribution made for, or an agreement to subscribe/contribute entered into towards, any plate, prize or sum of money, of the value or amount of Rs. 500 or more, to be awarded to the winner of a horse race, is —

(A) voidable.

(B) void.

(C) valid.

(D) unenforceable.

617. Prize Competitions which involves skill, e.g. picture puzzles, crossword competitions, athletic competitions, etc. are—

(A) Wagering Agreements.

(B) Not Wagering Agreements.

(C) Void Agreements.

(D) Voidable Agreements.

618. A and B bet as to whether it would rain on a particular day or not — A promising to pay Rs. 100 to B if it rained, and B promising an equal amount to A, if it did not. This is an example of—

(A) Voidable Agreement.

(B) Unlawful Agreement.

(C) Illegal Agreement.

(D) Wagering Agreement.

☞ Restitution

619. 'A' contracts to sing for 'B' at a concert for Rs. 5,000, which is paid in advance, 'A' is too ill to sing. Decide best.

(A) A must refund the advance of Rs. 5,000 to B.

(B) A is not liable to refund the money.

(C) 'B' should force 'A' to sing.

(D) 'A' is liable to refund only 50% of advance money to B.

620. A party receiving benefits under a void contract is liable to restore the benefits to the party from whom the benefits are received.

(A) True

(B) Partly true

(C) False

(D) None of the above

ANSWERS TO MULTIPLE CHOICE QUESTIONS

1. C	**36.** B	**71.** B	**106.** A	**141.** B
2. B	**37.** B	**72.** D	**107.** C	**142.** B
3. A	**38.** B	**73.** A	**108.** A	**143.** B
4. A	**39.** D	**74.** A	**109.** B	**144.** A
5. B	**40.** B	**75.** A	**110.** C	**145.** A
6. D	**41.** C	**76.** A	**111.** A	**146.** D
7. D	**42.** A	**77.** D	**112.** D	**147.** A
8. C	**43.** C	**78.** A	**113.** C	**148.** A
9. C	**44.** C	**79.** C	**114.** B	**149.** D
10. C	**45.** C	**80.** A	**115.** A	**150.** B
11. A	**46.** A	**81.** D	**116.** B	**151.** D
12. C	**47.** B	**82.** A	**117.** B	**152.** C
13. B	**48.** B	**83.** B	**118.** A	**153.** D
14. B	**49.** D	**84.** C	**119.** D	**154.** C
15. A	**50.** B	**85.** A	**120.** B	**155.** C
16. D	**51.** D	**86.** C	**121.** D	**156.** C
17. A	**52.** C	**87.** D	**122.** D	**157.** A
18. B	**53.** B	**88.** C	**123.** C	**158.** D
19. D	**54.** D	**89.** A	**124.** A	**159.** C
20. D	**55.** A	**90.** C	**125.** B	**160.** C
21. A	**56.** D	**91.** D	**126.** D	**161.** A
22. B	**57.** D	**92.** A	**127.** B	**162.** A
23. B	**58.** A	**93.** D	**128.** C	**163.** A
24. A	**59.** A	**94.** D	**129.** D	**164.** A
25. C	**60.** C	**95.** B	**130.** A	**165.** A
26. A	**61.** B	**96.** C	**131.** C	**166.** A
27. A	**62.** B	**97.** A	**132.** C	**167.** D
28. B	**63.** A	**98.** A	**133.** D	**168.** A
29. D	**64.** A	**99.** C	**134.** B	**169.** A
30. A	**65.** A	**100.** A	**135.** A	**170.** B
31. D	**66.** C	**101.** B	**136.** A	**171.** A
32. D	**67.** B	**102.** B	**137.** A	**172.** B
33. D	**68.** A	**103.** B	**138.** B	**173.** A
34. A	**69.** A	**104.** A	**139.** C	**174.** B
35. C	**70.** B	**105.** C	**140.** B	**175.** B

176. C
177. B
178. A
179. B
180. A
181. D
182. D
183. A
184. D
185. D
186. D
187. D
188. D
189. D
190. A
191. B
192. B
193. A
194. A
195. B
196. B
197. B
198. A
199. B
200. A
201. B
202. B
203. A
204. B
205. A
206. C
207. C
208. B
209. A
210. B
211. B
212. C
213. B
214. A
215. B
216. A
217. D
218. C
219. A
220. C
221. A
222. C
223. A
224. A
225. A
226. D
227. A
228. C
229. B
230. A
231. B
232. A
233. B
234. B
235. D
236. C
237. C
238. D
239. C
240. A
241. A
242. B
243. A
244. B
245. A
246. C
247. D
248. C
249. B
250. C
251. C
252. A
253. D
254. A
255. C
256. B
257. C
258. A
259. B
260. D
261. B
262. A
263. D
264. B
265. A
266. C
267. A
268. C
269. A
270. A
271. D
272. C
273. D
274. A
275. A
276. A
277. B
278. B
279. C
280. C
281. A
282. B
283. A
284. C
285. A
286. A
287. C
288. D
289. A
290. D
291. C
292. A
293. D
294. C
295. A
296. C
297. C
298. D
299. B
300. D
301. B
302. A
303. D
304. C
305. D
306. A
307. B
308. D
309. A
310. D
311. B
312. B
313. B
314. A
315. B
316. A
317. D
318. B
319. C
320. D
321. A
322. C
323. A
324. C
325. B
326. B
327. A
328. A
329. A
330. C
331. D
332. A
333. D
334. B
335. A
336. C
337. A
338. A
339. B
340. B
341. C
342. D
343. B
344. C
345. D
346. D
347. C
348. B
349. A
350. B
351. C
352. A
353. A
354. B
355. D
356. A
357. B
358. B
359. C
360. C
361. C
362. C
363. A
364. B
365. C
366. C
367. B
368. C
369. D
370. B
371. C
372. B
373. A
374. A
375. D
376. D
377. D
378. A
379. D
380. C
381. B
382. B
383. A
384. A
385. A
386. A
387. B
388. B
389. B
390. B
391. A
392. B
393. A
394. C
395. B
396. B
397. A
398. A
399. C
400. A
401. D
402. B
403. D
404. B
405. C
406. D
407. C
408. A
409. D
410. A
411. C
412. A
413. D
414. D
415. B
416. D
417. B
418. A
419. D
420. A
421. A
422. C
423. C
424. D
425. B
426. A
427. B
428. A
429. B
430. B
431. A
432. B
433. B
434. A
435. C
436. C
437. D
438. C
439. B
440. D
441. B
442. C
443. A
444. A
445. A

446. A
447. C
448. A
449. C
450. A
451. D
452. D
453. B
454. A
455. C
456. D
457. A
458. C
459. C
460. C
461. D
462. B
463. B
464. A
465. A
466. A
467. C
468. A
469. D
470. A
471. B
472. B
473. D
474. A
475. D
476. A
477. B
478. B
479. B
480. D
481. A
482. B
483. B
484. C
485. A
486. B
487. C
488. B
489. A
490. D
491. C
492. B
493. A
494. D
495. A
496. B
497. C
498. D
499. D
500. D
501. B
502. B
503. B
504. A
505. A
506. C
507. A
508. B
509. C
510. C
511. A
512. A
513. B
514. C
515. D
516. A
517. C
518. C
519. A
520. B
521. D
522. A
523. C
524. A
525. C
526. A
527. A
528. D
529. D
530. C
531. A
532. D
533. B
534. B
535. C
536. C
537. A
538. C
539. B
540. C
541. B
542. C
543. C
544. A
545. B
546. B
547. D
548. B
549. B
550. D
551. D
552. A
553. B
554. C
555. D
556. B
557. D
558. D
559. A
560. A
561. A
562. A
563. C
564. D
565. D
566. D
567. C
568. D
569. D
570. A
571. D
572. D
573. C
574. B
575. B
576. B
577. C
578. C
579. B
580. A
581. B
582. D
583. A
584. A
585. A
586. B
587. A
588. B
589. D
590. A
591. B
592. A
593. B
594. A
595. D
596. B
597. C
598. C
599. A
600. C
601. A
602. C
603. B
604. A
605. C
606. C
607. B
608. C
609. B
610. B
611. C
612. D
613. A
614. B
615. C
616. C
617. B
618. D
619. A
620. A

Chapter 2

PERFORMANCE OF CONTRACT

TYPES OF PERFORMANCE OF CONTRACT

(1) Actual Performance:

- ⇨ ***Meaning:*** When the parties have fulfilled their obligations under the contract.
- ⇨ ***Example:*** A agrees to sell his Car to B for Rs. 2 lakh. A delivers the car and B makes the payment. There is actual performance.
- ⇨ ***Effect:*** Actual performance discharges the contract.

(2) Attempted Performance (Tender):

- ⇨ ***Meaning:*** When one of the parties to the contract offers to perform the contract, but the other party does not accept it. It is also known as 'tender'.
- ⇨ ***Example:*** A agrees to sell his car to B for Rs. 2 lakh. A offers to deliver the car, but B does not accept it.
- ⇨ ***Effect:*** An attempted performance discharges the person who makes the attempted performance.

Essentials of a valid tender

1. It must be unconditional.

For Example: A sold his car to B. A offers to deliver the car to B, provided his father permits. It is a conditional offer and, therefore not a valid tender.

2. It must be made at a fixed time and place. If no such time and place has been agreed upon, then it should be during the business hour and at the place of business.

3. It must be made by a person, who is able and willing to perform the contract.

4. Tender must be for the quality and quantity agreed upon: The buyer is not bound to accept the deli very of goods in instalments. *Similarly*, if the goods are less or more than the quantity agreed, the buyer can refuse to accept the goods.

However, the buyer cannot reject the goods, if the variation is immaterial.

5. Reasonable opportunity must be given to the other party to examine the goods.

6. It must be made to the promisee or his authorised Agent: A tender made to a stranger is not valid.

7. It may be made to anyone of the joint promises.

8. In case of tender of money, the payment must be made in legal tender money. The creditor is not bound to accept payment by cheque. Where the debtor (promisor) makes a valid tender, i.e., offers to pay the amount to the creditor and the creditor refuses to accept the same, the debtor is not discharged from his liability to pay the amount. However, the debtor will not be liable to pay any interest from the date of the tender in case the tender was a valid one. Further, if the creditor files a suit against, the Court can also award the cost of defending the suit to the creditor.

EFFECT OF REFUSAL OF A PARTY TO PERFORM PROMISE WHOLLY

Where a party to a contract refuses to perform his promise, the other party (i.e. promisee) may put an end to the contract, unless the promisee has signified by words or conduct his consent in its continuance. (Section 39).

Example: A, a singer enters into a contract with B to sing at marriage party for three days. B engages to pay him Rs. 10,000 for each night's performance. On the second night, A willfully absents herself from the theatre. B is at liberty to put an end to the contract.

Suppose, A, with the consent of B, sings on the third night. B has signified his acquiescence in the continuance of the contract and cannot now put an end to it. However, he is entitled to the damages which he has sustained because of A's absence to sing on the second night.

WHO MUST PERFORM THE PROMISE (Secs. 37 & 40 to 43)

1. By the Promisor himself (Sec. 40) :	Where the contract is of a personal nature, then it must be performed by the promisor himself. Contracts of personal nature come to an end with the death of the promisor. ***Example***: A engages a singer to sing a song on his birthday party. The singer dies before the day of the party. Legal representatives are not liable to sing after the death of the singer.
2. By the Agent (Sec. 40) :	Where a contract is not of a personal nature, it may be performed by the promisor himself or by his agent.
3. By the Legal Representative (Sec. 37) :	After the death of the promisor, his legal representatives are bound to perform the contract. *However*, their liability is limited to the value of the property left by the deceased. ***Example:*** A borrowed Rs. 10,000 from B. A dies before the loan is repaid. A left an estate whose value is Rs. 6,000. A's representatives are liable to the extent of Rs. 6,000 only.
4. By third parties (Sec. 41) :	Where a promisee accepts performance from a third party, he cannot afterwards enforce it against the promisor.
5. By joint promisors: (Sec. 42, 43, 44)	Refer to next Topic

LIABILITY OF JOINT PROMISOR

1. **Voluntarily discharge of obligation (Sec. 42):** *Unless a contrary intention appears from the contract,* all such persons must perform the promise jointly.

   After the death of any of them, his representative jointly with the other survivor or survivors must perform the promise. If all the promisors die, the representatives of all of them must perform the promise jointly.

2. **If joint promisors do not voluntarily discharge their obligation, then Sec. 43 will come into operation.—**

   (i) **Joint and several liability :**

   Example: A, B and C borrow Rs. 3,00,000 from D. D can ask any of them to pay Rs.3,00,000.

   (ii) **Right of equal contribution :** Where any of the joint promisors has been compelled to pay the whole amount, he can ask for equal contribution from the others.

   Example: In the above case, if D recovered Rs. 3,00,000 from A, then A can ask for Rs. 1,00,000 each from B and C.

   (iii) **Liability to bear the loss due to default of other joint promisors equally:**

   Example: In the above example, if nothing is received from B who has become insolvent, then A and C shall be liable to bear B's loss equally, i.e., Rs. 50,000 each. *Thus*, A and C shall contribute Rs. 1,50,000 each towards the repayment of the loan

3. **Release of a joint promisor (Sec. 44):** A release of one of the joint promisors does not discharge the other joint promisors. The joint promisor so released continues to be liable to other joint promisors.

Example: A, B and C jointly borrowed a sum of Rs. 1,00,000 from D. D releases C and files a suit against A and B for recovery of the loan. A and B are not released from their liability, nor is C discharged from his liability towards A and B for contribution.

WHO CAN DEMAND PERFORMANCE?

1. Promisee
2. In case of death of the single promisee, his legal representative can demand performance.

   Example: A gave a loan to B. After A's death, his legal representative can demand the repayment of loan from B.
3. *In case*, there are more than one promisee, then the right to demand performance is to be exercised jointly by the surviving joint promisees and the legal representative of the deceased joint promisees.

   If all the promisees die, then the right to demand performance rests with all the legal representatives jointly.

   Example: B and C jointly lend Rs. 5,00,000 to A. B dies. The right to claim performance rests with B's representative jointly with C so long as C is alive. After C's death, representatives of B and C jointly can demand Rs. 5,00,000.

TIME & PLACE OF PERFORMANCE (Secs. 46 to 50)

Parties are free to determine the time and place of performance by agreement between themselves. These rules are summarised as follows:

1. Where no time is fixed and the performance is to be done without any request from the promisee (See 46): In this case, the promise must be performed within a reasonable time. The question what is a reasonable time is a question of fact.

2. Where time is fixed and the performance is to be done without any request from the promisee (See 47): In this case, the promisor may perform it at any time during the usual hours of business on such day and at the place at which the promise should be performed.

For Example: A, promises to deliver goods at B's godown on 1st Jan. On that day, A brings the goods to B's godown after the usual hours of business and they are not received, A has not performed his promise.

3. Where time is fixed and the performance is to be done at the request of the promisee (See 48): In this case, the promisee must apply for performance at a proper place and within the usual hours of business,

4. Where no place is fixed and the performance is to be done without any request from the promisee (See 49): In this case, it is the duty of the promisor to apply to the promisee to appoint a reasonable place for the performance and to perform it at such place (Sec. 49).

For Example: A undertakes to deliver one ton coal to B on 1st Jan. A must ask B to appoint a reasonable place for the delivery of the coal and must deliver it to him at such place.

5. Performance to be made in the manner and time prescribed (Sec. 50): The performance of any promise may be made in any manner or at any time which the promisee prescribes.

For Example: B owes A Rs. 2,00,000. A asks B to deposit the amount in A's account with C Bank. B deposits the amount in A's account with C Bank. Afterwards, and before A knows of the transfer, C Bank fails. There has been a good payment by B.

✎ Effect of failure to perform within the stipulated time

1. When time is of the essence (Sec. 55): When time is an essential factor in a contract and the contract is not performed within that time, the contract becomes voidable at the option of the other party.

For Example: A agrees to supply a coat for B's marriage to take place on 1st January. A fails to deliver the coat by 1st January. The contract is voidable at the option of B.

2. When time is not of the essence (Sec. 55): When time is not an essential factor in a contract and the contract is not performed within that time, the contract does not become voidable at the option of the other party. However, damages or compensation can be recovered for any loss caused to the promisee due to such non-performance.

RECIPROCAL PROMISES (Secs. 51 to 54)

"Promises which form the consideration or part of the consideration for each other, are called reciprocal promises." **--- *See.* 2(*f*)**

A reciprocal promise implies a mutual promise.

For example, A agrees to sell his car for Rs. 5,00,000. For A, 'delivery of car' is a promise. For B, 'payment of Rs. 5,00,000' is the promise.

Types of Reciprocal Promises

1. Mutual and Independent: In case each party has to perform its promise independently and irrespective of the fact whether the other party has performed it or not.

For Example: A agrees to deliver goods to B on 1st January and B agrees to make the payment on 10th January, the promise made by each party is independent of the promise of the other. Even if A does not deliver the goods on 1st January, B must make payment on 10th January. Of course, B can file a suit to recover the goods or any loss which he suffers because of non-delivery of goods by A in time, afterwards.

2. Conditional and Dependent: In case the performance of the promise by one party depends upon the prior performance of the promise by the other party, the promises are conditional and dependent.

For Example: A agrees to stitch a coat for B, provided B supplies the necessary cloth. B does not supply the cloth. A need not and cannot stitch the coat.

3. Mutual and Concurrent: In case the promises are to be performed by both the parties simultaneously, the promises are mutual and concurrent.

For Example: A agrees to buy a radio from B for cash. Payment by A and delivery of radio by B must be simultaneous.

Rules regarding the Performance of Reciprocal Promises

1. Simultaneous Performance (Sec. 51): Reciprocal promises should be performed simultaneously. Thus, no party need perform its promise, unless the other party is ready and willing to perform its promise.

For Example: A agrees to deliver certain goods to B to be paid on delivery. A need not deliver the goods unless B is ready and willing to make the payment. B need not make the payment unless A is ready and willing to deliver the goods.

2. Order of Performance of Reciprocal Promises (See. 52):

- ⇨ Where the order of performance is expressly fixed by the contract, they shall be performed in that order.
- ⇨ However, where the order is not expressly fixed, they will be performed in that order which the nature of the transactions require.

3. Consequence where a party prevents performance (Sec. 53): If one party prevents the other from performing his part, the contract is voidable at the option of the party so prevented. The party so prevented is entitled to compensation from the other party for any loss sustained due to the non-performance of the contract.

For Example: A and B contract that B shall execute certain work for A for Rs. 1,000. B is ready and willing to execute the work accordingly, but A prevents him from doing so. The contract is voidable at the option of B and if he elects to rescind it, he is entitled to recover from A compensation for any loss, which he has incurred by its non-performance.

4. Effect of default as to promise to be performed first (Sec. 54): Where the contract consists of reciprocal promises in such a manner that—

– one of them cannot be performed, until the other party has been performed, and

– the other party fails to perform it.

Then, such other party cannot claim the performance of the reciprocal promise from the first party and must compensate the first party for any loss.

APPROPRIATION OF PAYMENT (Secs. 59 to 61)

When a debtor owes several distinct debts to one creditor and makes a part payment, a problem may arise – 'to which particular debt should the payment be applied?' In this regard, the provisions are as under:

1. When the debtor expressly indicates the manner of appropriation, the creditor must apply the payment as requested by the debtor. (Sec. 59)

For Example: A owes B three debts of Rs. 1,000, 2,000 and 3,000 respectively. A pays Rs. 3,000 and asks B to apply these Rs. 3,000 to the third debt. B must apply Rs. 3,000 to the third debt.

2. Where there is an implied indication, the payment must be applied accordingly. (Sec. 59)

For Example: A owes B among other debts a sum of Rs. 567. B writes a letter to A demanding the payment of this sum. A sends Rs. 567. The circumstances in this case show that the payment is to be applied to the discharge of the debt of which B had demanded payment.

3. When there is neither any express nor implied indication (Sec. 60): In such a case, the creditor has the right of applying it at his discretion to any lawful debt actually due, even if it is time-barred by the Law of Limitation.

4. Where neither party appropriates (Sec. 61): Where neither party makes any appropriation, the payment shall he applied in discharge of the debts in order of time, even to the debts barred by the Law of Limitation.

If the debts are taken at the same time and date, the payment shall be applied in discharge of each debt proportionately.

5. Where both principal and interest are due: Where interest is payable and the debtor does not specify whether the payment is towards interest or principal, the payment should be applied in the first instance towards the payment of interest and the balance to the principal amount.

—*Harish Chandra* v *Kailash Chandra* (1975)

6. Clayton's Law: Where parties have a current account, the rule in *Clayton's* case is applicable. According to this rule, *in the absence of a contrary intention*, the items on the credit side of an account must be appropriated against the items on the debit side in order of date.

7. Rule in *Hallett's Estate* Case: Where a trustee keeps his own money as well as trust funds in one and the same bank account and mis-appropriates trust funds, this rule is applicable. According to this rule, where a series of withdrawals and deposits were made and trust funds misappropriated, the deposits would be credited first to the trust fund and then to his own fund; the withdrawals are to be debited first to his own money and then to the trust funds. The order of deposits and withdrawals appearing in the account will not be taken into account.

ASSIGNMENT OF CONTRACTS

Assignment of a contract means transfer of rights and liabilities arising out of a contract to a third party. Assignment is not possible where the contract is of personal nature. ***For example***, if A has engaged B to sing songs in his theatre, B cannot assign the contract to C or anyone else.

However, where the contract is not dependent upon the personal skill, it may be assigned subject to certain conditions. A contract can be assigned in two ways:

1. Assignment by Act of Parties:

(i) Novation: A contract which is not of a personal nature may be assigned, if both parties to the agreement agree.

For Example: A owes B Rs. 2 lakh. A and B, by an agreement with C, can agree that now C will pay Rs. 2 lakh to B. By this agreement, the liability of B to pay the debt is transferred from A to C.

☞ ***Exceptions:***

(a) A person cannot become a creditor of another without his consent.

Example: A owes B Rs. 1,000. B assigns his debt to C. C cannot recover the amount from A as C cannot become A's creditor without A's consent.

(b) A person is under no obligation to accept a stranger as his debtor.

Example: A owes Rs. 1,000 to B. A cannot ask B to recover the amount from C without the consent of B and C.

(ii) Performance of contract through Agent: Where the contract is not of a personal nature, a party can perform the contract through a competent agent, provided the contract does not expressly or impliedly require performance only by the promisor.

(iii) Assignment of Actionable Claim: Actionable claims can be assigned by an instrument in writing. Examples of actionable claims are as under: (1) Right of action arising out of a contract; (2) Money debts, i.e. a certain sum of money: (3) Book debts; (4) A share in a partnership firm.

2. Assignment by operation of Law:

(i) Death:

⇨ Where the contract is not of a personal nature – assignment to legal representative with limited liability.

⇨ Where the contract is of personal nature – contract comes to an end and becomes void.

(ii) Insolvency: Under the insolvency law, the rights and liabilities of an insolvent pass on to the official receiver or assignee.

☑☑☑

MULTIPLE CHOICE QUESTIONS

1. A, B and C Jointly promised to pay Rs. 30,000 to D. For recovery of this amount, D filed a suit against A only. Is he justified?

(A) Yes, as the liability of joint promisors is joint and several.

(B) No, as the liability of joint promisors is joint only.

2. A, B and C jointly promised to pay Rs. 6,000 to D. A was compelled by D to pay the entire amount of Rs. 6,000. *Here* –

(A) A can file a suit against D for recovery of amount exceeding his share.

(B) A is entitled to recover Rs. 2,000 each from B and C.

(C) On payment by A, the contract is discharged and B and C are also not liable to A.

(D) D is not justified here, and is liable to refund the entire amount to A.

3. Can a time barred debt be adjusted by a creditor, where the debtor makes the payment without indicating the debt to be adjusted?

(A) Yes, in such a case the creditor is at liberty to do this.

(B) No, as a time-barred debt cannot be recovered

(C) No, as there is absence of consideration.

(D) None of above.

4. Ram, Rohit and Kiran jointly borrowed Rs. 2,00,000 from Rahim by executing a promissory note. Rohit and Kiran are not traceable. Rahim wants to recover the entire amount from Ram. Ram objects this move by saying he is liable to pay 1/3 of the debt only. Which of the following statement(s) is correct?

(A) Rahim can recover the entire amount from Ram.

(B) Rahim can only recover 1/3 of Rs. 2,00,000 from Ram.

(C) Rahim cannot recover any amount from Ram.

(D) The promissory note is not executable against Ram as Rohit and Kiran are not traceable.

5. A, B and C jointly promise to pay D Rs. 3,000. Can D compel either A or B or C to pay him Rs. 3,000 ?

(A) Yes

(B) No

6. A, B and C are under a joint promise to pay D Rs. 30,000. C is unable to pay anything and A is compelled to pay the whole. Is A entitled to receive Rs. 15,000 from B ?

(A) Yes

(B) No

7. Which of the following persons can perform the contract?

(A) Promisor alone.

(B) Legal representatives of the promisor.

(C) Agent of the promisor.

(D) All of these.

8. A, B and C jointly promised to pay Rs. 60,000 to D. Before performance of the contract, C dies. Here, the contract –

(A) becomes void on C's death.

(B) should be performed by A and B along with C's legal representatives.

(C) should be performed by A and B alone.

(D) should be renewed among A, B and D.

9. Contracts classified on the basis of performance are of the following types–

(A) Executed contracts.

(B) Executory contracts.

(C) Partly executed or partly executory contracts.

(D) All of the above

10. When after the formation of a valid contract, an event happens, which makes the performance of contract impossible, the contract becomes–

(A) Void.

(B) Voidable.

(C) Valid.

(D) Illegal.

11. A promises to paint a picture for B by a certain day, at a certain price. A dies before that day. Can the contract be enforced either by A's representatives or by B?

(A) Yes

(B) No

12. A, a singer, enters into a contract with B, the manager of a theatre, to sing at his theatre for two nights in every week during the next two months and B engages to pay her Rs. 100 for each night's performance. On the sixth night, A willfully absents herself. Can the singer be sued?

(A) Ycs

(B) No

13. Where the performance of a promise by one party depend on the prior performance of promise by the other party, such reciprocal promises fall under the category of –

(A) Mutual and concurrent.

(B) Conditional and dependent.

(C) Mutual and independent.

(D) Both (A) and (B)

14. G books a ticket with Indian Airlines from Delhi to Chennai on 16th June, date of travel being 16th July. Indian Airlines has to perform its part of contract on 16th July. This is an example of—

(A) Void Contract.

(B) Illegal Contract.

(C) Unilateral Contract.

(D) Bilateral Contract.

15. Where time of performance is specified in the contract and the Promisee has accepted performance at any time other than the agreed time, the Promisee —

(A) cannot claim compensation for any loss occasioned by the non-performance of the promise at the time agreed.

(B) can claim compensation for any loss occasioned by the non-performance of the promise at the time agreed.

(C) cannot claim performance of the promise at all.

(D) is entitled to rescind the contract.

16. Only the Promisor should perform the promise personally in the following situations—

(A) Where the parties intended performance of the promise by the Promisor himself.

(B) Where performance involves the exercise of personal skills by the Promisor.

(C) Where the promise is founded on personal confidence between the parties.

(D) All of the above

17. When two or more persons have made a joint promise, then unless a contrary intention appears from the contract, all such persons must fullfill the promise—

(A) Jointly.

(B) Severally.

(C) jointly and severally.

(D) jointly or severally.

18. In case of death of the Promisor before performance, the Representatives of the Promisor are not bound when—

(A) it involves the personal skill of the Promisor.

(B) there is no such provision in the contract.

(C) either (A) or (B)

(D) neither (A) nor (B)

19. A promises to deliver goods to B's warehouse on 1st January. On that day, A brings the goods to B's warehouse, but after the usual hour for closing the warehouse and they are not received. Has A performed his promise?

(A) Yes

(B) No

(C) Partly Yes

(D) None of the above

20. In which of the following cases, the Promisor is at fault?

(A) Promisee does not give reasonable facilities for performance.

(B) Promisor has disabled himself from performing his promise in entirety.

(C) Promisor has refused to perform his promise in entirety.

(D) Both (B) and (C)

21. When a person has made a promise to two or more persons jointly, then unless a contrary intention appears from the contract, and, after the death of all of them, the right to claim performance rests with—

(A) by the Representatives of all the Promisees jointly.

(B) by the Representative of a majority of the Promisees.

(C) by the Representatives of any one of the Promisees.

(D) any one of the above

22. The Offer or Promisor to perform must be made to—

(A) The Promisee.

(B) Any one of the Joint Promisees.

(C) Authorised Agent(s) of (A) or (B).

(D) Any one of the above

23. A promises to paint a picture for B. B afterwards forbids him to do so. In such case—

(A) A is no longer bound to perform the promise.

(B) A can claim specific performance.

(C) B can sue A.

(D) All of the above

24. A contract to marry a person shall be performed by—

(A) Promisor himself.

(B) Representative of the Promisor competent to perform.

(C) A third person.

(D) Any of the above

25. If any one of Joint Promisors makes default in such contribution, remaining Joint Promisors must share the loss arising from such default—

(A) Equally.

(B) In the Agreed ratio.

(C) In the ratio of their properties.

(D) Any one of the above

26. A, B and C are under a Joint Promise to pay D Rs. 30,000. C is unable to pay anything and A is compelled to pay the whole. How much can A recover from B?

(A) Rs. 30,000

(B) Rs. 15,000

(C) Rs. 10,000

(D) Nothing at all

27. When one of the parties to the contract has performed its part of the promise, it is known as—

(A) Past Consideration.

(B) Executed Consideration.

(C) Executory Consideration.

(D) Future Consideration.

28. A, B and C Jointly promised to pay Rs. 50,000 to D. For recovery of this amount, D filed a suit against A only. Is he justified?

(A) Yes, as the liability of joint promisors is joint and several.

(B) No, as the liability of joint promisors is joint only.

(C) Both (A) and (B).

(D) None of the above

29. A owes B Rs.1,000 under a contract, B owes C Rs. 1,000. B orders A to credit C with Rs. 1,000 in his books, but C does not assent to the arrangement. Does B still owe C Rs. 1,000?

(A) Yes

(B) No

30. A contracts with B to execute certain builder's work for a fixed price. B supplying the scaffolding or timber, necessary for the work. B refuses to furnish any scaffolding or timber, and the work cannot be executed. Should A execute the work ?

(A) Yes

(B) No

31. Sohan induced Suraj to buy his motorcycle saying that it was in a very good condition. After taking the motorcycle, Suraj complained that there were many defects in the motorcycle. Sohan proposed to get it repaired and promised to pay 40% cost of repairs after a few days, the motorcycle did not work at all. In this case, Suraj—

(A) can rescind the contract.

(B) has affirmed to the contract and cannot rescind the contract.

(C) can return the motorcycle.

(D) all of the above

32. X owes Rs. 1,500 to his friend Y. Y assures X that he will not file a suit against him. Does this assurance of Y constitute 'proposal' in the legal sense of the term?

(A) Yes

(B) No

33. In commercial transactions, time is considered to be of the essence of the contract, and if the party fails to perform the contract within specified time, the contract becomes—

(A) Void and cannot be enforced

(B) Voidable at the option of the other party

(C) Illegal for non-compliance of legal terms

(D) Enforceable in higher court only.

34. Where a contract contains reciprocal promises and one of them cannot be performed or its performance cannot be claimed till the other promise is performed; and there is a failure to perform the promise which is to be performed first —

(A) Defaulting promisor cannot claim performance of the reciprocal promise.

(B) Defaulting Promisor shall compensate the other party to the contract for any loss suffered by him as a result of his non-performance.

(C) Both (A) and (B)

(D) The Contract becomes voidable at the option of the aggrieved party.

ANSWERS TO MULTIPLE CHOICE QUESTIONS

1. A	**8.** B	**15.** B	**22.** D	**29.** A
2. B	**9.** D	**16.** D	**23.** A	**30.** B
3. A	**10.** A	**17.** A	**24.** A	**31.** A
4. A	**11.** B	**18.** C	**25.** A	**32.** A
5. A	**12.** A	**19.** B	**26.** B	**33.** B
6. A	**13.** B	**20.** D	**27.** B	**34.** C
7. D	**14.** C	**21.** A	**28.** A	

Chapter 3

Discharge of Contract

DISCHARGE OF CONTRACT

(1) By Performance
- (a) Actual
- (b) Attempted

(2) By Agreement or Consent
- (a) Novation
- (b) Rescission
- (c) Alteration
- (d) Remission
- (e) Waiver
- (f) Merger

(3) By Impossibility of Performance
- (a) Impossibity existing at the time of formation of contract
  - – Known to Parties
  - – Unknown to parties
- (b) Impossibity arising after formation of contract **(Supervening Impossibility)**

An Excuse
- (a) Death
- (b) Personal Disability
- (c) Destruction of subject-matter
- (d) Object becoming Illegal
- (e) Out-break of war

Not an Excuse
- (a) Difficulty of performance
- (b) Commercial Impossibility
- (c) Default by third party on whom the promisor relies.
- (d) Strikes, lock-outs, civil riots, disturbance, etc.
- (e) Failure of one of the objects

(4) By Lapse of Time

(5) By Operation of Law
- (a) By merger
- (b) By death
- (c) By lapse of time
- (d) By insolvency
- (e) By unauthorised alteration
- (f) Rights and liability vesting with same person

(6) By Breach of Contract
- **Actual**
- **Anticipatory**
  - (a) Express
  - (b) Implied

1. Discharge by Performance (Sec. 37)

Performance is of two types:

⇨ ***Actual Performance:*** Both parties to the contract discharge.

⇨ ***Attempted Performance:*** In this case, the tenderer is discharged from his liability.

2. Discharge by Agreement/Consent

Just as a contract is created by an agreement, so also it can be discharged by an agreement.

Example: A agrees to repair car for B. Later on, B asks A not to repair the car. A does not object to it and returns the car. The old contract is discharged by the new agreement.

Other examples

(a) Discharge by Novation (Sec. 62): To create a new contract in discharge of old contract. For valid novation, mutual consent of all parties concerned is required.

Examples: (i) *A* borrows Rs. 500 and writes a promissory note in favour of *B* for one month. After one month, *A* goes to *B* and expresses his inability to pay the amount. *A* writes a new promissory note for Rs. 500. The old promissory note is discharged by the new one. This novation is between the old parties, *i.e., A* and *B*.

(ii) *A* borrows Rs. 500 from B. A, B and C agree that the debt will be discharged by C. Now, a contract between B and C is formed and the old contract between A and B will come to an end.

(b) Discharge by Rescission (Sec. 62): Rescission means cancellation. All or some of the terms of a contract may be cancelled. It may be—

- By the mutual consent of parties,
- When one party fails to perform the contract the other party may rescind the contract and claim compensation.

Examples: (i) *A* agrees to supply 50 tons of wheat to *B*. *A* and *B* agree that no wheat need be supplied. The contract is rescinded by mutual consent.

(ii) A agrees to sell his scooter to B. The delivery is to be made on 10-Jan, and the payment on 15-Jan. In this case, if Mr. A fails to deliver the scooter on 10-Jan, Mr. B can repudiate the contract and claim compensation.

(c) Discharge by Alteration (Sec. 62): Alteration means changing 'the terms of contract'. It should be noted that novation includes alteration, but alteration does not include novation. In alteration, there is change in terms only and not in parties, but in novation, there may be change in terms as well as parties.

⇨ *Bilateral Alteration*, i.e. alteration with the consent of both parties.

Example: *A* agrees to supply cotton of Grade-I to *B*. Before delivery, *A* and *B* agree that in place of Grade-I, the cotton of Grade-II will be supplied. There is bilateral alteration.

⇨ *Unilateral Alteration*, i.e. alteration by only one party without the consent of the other party. Unilateral alteration of material nature will discharge the other party from his liability.

Example: Alteration in negotiable instrument.

(d) Discharge by Remission (Sec. 63): Remission literally means exemption, *i.e.,* exempting the party from performing the contract. This remission may be full or partial.

Example: A has borrowed Rs. 500 from B. B agrees not to demand Rs. 500 from A. The contract is discharged.

(e) Discharge by Waiver: Waiver means giving up certain rights. Remission and waiver imply more or less the same thing.

(f) Discharge by Merger: When inferior rights of a person under a contract merge with the superior rights under a new contract, the contract with the inferior rights will come to an end.

Example: A was a tenant of B's house. A purchased B's house. A's tenancy rights are merged with his ownership rights, i.e., the tenancy agreement will come to an end.

3. Discharge by 'impossibility of Performance' (Sec. 56)

A. Impossibility existing at the time of formation of Contract:

(a) Known to the parties (absolute impossibility)– Agreement is *void ab initio*.

Example: A agrees with B to discover a treasure by magic. The agreement is *void ab initio*.

(b) Unknown to the parties- Agreeement is *void ab initio* on the ground of mutual mistake.

B. Impossibility arising subsequent to the formation of the Contract (i.e. Supervening Impossibility):

Such a contract shall become void. The following are some examples—

(a) Discharge by Death (Sec. 37): A contract of personal nature comes to an end by the death of the promisor. However, contracts, which are not of personal nature, do not come to an end. The legal representative is liable to the extent of the property inherited by him.

(b) Discharge by Personal Disability/Incapacity: Same as above.

(c) Discharge by destruction of subject-matter

(d) Discharge by object becoming illegal or unlawful.

(e) Discharge by outbreak of war.

'The rule that contract shall become void in case of supervening impossibility' is known as doctrine of frustration in English Law.

✍ **Exception, where impossibility does not discharge the contract:**

(a) Difficulty of Performance: A contract is not discharged merely because the performance has become difficult.

– Tsakir Oglou & Co. Ltd. v. Nobiee and Thorl. (1962)

Facts of Case:	A agreed to sell to B 300 tons of Sudan groundnuts. The usual and the normal route at the date of the contract was via Suez Canal. The Shipment was to be in November/ December, 1956. But on 2nd Nov. 1956, the Canal was closed to traffic and it was not reopened until the following April. It is stated that A could have transported the goods via another route, i.e. the Cape of Good Hope. The question now is whether by reason of the closing of the Suez route, the contract had been terminated.
Decision of Case	Held, A cannot claim the impossibility of performance and bound to deliver the goods via another route by the Cape of Good Hope, although it might be costlier.

(b) Commercial Impossibility: Again, a distinction has to be made between absolute impossibility and commercial impossibility. Commercial impossibility means only that the performance of the contract has become costlier in terms of money or labour.

(c) Default by third party on whom the promisor relies.

Example: D agreed with E to sell 10 tons of oil to be received from P. No supply could be received from P. D is not discharged and must pay damages to the buyer.

(d) Strikes, Lock-outs, Civil Riots, Disturbance, etc.

(e) Failure of one of the objects– When a contract is entered into for several objects, the failure of one of them does not discharge the contract.

4. Discharge by Lapse of Time specified in the Limitation Act

(Already discussed)

5. Discharge by Operation of Law:

(a) By merger
(b) By death
(c) By lapse of time
(d) By insolvency
(e) By unauthorised alteration
(f) Rights & liabilities vesting with same person

6. Discharge by Breach of Contract (Sec. 39)

Breach of contract may be of two types:

(a) Discharge by Actual Breach: Actual breach takes place when the party refuses to perform the contract on the due date of the contract. The promisee is discharged, but the promisor is not.

Example: A agrees with B to paint a picture on 1st March. On 1st March, A does not paint the picture. It is an actual breach. B is discharged, but not A.

(b) Discharge by Anticipatory Breach: It takes place before the due date of actual performance. Anticipatory breach may be of two kinds:

⇨ *Express-* When the promisor informs the promisee that he will not perform the contract.

⇨ *Implied-* When the promisor does an act which renders the perfomance impossible. For example, A agrees to sell his car to B for Rs. 10,000 on 10th January. Before 10th January, A sells the car to C. In this case, there is an implied anticipatory breach.

- Consequences of Anticipatory Breach:

1st Option: The promisee may treat the anticipatory breach as actual breach and claim for damages. Damages will be equal to the difference between the contract and market price on the date of anticipatory breach.

Example: A agrees to sell 100 kg. of wheat to B on 20th March @ Rs. 10 per kg. On 1st March, A informs B that he will not sell the wheat. On 1st March, the market price of the wheat was Rs. 12 per kg. If B treats it as actual breach and files a suit for damages, B will be entitled to damages @ Rs. 2 per kg., being the difference between the market price on the date of anticipatory breach and the contract price.

2nd Option: The promisee may keep the contract open and wait till the actual date of performance.

In this case, the contract is alive for the benefit of both the parties. *Hence*, if in the meantime, the performance of the contract becomes impossible, the promisor can take the benefit of such impossibility, and will be discharged from his liability. It should be noted that the promisee will not be entitled to any damages in such a case.

☑☑☑

MULTIPLE CHOICE QUESTIONS

1. A owes money to B under a contract. It is agreed between A, B and C that B shall henceforth accept C as his debtor instead of A. Does the old debt of A to B come to an end in this manner?

(A) Yes

(B) No

2. Commercial impossibility means that the performance will result in a loss to the promisor. In case of such Commercial Impossibility—

(A) Performance cannot be excused.

(B) Parties are not discharged from performance.

(C) Neither (A) nor (B)

(D) Both (A) and (B)

3. Each party to a contract is bound to perform his part of the obligation. After the parties have made due performance of the contract, their liability under the contract comes to an end. In such a case, the contract is said to be discharged—

(A) By breach of contract.

(B) By impossibility of performance.

(C) By agreement and novation.

(D) By performance of contract.

4. A Stationer agreed to supply white paper at a single rate contracted for one year. Later, due to steep increase in market price, contractor stated that he would suffer very heavy loss by supplying at the contracted rates. Under the contract, rates were to be firm except for statutory levies. In this case—

(A) Stationer cannot claim that contract had become impossible of performance.

(B) Stationer can claim that contract had become impossible of performance.

(C) Stationer can claim revision of contract rates.

(D) All of the above

5. Where consideration is illegally or physically impossible, uncertain or ambiguous, it shall not be —

(A) Transferable by law.

(B) Applied by law.

(C) Enforceable by law.

(D) Admitted by law.

6. A contract is discharged by Novation, which means the—

(A) cancellation of the existing contract.

(B) change in one or more terms of the contract.

(C) substitution of existing contract for a new one.

(D) none of these

7. A contract is discharged by Rescisson which means the—

(A) change in one or more terms of the contract.

(B) acceptance of lesser performance.

(C) abandonment of rights by a party.

(D) cancellation of the existing contract.

8. On the valid performance of the contractual obligations by the parties, the contract—

(A) is discharged.

(B) becomes enforceable.

(C) becomes void.

(D) none of these.

9. X owes Rs. 500 to his friend Y. Y assures X that he will not file a suit against X. Does this assurance of Y constitute "A valid proposal" in the legal sense of the term?

(A) Yes, there is a valid proposal.

(B) No, there is no consideration.

(C) No, it interferes with the course of law.

(D) We cannot conclude with this information.

10. Novation means—

(A) Substituting a new contract for the old one.

(B) Cancellation of the old contract.

(C) Modifying or altering the terms of contract such that it has the effect of substituting a new contract for the old one.

(D) Dispensing away the performance of the promise made by the other party.

11. Which of the following is correct?

(A) Recission must be communicated to the other party in the same manner as a proposal is communicated.

(B) Recission must be revoked in the same manner as a proposal is communicated.

(C) Communication of recission is optional.

(D) Both (A) & (B)

12. Where only one party performs his promise and the other does not, he alone gets discharged and has a right of action against the other party –

(A) True

(B) Partly True

(C) False

(D) None of the above

13. A contacts to sell his car to B for Rs. 4,00,000 and B agrees to pay on delivery. Once the car is delivered to B and B pays Rs. 4,00,000, contract comes to an end. This is called —

(A) Waiver of a Contract.

(B) Breach of a Contract.

(C) Rescission of a Contract.

(D) Discharge of a Contract.

14. A promises to paint a picture for B at a certain price. Which of the following is not correct?

(A) A is not bound to perform the promise himself.

(B) A can appoint some other painter to paint the picture on his behalf.

(C) A dies before painting the picture, the contract can be enforced either by the representatives of A or by B.

(D) All of the above are incorrect.

15. Which of the example is the case of contracts need not be performed?

(A) a party substitutes a new contract for the old.

(B) when the parties to a contract agree to rescind it.

(C) when the parties to a contract agree to alter it.

(D) All of these

16. Rights and obligations under a contract can be enforced only within a specified period, called–

(A) Period of Performance.

(B) Period of Limitation.

(C) Period of Guarantee.

(D) Period of Rights.

17. Limitation period to recover a debts is—

(A) 2 years.

(B) 2.5 years.

(C) 3 years.

(D) 3.5 years.

18. If a debt is not recovered within 3 years of its becoming due, the debt becomes time-barred and is discharged by –

(A) performance.

(B) lapse of time.

(C) breach .

(D) inaction.

19. In which of the ways can a contract be discharged by operation of law?

(A) Unauthorised alteration of terms of a written document.

(B) Vesting of rights and liabilities in the same person.

(C) Neither (A) nor (B)

(D) Both (A) and (B)

20. ______signifies that the parties are not further bound under the contract.

(A) Waiver of a Contract

(B) Breach of Contract

(C) Rsscission of a Contract

(D) Discharge of a Contract

21. When a contract ceases to bind the parties to it, it is said to be —

(A) Discharged.

(B) Performed.

(C) Obliged.

(D) Rescinded.

22. In which of the ways can a contract be discharged?

(A) By Performance

(B) By Operation of Law

(C) By Lapse of Time

(D) By all the above

23. A contract can be discharged by—

(A) frustration of the contract.

(B) performance of the contract.

(C) both (A) & (B)

(D) neither (A) nor (B)

24. A Promisee may dispense with the performance of a promise—

(A) wholly.

(B) in part.

(C) either (A) or (B)

(D) neither (A) nor (B)

25. An obligation under a contract stands discharged by—

(A) dispensing with the performance

(B) impossibility of performance

(C) death of the contracting party, if the contract is personal in nature

(D) all the above

26. A contract stands discharged—

(A) By performance of the contract.

(B) By breach of the contract.

(C) By agreement and novation.

(D) By all of these.

27. A Contract can be discharged by performance in which of the following ways?

(A) Actual performance

(B) Offer to Perform *i.e.* Tender

(C) Either (A) or (B)

(D) Both (A) and (B)

28. For a valid novation, substitution must be made—

(A) before making of the original contract.

(B) during the continuance of the original contract.

(C) after the conclusion of the original contract.

(D) any of the above

29. Novation may happen between—

(A) the same parties as the original contract.

(B) different parties.

(C) either (A) or (B)

(D) neither (A) nor (B)

30. In discharge of contract by novation, the consideration for the new contract is —

(A) the discharge of the Original Contract.

(B) to be separately identified.

(C) to be decided by the parties.

(D) all of the above

31. A owes money Rs. 50,000 to B under a contract. It is agreed between A, B & C that B shall henceforth accept C as his Debtor instead of A for the same amount. Old debt of A is discharged, and a new debt from C to B is contracted. This is called —

(A) rescission of contract.

(B) novation of contract.

(C) alteration of contract.

(D) all of the above

32. A contracts with B to supply certain goods at B's warehouse by 15th May and B agrees to pay on delivery. Both of them may agree to modify the terms, say, delivery on 18th May and payment one week since delivery. The original contract is discharged by—

(A) alteration of contract .

(B) novation of contract.

(C) remission of contract.

(D) rescission of contract.

33. In which of the ways can a contract be discharged by impossibility of performance?

(A) Initial Impossibility

(B) Supervening or Subsequent Impossibility

(C) Either (A) or (B)

(D) Neither (A) nor (B)

34. In which of the ways can a contract be discharged by agreement between parties?

(A) Remission

(B) Waiver

(C) Either (A) or (B)

(D) Neither (A) nor (B)

35. Partial Rescission of a contract occurs where the original contract is varied by—

(A) rescinding some terms of the contract.

(B) substituting new terms for those rescinded.

(C) adding new terms without any rescinding the original terms.

(D) all of the above

36. A contract stands discharged—

(A) By performance of the contract.

(B) By breach of the contract.

(C) By agreement and novation.

(D) By all of these

37. Novation can be made by—

(A) change in the terms of the contract

(B) change in the Contracting Parties

(C) either (A) or (B)

(D) neither (A) nor (B)

38. No consideration is necessary for remission–

(A) True

(B) Partly True

(C) False

(D) None of the above

39. A owes B Rs. 50,000. Due date for payment is 25th March. A pays to B Rs. 30,000 on 25th March, who accepts it in full satisfaction of the debt. The debt is discharged on account of—

(A) remission of part of the performance of a promise.

(B) extension of time of performance.

(C) acceptance of any other satisfaction instead of performance.

(D) all of the above

40. A owes B Rs. 50,000. Due date for payment is 25th March. On 25th March, B extend time of payment by two months. The contract to pay on 25th March is discharged on account of—

(A) remission of part of the performance of a promise.

(B) extension time of performance.

(C) acceptance of any other satisfaction instead of performance.

(D) all of the above

41. A owes B Rs. 50,000. Due date for payment is 25th March. On 25th March, B agrees to take a piece of land belonging to A worth Rs. 40,000 in satisfaction of the debt. The debt is discharged on account of—

(A) remission of part of the performance of a promise.

(B) extension time of performance..

(C) acceptance of any other satisfaction instead of performance.

(D) all of the above

42. Abandonment or intentional relinquishment of a right under the contract is called—

(A) Waiver.

(B) Breach.

(C) Rescission.

(D) Alteration.

43. No consideration is necessary for a waiver.

(A) True

(B) Partly True

(C) False

(D) None of the above

44. When a party waives his rights under a contract, the other party is—

(A) entitled to sue the first party for damages

(B) released from his obligations

(C) either (A) or (B)

(D) neither (A) nor (B)

45. A contracts with B to deliver 90 kg of material X on 15th June. A does not deliver on 15 June. B may rescind the contract. The contract is rescinded due to—

(A) Mutual decision.

(B) A's failure to perform.

(C) Impossibility of Performance.

(D) Revocation of proposal.

46. When the parties mutually agree to change certain terms of contract, it terminates the original contract. This is called—

(A) rescission of contract.

(B) novation of contract.

(C) alteration of contract.

(D) remission of contract.

47. In case of alteration, there is a change in the parties and new parties may be included.

(A) True

(B) Partly true

(C) False

(D) None of the above

48. If a person accepts a lesser sum of money that what was contracted for in discharge of the whole debt, it is known as—

(A) Waiver.

(B) Remission.

(C) Alteration.

(D) Rescission.

49. Remission is the acceptance of—

(A) a lesser sum than what was contracted for.

(B) a lesser fulfilment of the promise made.

(C) either (A) or (B)

(D) neither (A) nor (B)

50. Under remission, a Promisee may—

(A) remit the whole or part of the performance of a promise.

(B) extend time of performance.

(C) accept any other satisfaction instead of performance.

(D) all of the above

51. A Creditor agrees with his Debtor and a third party to accept that third party as his Debtor. The contract is discharged by—

(A) Performance.

(B) Alteration.

(C) Waiver.

(D) Novation.

52. For discharge of a contract by Novation, consent of _________is required.

(A) majority parties to the original contract

(B) all the parties to the original contract

(C) atleast two of the parties to the original contract

(D) any one of the above

53. A promises to supply 50 sets of Men's Suit of a particular type to B three months hence. By that time there is no demand for those suits. A & B can rescind the contract. This is called—

(A) Mutual Rescission.

(B) Breach.

(C) Impossibility of performance.

(D) Revocation of proposal.

54. In which of the ways can a contract be discharged by operation of law?

(A) Death of Promisor

(B) Insolvency of Promisor

(C) Merger of Rights

(D) All of the above

55. On the valid performance of the contractual obligations by the parties, the contract—

(A) is discharged.

(B) becomes enforceable.

(C) becomes void.

(D) becomes illegal.

56. In cases of refusal to perform by any one party, the other party can—

(A) ignore the notice of refusal for the time being and wait till the time when the contract is to be executed.

(B) waive his right to rescission by acquiescence.

(C) treat the repudiation as wrongful putting an end to the contract.

(D) all of the above

57. L contracts to sell 100 bags of sugar to M. Due to heavy loss by a major fire which leaves nothing to sell, L applies for insolvency and is adjudged insolvent. the contract is discharged due to —

(A) Performance.

(B) Breach.

(C) Operation of Law, i.e. Insolvency.

(D) Impossibility of Performance.

58. Rescission may be —

(A) Total.

(B) Partial.

(C) either (A) or (B)

(D) neither (A) nor (B)

59. Where a party under a voidable contract, decides to rescind the same, the other party is—

(A) guilty of breach of contract.

(B) discharged from his promise.

(C) entitled for damages.

(D) all of the above

60. The party rescinding a Voidable Contract shall restore benefits received, if any, to the person from whom it was received.

(A) True

(B) Partly True

(C) False

(D) None of the above

61. Rescission of a Voidable Contract may also be revoked and the parties can get back on the original contract.

(A) True

(B) Partly True

(C) False

(D) None of the above

62. Rescission of a voidable contract shall be communicated or revoked in the same manner as the communication or revocation of—

(A) Breach.

(B) Acceptance.

(C) Proposal.

(D) Impossibility.

63. Total substitution of new contract in place of the old contract takes place in case of –

(A) Remission.

(B) Recission.

(C) Novation.

(D) Alteration.

64. A Bill of Exchange which was accepted by K, reaches K's hands after being negotiated and endorsed through 4 other parties. The contract is discharged due to—

(A) Merging of inferior right in a superior right.

(B) Debt barred by law of limitation.

(C) Rights and liabilities vesting in the same person.

(D) Breach of contract.

ANSWERS TO MULTIPLE CHOICE QUESTIONS

1. A	**14.** D	**27.** C	**40.** B	**53.** A
2. D	**15.** D	**28.** B	**41.** C	**54.** D
3. D	**16.** B	**29.** C	**42.** A	**55.** A
4. A	**17.** C	**30.** A	**43.** A	**56.** D
5. C	**18.** B	**31.** B	**44.** B	**57.** C
6. C	**19.** D	**32.** A	**45.** B	**58.** C
7. D	**20.** D	**33.** C	**46.** C	**59.** B
8. A	**21.** A	**34.** C	**47.** C	**60.** A
9. A	**22.** D	**35.** D	**48.** B	**61.** C
10. A	**23.** C	**36.** D	**49.** C	**62.** C
11. D	**24.** C	**37.** C	**50.** D	**63.** C
12. A	**25.** D	**38.** A	**51.** D	**64.** C
13. D	**26.** D	**39.** A	**52.** B	

Chapter 4

Remedies For Breach Of Contract

1. Right to claim compensation/damages (Sec. 73)

The rules regarding damages are as follows:

(1) Ordinary Damages:

⇨ ***Meaning:*** Such damages arise *directly and naturally* as a result of a breach of contract. This means that the damages must be the result of a breach of contract.

⇨ ***Measurement of damages, in case of breach of contract for sale of goods***

Damages = The difference between contract price and market price on the date of breach

Example: A agrees to sell to B 100 quintals of cotton at Rs. 100 per quintal on a certain day. On the day appointed, B refuses to buy the cotton. On that day, the price of the cotton ruling in the market was Rs. 90 per quintal. Loss suffered by B will be Rs. 10 (Rs. 100-90) per quintal.

If after the day of breach the price of the cotton further goes down to Rs. 80 per quintal, A would not be entitled to damages at the rate of Rs. 20 (100-80) but only at the rate of Rs. 10 (100-90) per quintal.

Further, if the price of the cotton after the day of the breach goes up to Rs. 110 per quintal, then the seller can claim the loss on the date of the breach, i.e., Rs. 10 per quintal as well as keep with him the profit of Rs. 10 (110-100) per quintal.

⇨ ***Measure of damages, where the same types of goods are not available-***

(i) In such a case, the price of the nearest and best available substitute may be taken into account.

(ii) In case the goods are rare, then monetary compensation will not be an adequate remedy and the Court in such a case can order *specific performance.*

⇨ **No damages for remote/indirect loss**

Examples: A contracts to pay a sum of money to B on a day specified. A fails to pay the amount on that day; consequently, B is unable to pay his creditors. A is not liable to make good to B anything except the principal sum he contracted to pay together with a reasonable rate of interest upto the day of payment from the date of breach.

(2) Special/particular damages:

These damages are indirect damages which both the parties knew *at the time of making the contract*, to be likely to result from the breach of the contract. Such damages can be claimed by the aggrieved party.

Examples: (1) A, a taxi driver, gave his taxi for repair to a mechanic, informing him that an unreasonable delay will result in a loss of income of Rs. 500 per day. The mechanic unreasonably delays the repair of the taxi. A is entitled to recover the loss of income at the rate of Rs. 500 per day.

(2) A tailor gave his sewing machine to a transport company informing that his machine should be transported to a nearby town on a particular day on which a mela was being held, otherwise he will lose an income of Rs. 1,000. If the transport company does not transport the machine on the day appointed, the tailor is entitled to get Rs. 1,000 as special damages.

(3) Vindictive/exemplary/punitive damages:

These damages are very heavy. The object of granting vindictive damages is to punish the party and set an example before others so that they may not commit breach of contract.

Therefore, such damages do not come within the purview of the Contract Act. Under the Contract Act, damages are granted as a compensation for the loss suffered, but not as a punishment.

Examples: Vindictive damages are generally granted by the Courts in the following cases:

(i) Where there is a breach of a promise to marry.

(ii) Where a banker wrongfully dishonours the cheque of his customer, who happens to be a trader or businessman, the banker is liable to pay heavy (exemplary) damages for the loss of credit suffered by the customer.

(4) Nominal damages:

Where a party does not suffer any loss due to a breach of contract, the Court may grant nominal damages, i.e., say one rupee or one penny. It is done to uphold the right of a party given by the law.

(5) Damages for personal inconvenience:

Damages are also awarded for personal inconvenience caused directly by breach of contract.

Example: A passenger was transported to a wrong place, where he could not get conveyance and had to walk down several miles to reach his destination. *Held*, he was entitled to damages for the inconvenience suffered.

—*Hamlin* v *G. N. Rly. Co.* (1856)

However, in the above case the passenger would not be entitled to any damages for illness caused by walking or for any loss of business due to his failure to reach his destination in time.

(6) Damages for Breach of Warranty:

In case there is a breach of warranty, the buyer is entitled to claim all damages directly caused by such breach.

Example: A purchased milk from B. The milk contained typhoid germs. A's wife got infected after taking the milk and died.

Held, A can recover the expenses incurred for employing extra servants, because of the loss of his wife's services during her illness, medical expenses and pecuniary loss caused to him due to his wife's death.

—*Jackson* v *Watson & Sons* (1909)

Duty to Mitigate Damages:

The injured party should take all reasonable steps to minimise its loss. It will not be allowed to claim any damages or loss caused to it by its own negligence to mitigate the loss.

Example: A, agreed to take on rent a shop and paid one month's rent in advance. However, B could not give possession of the shop to A in time. In the vicinity, other shops were available, but A preferred not to do business for eight months. A sued B.

Held, he was not entitled to any damages except refund of advance, as he failed to minimise his loss by not taking another shop available in the neighbourhood. —*Naki* v *Prabhu*

Certain Issues regarding Damages

– Whether difficulty of assessing damages prevents a party from claiming damages? No

Example: A promised to marry B. He married C. A must pay damages to B, although it is difficult to calculate the loss suffered by B because of breach of promise to marry.

– What is the difference between liquidated damages and penalty?

To avoid the difficulty of assessing damages, *generally*, parties fix in advance the amount of damages that would be payable in case of breach of contract. This amount may be called *'liquidated damages'* or *'penalty'*.

'Liquidated damages' represent a fair and reasonable estimate of the loss, which a party may suffer due to breach of the contract. On the other hand, 'penalty' is an unfair and unreasonable estimate of the loss, which is fixed with the intention of coercing or compelling the other party to perform the contract.

In India, no such distinction is made. The courts in India allow only 'reasonable compensation'.

Distinction between liquidated damages & penalty

(1) One should not go by the words or phrases used in the contract. The Court is not bound by the words used and, therefore should ascertain in each case whether the stipulation is really a penalty or liquidated damages.

(2) Object: The object of penalty is to create a terror in the mind of the promisor to complete his promise. The object of liquidated damages is a genuine pre-estimate of damages, which is likely to result due to breach of contract.

Example: A agrees to pay Rs. 1,000. If A fails to pay B Rs. 500 on a certain day it is a penalty.

(3) Facts and Circumstances: The question whether a sum stipulated is a penalty or liquidated damages is a question of fact and circumstances and to be decided on a case-to-case basis. Consider the following situations:

(i) Where there is a promise to pay a certain sum of money and in case of its breach, a larger sum is payable as damages than the sum to be borrowed, it is a penalty.

Example: A contracts with B to pay Rs. 1,000, if he fails to pay B Rs. 500 on a given day. It is a penalty.

(ii) Where the sum stipulated for is extravagant in amount in comparison to the greatest loss that would possibly be proved to have resulted from the breach, it will be a penalty.

Example: A agrees to pay B a sum of Rs. 500 on a certain day and in default to pay a sum of Rs. 10,000 as damages. This amount of compensation is extravagant in comparison to the loss that B might suffer on account of breach of contract. *Hence,* it is a penalty.

(iii) Where a single sum is payable by way of compensation on the happening of one or more events, some of them may cause minor damage, while the other severe damage, then it can be presumed that it is a penalty. In other words, in case the amount of damage has no relation to the amount of loss, it is a penalty.

– Whether payment of interest at an increased rate, in case of default, amounts to penalty?

The rules in respect of payment of interest are summarised below:

(1) Interest is payable only if there is an express or implied agreement or if there is a custom or usage of trade in this respect.

(2) Interest may be paid under the provisions of the Interest Act, 1839.

(3) A stipulation for increased rate of interest from the date of default shall be treated as a penalty, only if the rate of interest is abnormally high, *e.g.*, an increase from 12% to 50% is a stipulation by way of penalty, the court shall grant relief in such a case.

(4) A stipulation for increased rate of interest from the date of contract (not merely from the date of default) shall always be considered penalty.

(5) Payment of decreased rate of interest to ensure punctual payment is not regarded as a penalty.

Example: A bond provides that 18% interest will be charged instead of 24%, if the debtor pays interest punctually at the end of every year. Such a clause is not in the nature of penalty.

– Whether forfeiture of earnest money and security deposits amounts to penalty?

Generally, contracts provide for forfeiture of earnest money and security deposit, so as to ensure performance of contract.

⇨ Earnest money is a part of the purchase price agreed. Forfeiture of earnest money in case of a breach of contract does not amount to a penalty, if the amount to be forfeited is reasonable. However, if the amount of earnest money to be forfeited is unreasonable, it will amount to a penalty.

⇨ Security deposit is not a part of the purchase price. The forfeiture of security deposit is a penalty. Only a reasonable amount for loss can be claimed as compensation.

– Whether a stipulation that in default of payment of any instalment, the whole amount shall become due, amounts to penalty? No.

A borrows Rs. 1,00,000 from B payable in 10 monthly instalments with a condition that in case of default of any installment, the whole sum shall become due. It is not a penalty. However, where the amount to be returned is more than the amount borrowed, such a stipulation shall amount to a penalty.

– For purposes of claiming damages, a breach of contract and quasi-contract is treated at par.

2. *Quantum Meruit*

Quantum meruit implies a payment for the work done. A claim for *quantum meruit* may arise, when—

(a) a person has done some work under the contract, and

(b) the other party repudiates the contract or the work cannot be performed further due to impossibility or illegality.

The party which has performed the contract can claim reasonable remuneration for the work done.

– Essentials of Quantum Meruit:

(1) The party doing the work must have been prevented from performing the contract either by the other party or by impossibility or illegality and not of his own desire.

For Example: A engaged B to write a book to be published in instalments in a magazine. After a few issues, the magazine was abandoned. Held, B could ask for remuneration for the work done on the basis of *Quantum Meruit*.

(2) The contract must be divisible.

For Example: Mr. P agreed to pay Mr. C a lump sum payment of £ 30 for a complete voyage from Jamaica to Liverpool. Mr. C died before the voyage was completed.

Held, his widow could not claim on the basis of *Quantum Meruit*. —*Cutler* v *Powell* (1795)

☞ ***Examples of quantum meruit:***

(1) Void Agreement: Where an agreement is discovered to be void, the party who has taken any benefit under the agreement must restore it or repay it (Sec. 65).

For Example: A agreed to purchase B's horse and paid an advance of Rs. 1,000 to B. Later on, it was discovered that the horse was dead at the time of contract. Mr. B must return the sum of Rs. 1,000 to A.

(2) Badly performed contract: In case a contract (whether divisible or indivisible) is completely performed, but badly, the person who has performed the contract can claim the contract amount, but the other party can make a deduction for the bad work.

For example: A agreed to decorate B's flat for a lump sum of £ 750. A did the work, but badly. B got the defect removed by paying £294. Held, A could recover £ 750 less £294. —*Hoeing* v *Issacs* (1952)

(3) When something is done or delivered without an intention to do so gratuitously (Sec. 70)- Already discussed

3. Specific Performance

Damages are granted by way of monetary compensation. However, where monetary compensation is not an adequate remedy, the Court may direct the defaulting party to carry out his promise. In contracts for sale of immovable property like land and buildings etc. or rare articles i.e. which are not readily available in the market, specific performance may be granted by the Court.

Exception: However, this remedy is purely discretionary and in the following cases the Court will not grant specific performance:

(i) Where monetary compensation is an adequate remedy.

(ii) Where contract is of a personal nature, e.g., a contract to sing or marry.

(iii) Where it will be inequitable, e.g., against a minor,

(iv) Where a contract made by a company is *ultra vires* the company.

4. Injunction Order

Where a contract is of personal nature, specific performance is not ordered by the Court as it cannot supervise the performance. In such a case, there is an indirect remedy, i.e., injunction order. An injunction order is issued to restrain a person from doing something.

Example: A agrees to sing at B's theatre for one year and not to sing elsewhere. During the year A agrees to sing at C's theatre and thus refuses to sing at B's theatre.

In this case the contract is of a personal nature, therefore, the Court cannot order specific performance, but can grant injunction order restraining A from singing at C's theatre thus indirectly compelling A to sing at B's theatre.

5. Restitution (Already discussed)

6. Cancellation or Rectification

Where the terms of contract do not express the real intention of the parties, either party may file a suit to have the instrument rectified. In such a case, if the court finds that there has been a fraud or mistake, it may ascertain the real intention of the parties, and may in its discretion, rectify the instrument so as to express that intention. If rectification is not possible, the court orders for the cancellation of the contract.

Example: A fraudulently got a gift deed signed from his father. His (A's) father can apply to the Court to get the gift deed cancelled.

MULTIPLE CHOICE QUESTIONS

1. Mr. R invited all his close friends for a dinner on the occasion of the successful completion of his research. He wanted to take good care of his friends and accordingly he arranged a very lavish dinner in a star hotel. On the day, to his shock and surprise the friends could not turn up to the dinner, consequently all the dishes and money were wasted. He was terribly disappointed. In the above situation which of the following remedies is/are available to Mr. R for the loss caused to him?

(A) Mr. R can file a suit against his friends for not attending the dinner.

(B) Mr. R cannot have any remedy.

(C) Mr. R can recover the expenses incurred for the arrangements from his friends.

(D) Mr. R can file a suit for the special damages.

2. Suppose the time fixed for performance of the contract has expired, but the time is not essential. What is the remedy of the promisee in the circumstances?

(A) Can rescind the contract

(B) To claim compensation

(C) No remedy available

(D) None of these

3. Any breach of duty bringing gains to the Doer, by misleading another to his prejudice is a case of—

(A) Suppression of Facts.

(B) Breach of Contract.

(C) Fraud.

(D) Misrepresentation.

4. F promised to pay his son S a sum of Rs. 1 lakh if S passed C.A. exams in the first attempt. S passed the exam in the first attempt, but F failed to pay the amount as promised. S files a suit for recovery of the amount.

State where S can recover the amount under the India Contract Act, 1872.

(A) S can sue F for not honouring his words.

(B) S has to pay Rs. 1 Lakh to F.

(C) S has no remedy against F.

(D) S has to write exam again, to claim the reward.

5. No action can be taken for breach of an illegal agreement.

(A) True

(B) Partly True

(C) False

(D) None of the above

6. A party who rightfully rescinds the contract is also entitled to receive compensation from the defaulting party.

(A) True

(B) Partly true

(C) False

(D) None of the above

7. Where a party to the contract has suffered substantial physical discomfort and inconvenience as a result of breach of contract, he can file a suit for claiming compensation from the party at fault.

(A) True

(B) Partly true

(C) False

(D) None of the above

8. The special damages, i.e., the damages which arise due to so especial or unusual circumstances–

(A) Are not recoverable altogether.

(B) Are illegal being punitive in nature.

(C) Can be claimed as a matter of right.

(D) Cannot be claimed as a matter of right.

9. Which of the following statements is incorrect?

(A) Ordinary damages are recoverable.

(B) Special damages are recoverable, only if the parties knew about them.

(C) Remote or indirect damages are not recoverable.

(D) None of these statements are incorrect.

10. When prior to the due date of performance, the promisor absolutely refuses to perform the contract, it is known as –

(A) abandonment of contract.

(B) remission of contract.

(C) actual breach of contract.

(D) anticipatory breach of contract.

11. In case of anticipatory breach, the aggrieved party may treat the contract –

(A) as discharged and bring an immediate action for damages.

(B) as operative and wait till the time for performance arrives.

(C) exercise option either (A) or (B).

(D) only option (A) is available.

12. Sometimes, a party is entitled to claim compensation in proportion to the work done by him. It is possible by a suit for–

(A) Damages.

(B) Injunction.

(C) *Quantum meruit.*

(D) None of these

13. A contracts to indemnify B against the consequences of proceedings, which C may take against B in respect of certain sum of money. C obtains judgment against B for the amount. Without paying any portion of the decree amount B sues A for its recovery. Will B succeed?"

(A) Yes

(B) No

14. Generally, which of the following damages are not recoverable?

(A) Ordinary damages

(B) Special damages

(C) Remote damages

(D) Nominal damages

15. Which of the following is correct?

(A) Free consent is not important, if consideration is preset, even if the consideration is inadequate.

(B) Anticipatory breach and anticipatory bail are actually the same thing.

(C) The concept of damage allows one to make some gain out of it.

(D) All of the above are incorrect.

16. Remedies available for breach of contract are–

(A) Dissolution of the firm.

(B) Charging extra fees from the party committing the breach.

(C) Suit for Specific Performance.

(D) None of the above.

17. ______________ does not exist.

(A) Liability for special damages

(B) Liability for exemplary damages

(C) Liability for nominal damages

(D) Liability for disciplinary damages

18. Suit for specific performance & suit for injunction –

(A) Are remedies which provide the same result.

(B) Are different remedies and they provide different results.

(C) Are not the correct way to act against the party committing the breach.

(D) Are the only correct way to act against the party committing the breach.

19. In case of breach of contract by the seller, the buyer has rights –

(A) For suit for damages.

(B) Suit for specific performance.

(C) Suit for breach of warranty.

(D) All of these

20. Which of the following statements is true?

(1) Even if, a proposal is not accepted properly it becomes a valid contract.

(2) The agreements which are against the public policy can be enforced if the parties are willing to contract.

(3) For breach of contract, a party can claim compensation for loss or damage.

(4) Two are more persons are said to consent, when they agree upon the same thing in the same sense.

(A) 1 & 2

(B) 2 & 3

(C) 3 & 4

(D) 1 & 4

21. In case of Gujrat & Maharashtra States, where a person enters into a wagering transaction through an agent, and the agent fails to carry out the Principal's instructions—

(A) Principal can sue Agent for breach of contract of agency.

(B) Principal cannot sue Agent for breach of contract of agency.

(C) Principal can sue Agent for damages.

(D) Principal can sue Agent to recover the betting moneys paid.

22. A contracts with B to deliver possession of a house under construction within a period of 6 months; failing which he would pay the monthly rental of B. The monthly rental payable by B for A is in the nature of—

(A) Exemplary Damages.

(B) Special Damages.

(C) Liquidated Damages.

(D) Penalty.

23. Breach of a Contract may be—

(A) Actual Breach.

(B) Anticipatory Breach.

(C) Either (A) or (B)

(D) Neither (A) nor (B)

24. A party entitled to rescind the contract, loses the remedy where —

(A) he has ratified the contract.

(B) third Party has acquired right in good faith.

(C) contract is not separable and recession is sought of a part only.

(D) all of these

25. Where the amount payable in case of breach is fixed in advance whether by way of liquidated damages or penalty, the aggrieved party may claim—

(A) a reasonable compensation for the breach.

(B) the amount so fixed in the contract.

(C) (A) or (B) whichever is lower

(D) (A) or (B) whichever is higher

26. In case of anticipatory breach, where the Promisee opts to keep the contract alive till the actual date of performance, the amount of damages = Price prevailing on the date of performance-Contract Price.

(A) True

(B) Partly true

(C) False

(D) None of the above

27. When there is breach of contract, special damages are awarded—

(A) Only when there are special circumstances.

(B) Only when there is special loss.

(C) Only when there is a notice of the likely special loss.

(D) In all cases

28. Vindictive Damages have been awarded—

(A) for a breach of promise to marry.

(B) for wrongful dishonour of a cheque by a banker possessing adequate funds of the customer.

(C) Either (A) or (B)

(D) Neither (A) nor (B)

29. In case of breach of contract of sale of some rare article or thing for which there is no substitute in the market, the Court may grant—

(A) *Quantum meruit*.

(B) Rescission.

(C) Specific Performance.

(D) Injunction.

30. Where the Buyer wrongfully neglects or refuses to accept and pay for the goods—

(A) Seller may sue Buyer for damages for non-acceptance.

(B) Seller cannot sue Buyer for damages for non-acceptance.

(C) Seller can sue Buyer's Banker for damages.

(D) Seller can sue Buyer's Solicitors for fraud.

31. Damages awarded to compensate the injured party for the actual amount of loss suffered by him for breach of contract are called—

(A) General/Ordinary Damages.

(B) Special Damages.

(C) Vindictive Damages.

(D) Nominal Damages.

32. Nominal Damages can be—

(A) claimed by the aggrieved party as a matter of right.

(B) awarded only at the discretion of the Court.

(C) should be specified/quantified in the contract.

(D) all of the above

33. *Quantum Meruit* is not applicable i.e. there is no right to sue, when—

(A) Contract is indivisible into parts and a lumpsum is to be paid on completion of total work.

(B) Person claiming compensation is himself guilty of breach.

(C) Work is performed gratuitously, i.e. there is no evidence of promise to pay for work done.

(D) All of the above

34. The phrase "*Quantum Meruit*" literally means—

(A) As much as earned.

(B) The fact in itself.

(C) A contract for the sale.

(D) As much as gained.

ANSWERS TO MULTIPLE CHOICE QUESTIONS

1.	B	**8.**	D	**15.**	D	**22.**	C	**29.**	C
2.	B	**9.**	D	**16.**	C	**23.**	C	**30.**	A
3.	D	**10.**	D	**17.**	D	**24.**	D	**31.**	A
4.	C	**11.**	C	**18.**	B	**25.**	C	**32.**	B
5.	A	**12.**	C	**19.**	D	**26.**	A	**33.**	D
6.	A	**13.**	A	**20.**	C	**27.**	C	**34.**	A
7.	A	**14.**	C	**21.**	B	**28.**	C		

Chapter 5

CONTINGENT And QUASI CONTRACT

CONTINGENT CONTRACT

☞ Meaning of Contingent Contract:

A contract may be an absolute contract or a contingent contract. An absolute contract is to be performed in every event without any condition. However, a contingent contract depends upon the happening or non-happening of an event.

> **A Contingent Contract is a contract to do or not to do something, if some event, collateral to such contract, does or does not happen.**

--- Sec. 31

For Example: (a) Mr. A promises to pay Rs. 10 lakh to Mr. B, if the ship "Victory" does not return. In this case, the contract can be enforced only if the ship does not return. However, if the ship returns, the contract cannot be enforced. Therefore, this is a contingent contract.

(b) A contracts to pay B Rs. 10,000, if B's House is burnt. This is a contingent contract.

☞ Essential characteristics of contingent contract:

1. The performance of the contract must depend upon the happening or non-happening of an event.
2. The happening of the event must be uncertain.
3. The event must be collateral and *forms no part of the reciprocal promises of which the contract consists.*

It is to be noted that insurance contracts, contracts of indemnity and guarantee are contingent contracts.

Rules Regarding the Contingent Contract

1. Contracts contingent on happening of a future uncertain event [Sec. 32]: Such contracts cannot be enforced by law, unless and until that event has happened. If the event becomes impossible, such contracts become void.

For Example: A contracts to pay B a sum of money when B marries C. C dies without being married to B. The contract becomes void.

2. Contracts contingent on the non-happening of a future uncertain event [Sec. 33]: Such contracts cannot be enforced by law, unless and until the happening of that event becomes impossible, and not before.

For Example: Mr. A promises to pay Rs. 10 lakh to Mr. B, if the ship "Victory" does not return. In this case, the contract can be enforced only if the ship does not return. However, if the ship returns, the contract cannot be enforced.

3. Contracts contingent on the future conduct of a living person [Sec. 34]: If the future event on which a contract is contingent is the way in which a person will act at an unspecified time, the event shall be considered to become impossible when such person does anything which renders it impossible that he should so act within any definite time, or otherwise than under further contingencies.

For Example: A agrees to pay B Rs. 10,000, if B marries C. C marries D. If bigamy is not allowed, then the marriage of B with C must be considered impossible, although it is possible that D may die and that C may afterwards marry B.

4. Contracts contingent on the happening of an event within a fixed time [Sec. 35(1)]: Such contracts become void, if—

(i) at the expiration of the time fixed, such event has not happened, or

(ii) before the time fixed, such event becomes impossible.

For Example: A promises to pay B a sum of money, if a certain ship returns within a year. The contract may be enforced, if the ship returns within the year and becomes void if the ship is sunk within the year.

5. Contracts contingent on the non-happening of an event within a fixed time [Sec. 35(2)]: Such contracts may be enforced by law, if –

(i) such event does not happen, or

(ii) before the time fixed, the happening of such event becomes impossible.

For Example: A promises to pay B a sum of money, if a certain ship does not return within a year. The contract may be enforced, if the ship does not return within the year or is sunk within the year.

6. Contracts contingent on the happening of an impossible event [Sec. 36]: Such contracts are void.

For Example: A agrees to pay B Rs. 100, if two parallel lines cut each other.

QUASI-CONTRACT

"Quasi-Contracts are the contracts which are created—

- neither by word spoken
- nor written
- nor by the conduct of the parties,
- but these are created by the Law."

In fact, these contracts depend upon the principle that nobody will be allowed to become rich at the expense of the others.

TYPES OF QUASI-CONTRACTS

The Indian Contract Act deals with the following types of 'quasi-contracts', as discussed in Secs. 68 to 72:

1. Necessaries supplied to a person incapable of contracting or on his behalf (Sec. 68):

If a person supplies the necessities of the life according to the living standard to—

- a person, who is incapable of entering into a contract, or
- any one whom such incapable person is legally bound to support,

then the supplier is entitled to be reimbursed from the property of such incapable person.

For Example: (1) A supplies B, a lunatic, with necessaries suitable to his condition in life. A is entitled to be paid out of B's property.

(2) A supplies the wife and children of B, a lunatic, with necessaries suitable to their condition in life. A is entitled to be reimbursed from B's property.

2. Reimbursement to the person paying money to another in the payment of which he is interested (Sec. 69):

If a person is legally bound to pay some money and the other person has some interest in that payment, so he makes the payment, then he is entitled to be reimbursed by the former.

For Example: B holds land in Bengal, on a lease granted by A, a Zamindar. The revenue payable by A to the government being in arrears, his land is advertised for sale by the government under the revenue law. The consequence of such sale will be the termination of his own lease. B, to prevent the sale and the consequent termination of his own lease, pays to the Government the sum due from A. A is bound to return to B the amount paid by B.

☞ ***Essential rules of Sec. 69 are as follows:***

(1) The payer should be interested in the payment. The interest should exist at the time of payment. If the person making the payment has no interest, he cannot recover the payment.

For Example: A purchased certain goods on credit. B, a friend of A, paid the amount on behalf of A without A's consent. B cannot recover the amount, as B is not interested in the payment.

(2) Another person must be bound by law to pay.

(3) The payer must not be bound himself to pay the amount.

(4) The payment must be made to some third party.

For Example: Certain land was held on lease by the forest department of the Government. Arrears of revenue were due from the landlord. The land was advertised for sale in order to realise the arrears. The forest department made the payment to save the land from being sold.

In this case, the payment was not made to any third party, but by one department of the government to another. Hence the Government could not recover under this section.

—*Secretary of State* v *Fernandes* (1907) Mad.

3. Non-Gratuitous Act (Sec. 70):

Where –

- a person lawfully does anything for another person, or delivers anything to him, and
- such person has no intention to do so gratuitously, and
- another person enjoys the benefit of his act,

then the latter is bound to make compensation to the former in respect of an act done or a thing delivered.

For Examples: (1) A, a trader, leaves goods at B's house by mistake. B treats the goods as his own. He is bound to pay A for them.

(2) A saves B's property from fire. A is not entitled to compensation from B, if the circumstances show that he saved the property without any intention of getting any reward.

☞ ***Essential rules of Sec. 70 are as follows:***

(1) The thing delivered or act done must be lawful

(2) The act must have been done with an intention to claiming the reward.

(3) The other party for whom the act was done or thing delivered must have enjoyed the benefit.

(4) This section does not apply to persons who are incompetent to contract. For example, minor etc.

4. Responsibility of the Finder of Goods (Sec. 71):

If a person finds goods belonging to another and takes them into his possession, then he is liable as a bailee. As a bailee, he is under an obligation to take reasonable care of the goods. He must make reasonable efforts to trace the real owner. *For example*, if the amount is substantial, he may give a public notice in a newspaper or if the address card is there in a purse found, he must contact the owner at that address.

However, until and unless the real owner is found, he remains the owner of the goods against the whole world.

5. Mistake or Coercion (Sec. 72):

If some money has been paid, or something has been delivered to a person by mistake or under coercion, then it becomes the duty of that person to repay or return it.

For Example: (a) A and B jointly borrow Rs. 10000 from C. A returns the amount to C. B, who does not know this fact, also pays the amount to C. Now, Mr. C is bound to return the amount so paid.

(b) A railway company demanded an unreasonable amount for carriage from a consignee before delivery. The consignee paid the sum in order to obtain the goods. He is entitled to recover the amount, which was unreasonable.

Note: The scope of section 72 is very wide. It covers not only a mistake of fact, but also a mistake of law.

For Example: (a) A Terminal tax was paid to the municipality under a mistake of law. Held, the tax payer was entitled to refund under section 72 of the Contract Act.

—*Nagar Mahapalika, Kanpur* v *Sri Ram Mahadeo Prasad* 1990 SC

(b) An insurance company paid the amount on a policy under a mistake that the goods had been destroyed. The goods in fact had been sold.

Held, the insurance company is entitled to recover the money.

—*Nowich Society Ltd.* v *Price (W.H.) Ltd.* (1934)

6. Claim on the basis of quantum meruit: Refer to Chapter-4

☑☑☑

MULTIPLE CHOICE QUESTIONS

☞ Contingent Contract

1. A contingent contract is—
(A) Void.
(B) Voidable.
(C) Valid.
(D) Illegal.

2. A contingent contract dependent on the happening of future uncertain event can be enforced, when the event –
(A) happens.
(B) become impossible.
(C) does not happen.
(D) either of these.

3. A agrees to pay Rs. One lakh to B, if he brings on earth a star from sky. This is a contingent contract and –
(A) Illegal.
(B) Valid.
(C) Voidable.
(D) Void.

4. The difference between contingent contract and wagering agreements are as follows–
(A) A wagering agreement consists of reciprocal promises, whereas a contingent contract may not contain reciprocal promises.
(B) In a wagering agreement the uncertain event is the sole determining factor, while in a contingent contract the event is only collateral.
(C) A wagering agreement is void, whereas a contingent contract is valid.
(D) All of the above

5. Which of the following are the characteristics of a contingent contract—
(A) The performance of a contingent contract depends upon the happening or non-happening of an uncertain event in future.
(B) The event must be uncertain.
(C) The event must be collateral to the main contract.
(D) All of the above

6. A wager means—
(A) A promise to give money or money's worth upon the determination or ascertainment of an uncertain future event.
(B) A promise to give money or money's worth upon the determination or ascertainment of a certain future event.
(C) A promise to give money or money's worth upon the happening of future event the outcome if which is pre determined.
(D) A promise to give money or money's worth upon the non-happening of certain future events the outcome if which is pre-determined.

7. Which of the following is correct—
(A) A wagering agreement is void.
(B) A contingent contract is valid.
(C) A wagering agreement is void while a contingent contract is valid.
(D) None of the above.

8. Which is the example of wagering agreement?
(A) To purchase a lottery ticket
(B) Speculative trading in stock exchange
(C) Horse–race
(D) All of these

9. A agrees to pay Rs. 500 to B if it rains, and B promises to pay a like amount to A if it does not rain, this agreement is called—
(A) Contingent Contract.
(B) Quasi Contract.
(C) Wagering Agreement.
(D) Voidable Contract.

10. A contingent contract dependent on the non-happening of a future uncertain event become void, when such event—

(A) Happens.

(B) Does not become impossible.

(C) Does not happen.

(D) Both (A) and (B)

11. Transactions for sale and purchase of stocks and shares or for sale and delivery of goods, with a clear intention to give and take delivery of shares or goods are—

(A) Wagering Agreements.

(B) Not Wagering Agreements.

(C) Contingent Contracts.

(D) Voidable Agreements.

12. A contract dependent on the happening or non-happening of future uncertain event, is a –

(A) Uncertain contract.

(B) Contingent contract.

(C) Void contract.

(D) Voidable contract.

13. A contingent contract dependent on the non-happening of specified uncertain event within fixed time can be enforced, if the event–

(A) does not happen within fixed time.

(B) becomes impossible before the expiry of fixed time.

(C) happens within the fixed time.

(D) both (A) and (B)

14. Performance of a contingent contract is dependent on the —

(A) happening of the collateral event.

(B) non-happening of the collateral event.

(C) either (A) or (B)

(D) neither (A) nor (B)

15. A contingent contract to do or not to do anything on the happening of an uncertain future event —

(A) is never enforceable.

(B) is enforceable since the time of making it.

(C) becomes enforceable in the immediate possibility of happening of that event.

(D) becomes enforceable only on the happening of that event.

16. Contracts contingent upon the non-happening of an Uncertain Future Event within a fixed time, can be enforced by law —

(A) when time fixed has expired and such event has not happened.

(B) before expiry of the time fixed, it becomes certain that such event will not happen.

(C) either (A) or (B)

(D) neither (A) nor (B)

17. A contingent contract dependent on the non-happening of specified uncertain event within fixed time can be enforced if the event —

(A) does not happen within fixed time.

(B) becomes impossible before the expiry of fixed time.

(C) happens within the fixed time.

(D) both (A) and (B)

18. In a contingent contract neither party should have interest in the happening (or non-happening) of the event other than —

(A) his honour or prestige.

(B) the sum or stake he stands to win or lose.

(C) either (A) or (B)

(D) both (A) and (B)

19. A agrees to pay Rs. 1000 to B, if a certain ship returns within a year. However, the ship sinks within the year. In this case, the contract becomes –

(A) valid.

(B) void.

(C) voidable.

(D) illegal.

20. A Collateral event is an event –

(A) The performance for which is neither directly promised nor it is the entire consideration for the promise.

(B) The performance for which is directly promised.

(C) It is the entire consideration for the promise.

(D) The performance which is agreed upon by the parties in a Court of Law.

☛ Quasi Contract

21. M, a minor makes a promissory Note in favour of D. On attaining majority, M makes out a fresh Promissory Note (P/N) in lieu of the old one. In this case—

(A) The original P/N is invalid but the fresh P/N is valid.

(B) The original P/N is valid but the fresh P/N is invalid.

(C) Both the original and fresh P/N are valid.

(D) Both the original and fresh P/N are invalid.

22. Sometimes, a person finds certain goods belonging to some other persons. In such a case, the finder –

(A) becomes the owner of the goods and can use them.

(B) is under a duty to trace the true owner and return the goods.

(C) can sell the perishable goods, if the true owner cannot be found.

(D) both (B) and (C)

23. Quasi-Contract rests on the principle of—

(A) Equality/equity.

(B) There cannot be unjust enrichment of a party at the expense of another.

(C) Neither (A) nor (B)

(D) Both (A) and (B)

24. A Quasi-contract—

(A) is a contract.

(B) is an agreement.

(C) has only a legal obligation.

(D) is not any of these.

25. Quasi-contracts are called contracts in facts and not contracts in law.

(A) True

(B) Partly true

(C) False

(D) None of the above

26. Quasi-Contracts or Implied Contracts are exceptional kinds of contracts by which

(A) One party is bound to pay money in consideration for something done or suffered by the other party.

(B) No contractual relation exists between the parties.

(C) No contract has been made by the parties.

(D) All of these

27. Sections 68 to 72 of the Indian Contract Act deal with—

(A) Performance of contract

(B) Discharge of contract

(C) Certain relations resembling those created by contract

(D) Breach of contract

28. The Indian Contract Act deals with the following quasi-contract obligations—

(I) Claim for necessaries supplied to a person incompetent to contract.

(II) Reimbursement of money paid due by another.

(III) Obligation of person enjoying benefit of non-gratuitous act.

(IV) Responsibility of the Finder of Goods.

(A) I and II

(B) II and III

(C) III and IV

(D) I, II, III and IV

29. To claim reimbursement of money paid on behalf of another person, the payment should be made bona *fide*, i.e. for protection of own interest of the payer.

(A) True

(B) Partly True

(C) False

(D) None of the above

30. The maxim "*in pari delicto, potior est condition defendentis*" means—

(A) the defendant can be pardoned if his condition demands so.

(B) Defendant has to prove his innocence beyond doubt.

(C) In cases of equal guilt, the defendant is in a better position.

(D) The law assumes that the defendant is innocent.

31. Hari owes Rs. 1 lakh to Jaya. Jaya is entitled to recover this amount from Hari. This is called—

(A) Rights in *personam.*

(B) Rights *in rem.*

(C) Constitutional right.

(D) There is no right at all.

32. The basis of "quasi-contractual relations" is the –

(A) Existence of a valid contract between the parties.

(B) Prevention of unjust enrichment at the expense of others.

(C) Provisions contained in section 10 of the Contract Act.

(D) Existence of a voidable contract between the parties.

33. Claim for necessaries supplied to a person incompetent to contract, from the property of such person is enshrined in ______ of the Indian Contract Act, 1872.

(A) Section 68

(B) Section 69

(C) Section 70

(D) Section 71

34. In case of necessaries supplied to a person incompetent to contract, which of the following is true?

(A) Only the property (movable and immovable) of the incapable person shall be liable.

(B) The incapable person cannot be held liable personally.

(C) Where the incapable person does not own any property, nothing shall be payable.

(D) All the above

35. Claim for necessaries of life supplied to a lunatic under section 68 of Indian Contract Act, can be enforced against—

(A) the lunatic personally when he ceases to be lunatic.
(B) the relative of the lunatic.
(C) the guardian of the lunatic.
(D) the lunatic's property or estate.

36. A supplies B, a lunatic, with necessaries suitable to his condition in life. A is—

(A) Not entitled to be reimbursed from B's property.
(B) Entitled to be reimbursed from B's property.
(C) Personally liable.
(D) Jointly and Severally liable.

37. A who supplies the wife and children of B, a lunatic, with necessaries suitable to their condition in life, is entitled to be reimbursed from—

(A) B's property.
(B) B personally.
(C) B's wife and children.
(D) the Court.

38. Quasi Contractual Obligations are also termed as—

(A) Certain Relations Resembling Those Created by Contracts.
(B) Law of Restitution.
(C) Either (A) or (B)
(D) Neither (A) nor (B)

39. There are situations in which a person may be required to conform to an obligation, although he has not entered into or broken any contract. Such obligations created by the law are called—

(A) Quasi Contracts.
(B) Contingent Contracts.
(C) Unforeseen Contracts.
(D) Deemed Contracts.

40. X leaves his goods at Y's place who consumes them. Y is bound to pay the price. Y's act of consumption of goods constitutes an implied promise to pay, under the principle of—

(A) Contractual obligations.
(B) Quasi-contractual obligations.
(C) Semi contractual obligations.
(D) Deemed contractual obligations.

41. A person to whom money has been paid, or anything delivered by mistake or under coercion, must repay or return it.

(A) True
(B) Partly true
(C) False
(D) None of the above

42. A and B jointly owe Rs. 10 lakhs to C.A alone pays the amount to C and B, not knowing this fact pays Rs. 10 lakh over again to C.

(A) C is bound to repay the amount to B.
(B) C is bound to repay the amount to B and A jointly.
(C) C is bound to repay the amount to A and B equally.
(D) C is not bound to repay the amount to B.

43. If sales-tax had been deposited with respect to an item on which, there was no levy, the depositor/ assessee is—

(A) not entitled to refund from the government.
(B) entitled to refund from the government.
(C) entitled to charge the same from customers.
(D) entitled to refund from the court.

44. By claiming to retain the tax that has been collected though the collection is not authorised by law, the Government cannot enrich itself. It becomes liability of the Government to make restitution to the person making payment under mistake or coercion.

(A) True
(B) Partly true
(C) False
(D) None of the above

45. In case of payment of an amount under mistake, the period of limitation starts from—

(A) date of payment under mistake.
(B) date the mistake is or could have been discovered.
(C) (A) or (B) whichever is earlier
(D) (A) or (B) whichever is later

46. A left certain goods at B's house by mistake and B used the goods as his own. Here, A can recover the price of goods from B.

(A) True, on the basis of quasi-contract
(B) No, there is no valid contract between them.
(C) No, the goods have to be returned in specie.
(D) The court may set aside the arrangement.

47. Quasi-contracts arise—

(A) Where obligations are created without a contract.
(B) Where obligations are created under a contract.
(C) Out of natural causes
(D) Out of man-made causes

48. A person, who finds goods belonging to another and takes them into his custody, is subject to the same responsibility as a—

(A) Bailee.
(B) True Owner.

(C) Thief.

(D) Trespasser.

49. A person to whom money has been paid, or anything delivered by mistake—

(A) Becomes the owner of such money or those goods.

(B) Must repay the money or return those goods.

(C) Is allowed to sell the goods and retain the money realized from such sale.

(D) Has no obligation to return the money, he may do so only a good gesture.

ANSWERS TO MULTIPLE CHOICE QUECTIONS

1. C	**11.** B	**21.** D	**31.** A	**41.** A
2. A	**12.** B	**22.** D	**32.** B	**42.** A
3. D	**13.** D	**23.** D	**33.** A	**43.** B
4. D	**14.** C	**24.** A	**34.** D	**44.** A
5. D	**15.** D	**25.** C	**35.** D	**45.** B
6. A	**16.** C	**26.** D	**36.** B	**46.** A
7. C	**17.** D	**27.** C	**37.** A	**47.** A
8. A	**18.** B	**28.** D	**38.** C	**48.** A
9. C	**19.** B	**29.** A	**39.** A	**49.** B
10. D	**20.** A	**30.** C	**40.** B	

DIVISION II
THE SALE OF GOODS ACT, 1930

Chapter 1

Formation, Conditions And Warranties

The Sale of Goods Act, 1930 has 7 Chapters.

☞ **Applicability:**

- This Act extends to whole of India, except the State of Jammu and Kashmir.
- This Act came into force w.e.f. 1-7-1930.
- The Indian Contract Act, 1872 shall continue to apply to contracts for the sale of goods, if they are not inconsistent with this Act. (Sec. 3)

The word 'Indian' was omitted from the title of this Act in 1963.

☞ **Definitions (Sec. 2):**

Parties to Contract of sale

Buyer [Sec. 2(1)]
A person, who buys or agrees to buy the goods

Seller [Sec. 2(13)]
A person who sells or agrees to sell the goods

Document of Title [*Sec. 2(4)*]

1. Bill of lading
2. Dock-warrant
3. Warehouse keeper's certificate
4. Wharfingers' certificate
5. Railway receipt
6. Multimodal Transport Document
7. Warrant/Order for the delivery of goods

Any other document used in the ordinary course of business-

(i) as proof of the possession of goods, or

(ii) authorising, either by endorsement or by delivery, the possessor of the document to transfer or receive goods

Document of Title* v. *Document showing the title: A document of title enables a person named therein to transfer the property by mere endorsement and delivery, whereas a document showing title does not confer any right to transfer by way of endorsement and delivery. *For example*, a share certificate shows that the person named therein is entitled to the shares represented by it, but does not allow transfer of the shares by mere endorsement and delivery of the certificate.

Meaning of 'Contract of Sale of Goods'

"A *contract of sale of goods* is a contract whereby the seller transfers or agrees to transfer the property in the goods to the buyer for a price."

- - - Sec. 4

SALE & BAILMENT

☞ **Sale** : In the case of sale, the ownership in the goods is transferred from the seller to the buyer. The buyer becomes the owner of the goods.

☞ **Bailment** : In the case of bailment, the possession of the goods is transferred from one person to another person. For example, a Car given to workshop for repair etc.

The bailee does not become the owner of the goods. The transfer of possession is only for some time and the goods are taken back as per the directions of the bailor.

SALE & CONTRACT FOR WORK / LABOUR

The crucial test is **'what is the object of the contract, i.e. whether it is for the supply of goods or exercise of skill and labour?'** In the first case it would be a sale and in the second case, a contract for work and labour.

Examples (1) A dentist agreed to supply a set of artificial teeth to a patient. The material was wholly found by the dentist. *Held,* it was a contract for the sale of goods.

(2) An artist was asked to paint a portrait. The material was supplied by the party and not by the painter. It was held to be a contract for work and labour and not of sale.

SALE & HIRE PURCHASE AGREEMENT

In the case of sale, the ownership in goods is transferred from the seller to the buyer immediately.

However, in a hire-purchase agreement, the ownership in the goods shall be transferred only on payment of all the instalments. Thus, if the hire-purchaser refuses or is unable to pay all the instalments, then the instalments paid are treated as hire charges for the use of the goods by the hire-purchaser.

Thus, hire-purchase agreement is a combination of a bailment and an agreement to sell.

SUBJECT MATTER OF CONTRACT OF SALE – GOODS

" Goods -

- *means* every kind of movable property other than actionable claims and money, and
- *includes* stock and shares, growing crops, grass and things attached to or forming part of land which are agreed to be severed before sale or under the contract of sale."

- - - Sec. 2(7)

– **Essential features of Goods**:

1. Goods must be movable property.
2. Actionable claims and money have been expressly excluded from the definition.
3. Stocks and shares, growing crops, grass, agreed to be severed before sale are included in goods.

Types of Goods

1. Existing Goods: Existing goods are the goods, which are owned and possessed by the seller at the time of sale. Only the existing goods can be sold. Existing goods may be of three types:

(a) Specific goods	:	There are the goods, which are ***identified and agreed upon*** by the parties ***at the time of contract of sale***. It should be noted that the goods must be both identified and agreed upon.
(b) Ascertained goods	:	There are the goods, which are identified after the formation of a contract of sale.
(c) Unascertained goods	:	These are the goods, which are not identified and agreed upon at the time of the contract of sale. These goods are merely described by the parties at the time of contract of sale.

For Example: Mr. A, a car dealer, has 50 cars. He contracts to sell one of the cars to B.

(a) If A shows a particular car to B at the time of contract, it will be a contract for the sale of specific goods. The car has been identified and agreed upon by the parties at the time of contract of sale.

(b) If car was not identified at the time of sale, but after the contract of sale, A informs B that he will sell a particular car and B consents to it, the car becomes ascertained goods.

(c) If at the time of contract, or even subsequently, the parties have not agreed which of the cars has to be sold, the car remains unascertained goods.

2. Future Goods: Future goods are those goods, which do not exist at the time of the contract of sale. These goods are to be manufactured or acquired by the seller after making of contract of sale. Future goods cannot be sold, but there can only be an agreement to sell.

3. Contingent Goods: Contingent goods are a kind of future goods. These goods are those goods, the acquisition of which is contingent upon the happening or non-happening of an uncertain event.

For Example: A agrees to sell the cargo loaded on the ship 'Victory", which is coming from London to Bombay. The ship may or may not arrive. So, these goods are called contingent goods.

Types of Goods

1. Existing goods
   (a) Specific Goods
   (b) Ascertained Goods
   (c) Unascertained Goods
2. Future goods
3. Contingent goods

CONSEQUENCES OF DESTRUCTION OF GOODS [Secs. 7 – 8]

1. Goods perishing before making of contract [Sec. 7]: Contract is *void-ab-initio*, due to mistake as to existence of subject matter.

It is to be noted that **if the seller has knowledge** about the destruction of goods, even then he enters into the contract of sale with buyer, then seller is bound to compensate to the buyer. (***Reason:*** *Fraud*)

2. Where a part of the goods is perished before making contract: If the goods was divisible, then the contract can be enforced partly and if the goods was indivisible, then the contract becomes *void-ab-initio*.

For Example: A contracted to sell one wagon containing 700 bags of groundnut to B. Unknown to A, 109 bags had been stolen at the time of sale. Therefore, A made a delivery of 591 bags.

Held, the sale was void and B could not be compelled to take the remainder.

3. Goods perishing after the 'Agreement to sell', but before 'Sale' [Sec. 8]:

Where there is a contract for the sale of specific goods, the contract is void, if—

(i) subsequently the goods have perished, and

(ii) there is no fault on the part of the buyer or seller in perishing of the goods.

For Example: A horse was delivered upon trial for 8 days. However, the horse died within 8 days, without the fault of buyer or seller. Held, the seller must bear the loss, as the contract was void.

> ***Note:*** *Secs. 7 and 8 applies only in the case of specific goods*, not in the case of unascertained goods. So, if the unascertained goods are destroyed, the contract will not become void.

For Example: Mr. A, car dealer, has 50 cars. He contracts to sell one of the cars to B. The car was not identified at the time of sale. Before the car could be identified, then A's godown caught fire and all the cars were destroyed.

In this case, the contract does not become void, as the sale is not of specific goods, so A must supply one car or pay damages.

PRICE [Secs. 9-10]

✍ **Mode of fixation of Price (Sec. 9):** The price may be fixed in any of the following manner:

1. By the contract
2. By the valuer
3. May be agreed to be fixed in the course of dealing between the parties.

Where the price is not fixed as above, the buyer shall pay the seller a reasonable price. '*What is a reasonable price*?' is a question of fact and circumstances.

✍ **Fixation of Price by Third Party (Sec. 10):**

1. **Failure to value by third party:** Where the price is to be fixed by the valuation of a third party and such third party cannot or does not make such valuation, the agreement can be avoided. However, if the goods or any part thereof have been delivered to the buyer, he shall pay a reasonable price therefor.
2. **Where such third party is prevented from making the valuation** by the fault of the seller or buyer, the party not in fault may maintain a suit for damages against the party in fault.

TIME [Sec. 11]

If the contract does not otherwise provide, then—

- **Stipulation as to time of payment** is not deemed to be essence of contract.
- **Stipulation as to time of delivery** is deemed to be essence of contract.

CONDITIONS AND WARRANTIES

Generally, at the time of sale, the seller makes some representations, statements or stipulations in the praise of his goods. This stipulation may be a condition or a warranty.

Basis	Condition	Warranty
1. Meaning :	A condition is a stipulation, which is **essential to the main purpose** of the contract. [Sec. 12(2)]	A warranty is a stipulation, which is **collateral**, i.e. which is not essential to the main purpose of the contract. [Sec. 12(3)]
2. Remedy :	A breach of condition gives— - a right to repudiate the contract, and - a right to claim damage.	A breach of warranty gives only a right to claim damages.
3. Root of Contract :	Condition goes directly to the root of the contract.	It does not go to the root of the contract.
4. Treatment :	A breach of condition may be treated as a breach of warranty.	However, a breach of warranty cannot be treated as a breach of condition.
Example	B asked a car dealer to suggest him a suitable car for touring purposes. The dealer suggested buying a **Buggatti car**. B	B buys a new car from S. The car is guaranteed against any manufacturing defect for two years and in the event of

Basis	Condition	Warranty
	accordingly purchased the car, but found it unfit for the touring purpose. Held, the suitability of the car for touring purposes is a condition. It was so important that its non-fulfillment defeated the very purpose of the buyer. Hence B could return the car and get back the price. – *Bardry* v *Marshall* (1925)	any manufacturing defect, there is a warranty for replacement of the defective part. If after six months, B finds that the head-lights of the car are not working properly, he cannot terminate the contract. He can get it repaired or replaced.

Whether a stipulation is a condition or a warranty, it will depend on the construction of the contract and the intention of the parties. The use of the terms, *i.e.* condition or warranty, by the parties is immaterial.

☞ **When a breach of condition to be treated as a breach of warranty [Sec. 13]?**

(i) **Voluntary:** The buyer may waive the condition, or

(ii) **Voluntary:** The buyer may elect to treat 'the Breach of the Condition' as 'the Breach of Warranty'.

(iii) **Compulsory:** Where the contract of sale is not severable and the buyer has accepted the goods or part thereof.

(iv) **Quasi:** Where the fulfillment of condition or warranty is excused by Law due to impossibility of the Law.

EXPRESS CONDITIONS AND WARRANTIES

The conditions and warranties may be express or implied. Express conditions and warranties are those, which the parties agree expressly, i.e. orally or in writing. *For example*, cash to be paid on delivery of goods, cash and carry, etc.

IMPLIED CONDITIONS

Implied conditions are those which are implied by the law in the absence of any agreement to the contrary. These are as follows:

1. Conditions as to Title [Sec. 14(a)]

In the absence of any contract to the contrary, there is an implied condition on the part of the seller that—

(i) *In the case of sale*, the seller has a right to sell the goods, and

(ii) *In the agreement to sell*, the seller will have a right to sell the goods at the time of passing of ownership in goods.

If the title of the seller turns out to be defective, the buyer must return the goods to the true owner and recover the price from the seller.

For Example: X purchased a motor car from Y and used it for four months. Y had no title to the car. A had to return the car to the true owner.

Held, X could get back the price as there was a breach of implied condition as to title.

—*Rowland* v *Divall* (1923)

2. Conditions as to Description [Sec. 15]

Where the goods are sold by description, there is an implied condition that the goods shall correspond to description.

> "If you contract to sell peas you cannot oblige a party to take beans. If the description of the article rendered is different in any respect, the other party is not bound to take it."

—*Bowes* v *Shand* (1877)

For Example: A machine was sold. The buyer has not seen the machine, but the seller described it as a new one. However, it was found to be a very old one. Held, the machine was not according to description.

— *Varley* v *Whipp* (1900)

3. Conditions as to Quality & Fitness [Sec. 16(1)]

Ordinarily, there is no implied condition as to quality or fitness. *In the absence of anything to the contrary*, the doctrine of **'Let the buyer beware'** applies.

However, the following points must be noted regarding the condition as to quality and fitness:

(1) Where the buyer, *expressly or impliedly*, tells the seller the particular purpose for which he needs the goods and relies on the skill or judgment of the seller, there is an implied condition that the goods shall be reasonably fit for such purpose. [Refer to the case of *Bardry* v *Marshall* (1925)]

(2) When the article can be used only for one particular purpose, the buyer need not inform the seller the purpose for which the goods are required.

For Example: P purchased a hot water bottle from a chemist. While the bottle was being used by A's wife, it burst and injured A's wife.

Held, the seller was liable for damages as the bottle was not fit for the purpose for which it was meant.

—*Priest* v *Last* (1903)

☞ **Exceptions to the Implied Condition as to Quality or Fitness:**

(1) 'The condition as to quality or fitness' will not apply, if the buyer is suffering from an abnormality, which renders the goods unsuitable for a particular purpose and the buyer does not inform the seller about that abnormality.

For Example: G purchased a coat. She had abnormally sensitive skin. By wearing the coat, she got skin complaint.

Held, there was no breach of condition, as she had not disclosed the abnormality of her skin.

—*Griffith* v *Peter Conway Ltd.* (1939)

(2) Where the goods can be used for a number of purposes, the buyer should inform the particular purpose for which such goods were required. If he does not disclose, there is no such condition of quality or fitness.

For Example: Certain cloth was sold to a tailor by sample. The tailor required the cloth for the particular purpose of making it into liveries. However, the tailor did not inform the dealer about his purpose. The cloth was according to sample, but was unfit for the purpose. However, it could be used for other purposes. Held, the buyer could not reject the cloth. —*Jones* v *Padgett* (1890)

(3) In case the goods are purchased under a patent name or other trade name, without disclosing the purpose of purchase, there is no implied condition as to quality or fitness. This is because, in such a situation, the buyer is not relying on seller's skill and judgment.

For Example: A asks a dealer to supply "Ambassador Car". If subsequently, the car turns out to be useless in a hilly area, the seller is not liable.

4. Conditions as to Merchantability [Sec. 16(2)]

Where goods are bought by description from a seller, who deals in goods of that description, there is an implied condition that the goods shall be of merchantable quality.

By the term 'Merchantability', we mean that there is no defect in the goods, which renders them unfit for sale. Thus, a watch that will not keep time and a pen that will not write cannot be regarded as merchantable.

For Example: A radio set was sold to a layman. The set was defective. It did not work in spite of repairs. Held, the buyer could return the set and claim refund. —*R.S. Thakur* v *HGE Corporation* (1971)

☞ **Exception to the Implied Condition as to Merchantability:** Apparent Defect.

5. Sale by Sample [Sec. 17]

Where the goods are sold by sample, the following are implied conditions:

(1) The bulk shall correspond to sample in quality.

(2) The buyer shall be given a reasonable opportunity to compare the goods with the sample.

(3) The goods shall be free from any defect, rendering them un-merchantable. It is to be noted that this implied condition applies only in the case of latent defects, i.e. those defects which cannot be discovered by ordinary inspection. In fact, such defects are discovered when the goods are put to use or by examination in laboratories. The seller is not liable for apparent or visible defects which can be discovered by examination.

(4) **Sale by description as well as sample:** If the sale is by sample as well as description, there is twin condition that the goods shall correspond not only to sample, but also to description.

For Example: A agreed to sell to C some oil described as "Foreign refined oil" and warranted only equal to sample. The goods supplied were equal to sample, but contained a mixture of hemp oil.

Held, C could reject the goods. —*Nichol* v *Godts* (1854)

6. Condition as to Wholesomeness

In the case of eatables and other provisions, there is an implied condition that the goods shall be wholesome, i.e., free from any defect which renders them unfit for human consumption.

Example: F purchased milk from B, a milk dealer. The milk contained typhoid germs. A's wife on taking the milk got infected and died. Held, A was entitled to get damages.

—*Frost* v *Aylesbury Dairy Co. Ltd.* (1905)

IMPLIED WARRANTIES

1. Implied warranty as to Quiet Possession [Sec. 14(b)]: *In the absence to any contract showing contrary intention*, there is an implied warranty that the buyer shall have and enjoy quiet possession of the goods. If the buyer is disturbed in the enjoyment of the goods, he can claim damages from the seller.

2. Implied warranty against encumbrances [Sec. 14(c)]: Unless the circumstances of the case are such as to show a contrary intention, there is an implied warranty that the goods shall be free from any charge or encumbrance in favour of any party not declared or known to the buyer before or at the time contract is made.

3. Warranty as to Quality and Fitness by Usage of Trade [Sec. 16(3)]: An implied warranty as to quality or fitness for a particular purpose may be annexed by the usage of trade.

4. Warranty to Disclose the Dangerous nature of Goods: In case of sale of dangerous goods, the seller is under an obligation to warn the buyer about the probable danger. Failure to do so will make the seller liable to pay damages.

For Example: A sold a tin of disinfectant to B, knowing that it was likely to be dangerous to B, if opened without special care. B opened the tin, whereupon disinfectant powder went into her eyes, causing injury.

Held, A was liable to damages to B, as he failed to warn B of the probable danger.

—*Clark* v *Army and Navy Society Ltd.* (1903)

DOCTRINE OF *CAVEAT EMPTOR*

The doctrine of '*Caveat Emptor*', i.e., let the buyer beware, means that the buyer while purchasing goods must act with a "**third eye and ear**", i.e.—

1. He should be careful to see that the goods purchased will serve his purpose well.
2. If the buyer is not careful and he finds later on that the goods do not serve his purpose, he cannot hold the seller liable for it.
3. The seller is under no obligation to tell the defects of his articles.

– Exceptions to this Doctrine:

1. Implied conditions as to quality or fitness
2. Sale of goods by description
3. Merchantable Quality

4. **Usage or custom of trade [Sec. 16(3)]:** An implied condition or warranty as to quality or fitness may be applied by usage or custom of trade.
5. **Consent by Fraud:** Although seller is under no obligation to tell the defects of his articles, yet he cannot fraudulently conceal defects, which on a 'reasonable examination' cannot be discovered. If he does so, the buyer has a right to reject the goods or/and claim damages.

MULTIPLE CHOICE QUESTIONS

☞ Applicability & Definitions

1. Which one of the following is true?

(A) The provisions of Sale of Goods were originally with the Indian Contract Act, 1872.

(B) The Sale of Goods Act, 1930 deals with mortgage.

(C) The Sale of Goods Act restricts the parties to modify the provisions of law.

(D) None of the above

2. A contract for the sale of goods, where property would pass to the buyer on payment of total price would be –

(A) Sale.

(B) Agreement to sell.

(C) Sale on approval.

(D) Hire-purchase contract.

3. In which form of the contract the property in the goods passes to the buyer immediately –

(A) Agreement to sell.

(B) Hire-purchase.

(C) Sale.

(D) Installment to sell.

4. Legally, a contract of sale includes–

(A) sale.

(B) agreement to Sell.

(C) barter.

(D) both (A) and (B)

5. Contract of Sale is –

(A) executory contract.

(B) executed contract.

(C) both of the above.

(D) none of the above.

6. A agrees to deliver his old car valued at Rs. 80,000 to B, a car dealer, in exchange for a new car, and agrees to pay the difference in cash it is–

(A) Contract of sale.

(B) Agreement to sell.

(C) Exchange.

(D) Barter.

7. The person who buys or agrees to buy goods is known as—

(A) Consumer.

(B) Buyer.

(C) Both (A) and (B)

(D) None of the above

8. The Sale of Goods Act, 1930 deals with –

(A) sale.

(B) mortgage.

(C) pledge.

(D) all of the above

9. Which one of the following is a document of title to goods?

(A) Railway receipt.

(B) Wharfinger's certificate.

(C) Warehouse keeper's certificate.

(D) All of the above

10. In a hire-purchase agreement, the hirer–

(A) has an option to buy the goods.

(B) must buy the goods.

(C) must return the goods.

(D) is not given the possession of goods.

11. In a contract of sale, the agreement may be–

(A) Expressed .

(B) Implied from the conduct of the parties.

(C) Quasi.

(D) All of the above

12. In a contract of sale, the consideration for sale must be received in –

(A) Another Goods.

(B) Money.

(C) Immovable Property.

(D) All of the above

13. If A agrees to deliver 1,000 kg. of sugar to B in exchange of 150 mts. of cloth, then it is–

(A) Contract of sale.

(B) Agreement to sell.

(C) Sale on Approval.

(D) Barter.

14. The Sale of Goods Act, 1930 came into force on–

(A) 1st March, 1930.

(B) 1st July, 1930.

(C) 31th July, 1930.

(D) 1st June, 1930.

15. Which of the following case laws relate to the definition of contract of sale?

(A) Rajlikhee Devi v. Bhoot Nath, 1900.

(B) State of Madras v. Gannon Dunkerly and Co. Limited, 1958.

(C) Khawaja Md. Khan v. Hussaini Begum, 1910.

(D) Suppu Ammal v. Subramanian, 1910.

16. A sale implies an agreement –

(A) Plus conveyance of property and creates *jus in personam*.

(B) Plus conveyance of property and creates *jus in rem*.

(C) No conveyance of property and creates *jus in rem*.

(D) No conveyance of property and creates *jus in personam*.

17. Where both parties to a contract of sale are under a mistake as to a matter of fact essential to such contract, then the contract is –

(A) Illegal.

(B) Void.

(C) Still enforceable.

(D) None of the above

18. 'Seller' means a person, who –

(A) Sells goods.

(B) Agrees to sell goods.

(C) Sells or agrees to sell goods.

(D) Has sold goods.

19. A person employed to do any act for another or to represent another in dealings with the third parties is–

(A) Principal.

(B) Agent.

(C) Servant.

(D) Bailee.

20. C.I.F. contract is –

(A) Contract for the sale of insured goods.

(B) Contract for the sale of document.

(C) Contract for the sale of goods.

(D) Contract for the sale of specific goods.

21. Which of the following is/are necessary constituent(s) of a contract of sale?

(1) Three distinct parties-seller, buyer and a mediator.

(2) Movable goods for a price

(3) Transfer of general property

(4) Exchanging of goods without money

(A) 1 & 2

(B) 2 & 3

(C) 2 & 4

(D) 3 & 4

22. Price consideration in a contract of Sale can be—

(A) Only by way of money.

(B) Only by way of goods in return.

(C) Partly by way of money or partly by way of goods in return.

(D) No consideration is required at all.

23. If X commissioned Y, an artist, to paint a portrait of A for 2000 dollars & Y uses his own canvas & paint then it is –

(A) Contract of sale.

(B) Contract of work.

(C) Sale on approval.

(D) Hire-Purchase agreement.

24. The term "Quality of Goods" in Section 2(12) of the Sale of Goods Act, has a reference to—

(A) Description.

(B) Fitness for a particular purpose.

(C) State or condition.

(D) None of the above

25. Under the Sale of Goods Act, "fault" means—

(A) non-payment of price by Buyer.

(B) non-delivery of goods by Seller.

(C) any wrongful act or default.

(D) any act or omission as decided by the Court.

26. In a contract of sale, the agreement may be expressed or implied from the conduct of the parties.

(A) True

(B) Partly True

(C) False

(D) None of the above

27. The Sale of Goods Act, 1930 has ____ Chapters.

(A) Four

(B) Seven

(C) Eight

(D) Five

28. The objective of the Sale of Goods Act, 1930 is to define and amend the law relating to—

(A) Sale of immovable properties.

(B) Sale of goods.

(C) Agreements to sell.

(D) All of the above

29. The Sale of Goods Act, 1930 extends to the whole of India, except the state of—

(A) Maharashtra.

(B) Jammu and Kashmir.

(C) Tamilnadu.

(D) Uttar Pradesh.

30. Section _____ of the Sale of Goods Act, 1930 defines the term "buyer".

(A) 2(1)

(B) 2(2)

(C) 2(3)

(D) 2(4)

31. A mate's receipt –

(A) Is a document of title to goods.

(B) Is an acknowledgement for the receipt of goods.

(C) Both the above

(D) None of the above

32. In case of sale, –

(A) Property in goods passes to the buyer.

(B) Risk in the goods passes to the buyer.

(C) Both the above.

(D) None of the above.

33. In case of a hire-purchase the hirer –

(A) Can pass a goods title to a *bona fide* purchaser.

(B) Cannot pass a goods title to a *bona fide* purchaser.

(C) Can choose whether to pass or not to pass the goods title to a *bona fide* purchaser.

(D) All of the above

☞ Goods & Consequences of destruction of Goods

34. Goods, which are in existence at the time of the Contract of Sale, are known as–

(A) Present Goods.

(B) Existing Goods.

(C) Specific Goods.

(D) None of the above

35. In a contract of sale, the subject matter of contract must always –

(A) Goods.

(B) Money.

(C) Immovable Property.

(D) All of the above

36. In a contract of sale, goods means–

(A) Only movable items.

(B) Only immovable items.

(C) B's Movable and Immovable items.

(D) None of the above

37. The term "goods" under the Sale of Goods Act, 1930 does not include—

(A) Goodwill.

(B) Actionable claims.

(C) Stocks and shares.

(D) Harvested crops.

38. X of Mumbai agreed to sell 1000 bales of cotton @ Rs. 999 per bale and to deliver within a fortnight at the buyer's godown at Karachi. X failed to supply these goods. If unknown to both the parties, the goods were destroyed at the time of agreement.

(A) Void on the ground of X's mistake

(B) Void on the ground of mutual mistake

(C) Void on the ground of supervening impossibility

(D) Void on the ground of commercial impossibility

39. In *Q. 38* above, If X knew the goods were destroyed by fire at the time of agreement, then agreement will be –

(A) Void on the ground of X's mistake.

(B) Voidable.

(C) Void but X should compensate the buyer for any loss that it sustains through non-performance.

(D) Void on the ground of supervening impossibility.

40. In *Q. 38* above, If war is declared between India & Pakistan, then contract will become –

(A) Void on the ground of supervening impossibility.

(B) Void on the ground of non-performance.

(C) Voidable.

(D) Void on the ground of commercial impossibility.

41. In *Q. 38* above, If these goods were to be manufactured by Z, who is ready to supply @ Rs. 1,111 per bale because of unexpected increase in the cost of material and labour, the contract will be –

(A) Valid on the ground of supervening impossibility.

(B) Valid on the ground of non-performance.

(C) Void on the ground of third-party default.

(D) Valid on the ground of commercial impossibility.

42. In *Q.38* above, If these goods could not be delivered because of strike of transport operators, then contract will be –

(A) Valid on the ground of supervening impossibility.

(B) Void on the ground of non-performance.

(C) Valid on the ground of third-party default.

(D) Void on the ground of commercial impossibility.

43. Necessary condition for existing goods is –

(A) They should be in existence at the time of the contract of sale.

(B) They should be owned or possessed by the seller.

(C) Both of the above

(D) None of the above

44. Future goods means goods to be manufactured or acquired by the seller–

(A) Before making the contract of sale.

(B) At the time of contract of sale.

(C) After making the contract of sale.

(D) All of these

45. A contract for the sale of "future goods" is–

(A) sale.

(B) agreement to sell.

(C) void.

(D) hire-purchase contract.

46. Which one of the following is not true?

(A) Document showing title is different from document of title.

(B) Bill of lading is a document of title to goods.

(C) Specific goods can be identified and agreed upon at the time of the contract of Sale.

(D) None of the above

47. Under Sale of Goods Act, 1930 the terms "Goods" means every kind of movable property and it includes –

(A) Stock and share.

(B) Growing crops, grass.

(C) Both (A) and (B)

(D) None of the above

48. The term 'goods' for the purpose of Sale of Goods Act, does not include –

(1) Money

(2) Actionable claims

(3) Stock & Shares

(4) Growing crops, grass

(A) 1 & 2

(B) 1 & 3

(C) 2 & 4

(D) 3 & 4

49. _____ under the Sale of Goods Act, means goods identified in accordance with the agreement after the contract of sale is made –

(A) Ascertained goods.

(B) Unascertained goods.

(C) Illegal goods.

(D) Contingent goods.

50. Specific performance of a contract of sale of goods can be sought in cases where the goods are —

(A) Future goods.

(B) Unascertained goods.

(C) Specific or Ascertained goods.

(D) Contingent goods.

51. Section 8 of the Sale of Goods Act, deals with cases of impossibility of performance of the contract—

(A) at the time of formation of the contract.

(B) subsequent to the formation of the contract.

(C) before the formation of the contract.

(D) all of the above

52. If a contract for sale of goods is for sale of two or more things under an entire contract, the perishing of some of them would avoid the whole contract.

(A) True

(B) Partly True

(C) False

(D) None of the above

53. If a contract for sale of goods is for sale of two or more things under a divisible contract, the perishing of some of them would _____ the whole contract.

(A) avoid

(B) invalidate

(C) not affect

(D) eliminate

54. Actual Sale of future goods is –

(A) Impossible.

(B) Possible through an agreement to sell.

(C) Illegal.

(D) A myth.

☞ Price of Time

55. P agrees to sell apples to Q at price to be fixed by R. Subsequently, R refuses to value the goods and fix the price. Decide –

(A) The agreement can be avoided.

(B) The agreement can not be avoided, because some other person may fix the price.

(C) The agreement can be avoided, because price may be fixed by parties by mutual agreement.

(D) Both (B) and (C)

56. If in *Q. 55* above, R was willing to value the apples, but was prevented from evaluating by the wrongful act of P. Could Q file a suit for damages against P?

(A) Yes

(B) No

57. In a contract of sale, the Price may be—

(A) fixed by the contract.

(B) agreed to be fixed in a manner thereby agreed.

(C) determined by course of dealings between the parties.

(D) all of the above

58. Where no price is fixed by express agreement or by implication, Buyer shall pay the Seller —

(A) Net Realisable Value.

(B) Reasonable Price.

(C) Resale Price.

(D) *Ad hoc* Price.

59. A and B both believe that a particular kind of rice is being sold in the market at Rs. 300 per quintal and A sells rice of that kind to B at Rs.300 per quintal. But, in fact, the market price was Rs. 400. The contract is –

(A) Valid.

(B) Void.

(C) Voidable.

(D) Illegal.

☞ Conditions & Warranty

60. The conditions and warranties may be in the form of–

(A) express.

(B) implied.

(C) either (A) or (B)

(D) none of the above

61. In case of goods sold by sample, the goods should correspond with the sample otherwise–

(A) buyer can reject the goods.

(B) buyer cannot reject the goods.

(C) contract is automatically terminated.

(D) seller is liable to punishment.

62. A sold a tin of disinfectant powder to K without warning knowing fully that if the tin was not opened with care, it is likely to cause injury. K was injured while opening the tin. Which of the following statement(s) is/are correct?

(A) A is not liable to K under the Doctrine of caveat emptor.

(B) A is liable for the damages.

(C) A has no duty to disclose the facts to K.

(D) The buyer has the responsibility to enquire about all the things before purchasing the goods.

63. M, a shopkeeper, sold a Television set to N, who purchased it in good faith. The set had some manufacturing defect and it did not work after a few days in spite of repairs. In this case, the television was not merchantable as it was not fit for ordinary usage.

(A) The buyer has no right to reject the television.

(B) The buyer has the right to reject the television and to have refund of the price.

(C) Either of the above

(D) None of (A) and (B)

64. In case of Breach of Warranty, the aggrieved party can claim –

(A) Only damages.

(B) Repudiation of contract.

(C) Both (A) and (B)

(D) None of the above

65. In a contract of sale of goods by description, the implied condition is that, the goods need not correspond with the description.

(A) True

(B) False

66. Where the buyer is deprived of the goods by their true owner then the buyer—

(A) may recover the price for breach of the condition as to title.

(B) cannot recover the price for breach of the condition as to title.

(C) either (A) or (B)

(D) none of the above

67. The implied condition that goods shall be fit to buyer's specific purpose, is applicable only where the buyer tells his purpose to the seller and relies upon seller's skill and judgement.

(A) True, as there is a condition as to description

(B) False, as it is buyer's duty to select goods which serve his purpose.

(C) True, as there is a condition as to Title

(D) None of these

68. The implied condition that goods shall be fit to buyer's specific purpose, is applicable only where the buyer tells his purpose to the seller and relies upon seller's skill and judgment.

(A) It is the requirement of Law

(B) It is buyer's duty to select goods, which serve his purpose.

(C) Seller can be silent.

(D) All of the above

69. In case, a condition is changed to the status of a warranty, then the buyer –

(A) loses the right to reject goods.

(B) retains right to claim damages only.

(C) both (A) and (B) are true

(D) both (A) and (B) are false

70. __________ is a stipulation essential to the main purpose of the contract –

(A) Condition

(B) Warranty

(C) Both (A) and (B)

(D) None of the above

71. M purchased a hot water bottle from a Chemist. The bottle burst and injured his wife. The Chemist is liable on account of—

(A) breach of express condition as to quality.

(B) breach of implied condition as to quality.

(C) personal injury caused to the Buyer's wife.

(D) hot water bottle sales are illegal.

72. P sold barley to B by sample delivery to be made at T railway station. B sold the barley to X. The barley was delivered at T railway station and B after inspecting a sample of it sent it to X. X rejected it as not being according to sample whereupon B seeks to reject the goods. Will B succeed?

(A) Yes

(B) No

73. Right to repudiate the contract exists in –

(A) Condition.

(B) Warranty.

(C) Both (A) and (B)

(D) None of the above

74. A breach of warranty may be treated as breach of condition.

(A) False

(B) True

75. Right to claim for damages exists in –

(A) Condition.

(B) Warranty

(C) Both (A) and (B)

(D) None of the above

76. A stipulation which is collateral to the main purpose of the contract is –

(A) Condition.

(B) Warranty

(C) Both (A) and (B)

(D) None of the above

77. A bought a motor car from B. He used it for 3 months and thereafter the car was detected to have been stolen. A was compelled to return it to the true owner. Decide –

(A) A can recover the sale price and compensation from B, as there is breachment of condition as to title.

(B) A can recover the sale price and compensation from B, as there is breachment of condition as to Description.

(C) A can recover the sale price and compensation from B, as there is breachment of condition as to Merchantability.

(D) A cannot recover anything from B.

78. X sold to Y certain quantities of 'foreign refined oil' warranted only equal to samples'. The samples consisted of 'refined oil' mixed with 'hemp oil'. The oil tendered corresponded with the samples, but it was not such as is known in the market as 'foreign refined oil'. Decide –

(A) Y is entitled to reject the goods, as there is breachment of condition as to Title.

(B) Y is entitled to reject the goods, as there is breachment of condition as to Merchantability.

(C) Y is entitled to reject the goods, as there is breachment of 'condition as to sale by Sample and description'.

(D) Y is not entitled to reject the goods, as the doctrine of caveat emptor will apply.

79. A contracts to sell Java Sugar according to the sample produced by him on the delivery of the sample to B, the buyer. It transpires that the sugar agrees with sample but is not Java Sugar. Will B be entitled to any remedies?

(A) B is entitled to reject the goods, as there is breachment of condition as to Title.

(B) B is entitled to reject the goods, as there is breachment of condition as to Merchantability.

(C) B is entitled to reject the goods, as there is breachment of condition as to sale by Sample and description.

(D) B is not entitled to reject the goods, as the doctrine of caveat emptor will apply.

80. X enters into a druggist's shop and asked for a hot water bottle. He is shown a bottle, which the proprietor of the shop say that it is meant for hot water. X buys the bottle, and one day while using it, it bursts and injures X's wife. Decide –

(A) X is entitled to claim compensation, as there is breachment of 'condition as to Title'.

(B) X is entitled to claim compensation, as there is breachment of 'condition as to Merchantability'.

(C) X is entitled to claim compensation, as there is breachment of 'condition as to Sale by Sample'.

(D) B is not entitled to claim compensation.

81. Which of the following is not an implied condition in a contract of sale?

(A) Condition as to title.

(B) Condition as to description.

(C) Condition as to free from encumbrance.

(D) Condition as to sample.

82. A stipulation which is collateral to the main purpose of the contract, and if proves false, gives the buyer only a right to claim damages, is known as –

(A) conditions.

(B) guarantee.

(C) warranty.

(D) none of these.

83. Which one of the following is not an implied warranty?

(A) Warranty as to undisturbed possession.

(B) Warranty as to existence of encumbrance.

(C) Disclosure of dangerous nature of goods.

(D) Warranty as to quality or fitness by usage of trade.

84. A stipulation in a contract of sale of goods whose violation by seller gives a right of rescission to buyer, is called –

(A) Guarantee.

(B) Warranty.

(C) Condition.

(D) Term.

85. Following conditions are implied in a contract of sale of goods, unless the circumstances of the contract show a different intention–

(A) Condition as to non-existence of encumbrances.

(B) Condition as to undisturbed possession.

(C) All of the above

(D) None of the above

86. The following may be treated as a breach of warranty–

(A) Breach of warranty.

(B) Breach of condition.

(C) Both the above

(D) None of the above

87. Following conditions are implied in a contract of sale of goods, unless the circumstances of the contract show a different intention–

(A) Condition as to title.

(B) Sale by description.

(C) Sale by sample.

(D) All of the above

88. Following conditions are implied in a contract of sale of goods unless the circumstances of the contract show a different intention–

(A) Condition as to wholesomeness.

(B) Sale by description as well as by sample.

(C) Condition as to quality or fitness.

(D) All of the above.

89. Where the goods are sold by sample as well as by description the implied condition is that the bulk of the goods supplied must correspond with–

(A) Sample only.

(B) The description only.

(C) Sample and description both.

(D) Sample, description and fair price.

90. In the case the goods correspond with the sample but do not tally with the description the buyer has right to –

(A) repudiate the contract.

(B) sue for damages caused to him.

(C) declare the contract as illegal.

(D) declare the contract as void.

91. A warranty is a stipulation essential to the main purpose of the contract—

(A) True

(B) False

92. A agrees to supply to B a certain quantity of timber of half inch thickness. The timber actually supplied varies in thickness. The timber is merchantable and commercially fit for the purpose for which it was ordered. B rejects the timber. Is his action justified?"

(A) Yes

(B) No

93. A lady, who knew that her skin was abnormally sensitive bought a tweed coat and developed skin trouble by using it. She did not disclose to the seller that her skin was abnormally sensitive. Is the seller liable?

(A) Yes

(B) No

94. Some mixed worsted coatings were sold by sample. The goods when supplied corresponded to the sample, but it was found that owing to a latent defect in the cloth coats made out of it would not stand ordinary wear and therefore unsaleable. The same defect existed in the sample also but could not be detected on a reasonable examination. Is buyer entitled to reject the goods?

(A) Yes

(B) No

95. Under the Sale of Goods Act, 1930 which of the following is/are the implied warranty(ies)?

(1) Warranty of quiet possession

(2) Warranty of freedom from encumbrances

(3) Warranty of title

(4) Warranty as to wholesomeness.

(A) 1 & 2

(B) 1 & 3

(C) 2 & 4

(D) 3 & 4

96. X sold to Y certain quantities of "foreign refined rapeseed oil warranted equal to samples". The samples consisted of rapeseed oil mixed with hemp oil. The oil tendered corresponded with the samples, but it was not such as is known in the market as "foreign refined rapeseed oil". Can Y avoid the contract?

(A) Yes

(B) No

(C) Partly Yes

(D) None of the above

97. Right to repudiate the contract exists both in conditions and warranties.

(A) True

(B) Partly True

(C) False

(D) None of the above

98. Which of the following is not an implied condition in case of sale by sample?

(A) Bulk of goods should correspond with sample in quality.

(B) Buyer should be given reasonable opportunity of inspection.

(C) Goods should be free from latent defects making them un-merchantable.

(D) Goods should be fit for the quality or purpose stated by the Buyer.

99. Where goods are brought by description from a seller who deals in goods of that description (whether he is the manufacturer or producer or not), there is an implied condition that the goods shall be of –

(A) decent quality.

(B) reasonable quality.

(C) tradeable quality.

(D) merchantable quality.

100. The implied condition that the goods are of merchantable quality, ________ where the buyer has actually examined the goods and there is apparent defect.

(A) is applicable

(B) is not applicable

(C) is presumed

(D) exists

101. Implied condition that the goods are of merchantable quality, is lost where the buyer has actually examined the goods. This is applicable in respect of —

(A) patent defects (those which such examination ought to have revealed).

(B) latent defects (those which cannot be identified on mere examination og goods).

(C) defects which arise subsequent to delivery of goods.

(D) defects which are pointed out by a Third Party.

102. An implied warranty or condition as to quality or fitness for a particular purpose cannot be annexed by usage of trade. This statement is—

(A) True

(B) Partly True

(C) False

(D) None of the above

103. An implied warranty or condition as to quality or fitness for a particular purpose may be annexed by the usage of trade.

(A) True

(B) Partly True

(C) False

(D) None of the above

104. An express warranty or condition does not negative a warranty or condition implied by this Act, unless inconsistent therewith. This statement is—

(A) True

(B) Partly True

(C) False

(D) None of the above

105. There was a sale by sample on 5th May, of two parcels of rice containing 500 and 100 bushels respectively. When, on the 12th May, the Buyer went to examine the bulk, the parcel containing 500 bushels was shown to him, but the Seller refused to show him the other parcel. Can the Buyer avoid the contract?

(A) Yes

(B) No

(C) Partly Yes

(D) None of the above

106. In a contract of Sale of Goods by description, the implied condition is that, the goods need not correspond with the description.

(A) True

(B) Partly True

(C) False

(D) None of the above

107. K owns a residential flat in Chennai. He is entitled to quiet possession and enjoyment of his property. This is called—

(A) Rights *in personam*

(B) Rights *in rem*

(C) Constitutional Right

(D) There is no right at all

☞ *Caveat Emptor*

108. The rule of *caveat emptor* does not apply in the case of –

(A) Fitness for buyer's purpose.

(B) Sale under a patent or trade name.

(C) Usage of trade or consent by fraud.

(D) All of the above

109. R, a grain merchant, displays wheat of different varieties. A after satisfying himself of the quality buys the wheat in the belief that the wheat is of earlier harvest. In fact, the wheat is of recent harvest. A wants to return the wheat and refuses to pay the price. Which of the following is /are true?

(A) A can return the wheat.

(B) A can refuse to pay the price.

(C) A cannot return the wheat.

(D) R cannot sue A to recover the money.

110. In case of sale of goods by sample, there is ______ that the goods shall correspond with the sample in quality.

(A) an implied warranty

(B) no implied warranty

(C) an implied condition

(D) no implied condition

111. In case of sale of goods by sample, there is an implied condition that _____ shall correspond with the sample.

(A) some of the goods

(B) bulk of the goods

(C) most of the goods

(D) all of the goods

112. The Principle of "*Caveat Emptor*" is found, in the Sale of Goods Act, under Section—

(A) 15

(B) 16

(C) 17

(D) 18

113. The general rule is that the Buyer of goods must keep his eyes open, his mind active, and be cautious while buying the goods. This doctrine is called—

(A) *Ignorantia juris non excusat*

(B) *Nemo dat quad non habet*

(C) *Quid Pro Quo*

(D) *Caveat Emptor*

114. In which of the following situations "*Caveat Emptor*" is applicable—

(A) Seller makes a misrepresentation and Buyer relies on it.

(B) Seller makes a false representation amounting to fraud, the buyer believes the same.

(C) Seller provides reasonable opportunity to the Buyer to examine the goods.

(D) Seller actively conceals a defect in the goods.

115. The principle of "*Caveat Emptor*" as found in section 16 of the Sale of Goods Act, means that the —

(A) Buyer must take care.

(B) Buyer must take a chance.

(C) Seller must take care.

(D) Seller must take a chance.

116. Doctrine of *Caveat Emptor* means–

(A) let the seller beware.

(B) let the creditor beware.

(C) let the buyer beware.

(D) none of the above.

117. Under the doctrine of *Caveat Emptor* the seller is—

(A) responsible for the bad selection of goods by the buyer.

(B) not responsible for the bad selection of goods by the buyer.

(C) either (A) or (B)

(D) none of the above

118. The doctrine of *Caveat Emptor* does not apply, when—

(A) the goods are bought by sample.

(B) the goods are bought by sample as well as description.

(C) the goods are purchased under its brand name.

(D) all of the above.

119. M at Calcutta sold to N 20 bags of "waste silk" on their way from Murshidabad to Calcutta. But when the bags reached N, he found that they contained "waste silk" no doubt but not of the quality he had in view. Would N be entitled to reject the goods?

(A) Yes

(B) No

(C) Partly Yes

(D) None of the above

120. M at Calcutta sold to N 20 bags of waste 'silk' then on their way from Murshidabad to Calcutta. But when the bags reached N, he found that they contained waste silk no doubt, but not of the quality he had in view. Decide –

(A) N is entitled to reject the goods, as there is breachment of condition as to Title.

(B) N is entitled to reject the goods, as there is breachment of condition as to Description.

(C) N is entitled to reject the goods, as there is breachment of condition as to Merchantability.

(D) N is not entitled to reject the goods, as the doctrine of caveat emptor will apply.

ANSWERS MULTIPLE CHOICE QUESTIONS

1.	A	**26.**	A	**51.**	B	**76.**	B	**101.**	A
2.	B	**27.**	B	**52.**	B	**77.**	A	**102.**	C
3.	C	**28.**	B	**53.**	C	**78.**	C	**103.**	A
4.	D	**29.**	B	**54.**	B	**79.**	C	**104.**	A
5.	C	**30.**	A	**55.**	A	**80.**	B	**105.**	A
6.	A	**31.**	B	**56.**	A	**81.**	C	**106.**	C
7.	B	**32.**	C	**57.**	D	**82.**	C	**107.**	B
8.	A	**33.**	B	**58.**	B	**83.**	B	**108.**	D
9.	D	**34.**	B	**59.**	A	**84.**	C	**109.**	C
10.	A	**35.**	A	**60.**	C	**85.**	D	**110.**	C
11.	D	**36.**	A	**61.**	A	**86.**	C	**111.**	B
12.	B	**37.**	B	**62.**	B	**87.**	D	**112.**	B
13.	D	**38.**	B	**63.**	B	**88.**	D	**113.**	D
14.	B	**39.**	C	**64.**	A	**89.**	C	**114.**	C
15.	B	**40.**	A	**65.**	B	**90.**	A	**115.**	A
16.	B	**41.**	D	**66.**	A	**91.**	B	**116.**	C
17.	B	**42.**	B	**67.**	A	**92.**	A	**117.**	B
18.	C	**43.**	C	**68.**	A	**93.**	B	**118.**	D
19.	B	**44.**	C	**69.**	C	**94.**	A	**119.**	B
20.	A	**45.**	B	**70.**	A	**95.**	A	**120.**	D
21.	B	**46.**	D	**71.**	B	**96.**	A		
22.	C	**47.**	C	**72.**	B	**97.**	C		
23.	B	**48.**	A	**73.**	A	**98.**	D		
24.	A	**49.**	A	**74.**	A	**99.**	D		
25.	C	**50.**	C	**75.**	C	**100.**	B		

Chapter 2

Transfer Of Property In Goods And Delivery

TRANSFER OF PROPERTY IN GOODS

1. Unascertained Goods/Future Goods (Sec. 18 and 23):

No property in the goods is transferred to the buyer, unless the goods are ascertained and appropriated.

- **Ascertained (Sec. 18):** It is the process to identify the goods.
- **Appropriated (Sec. 23):** The following is the manner of appropriation:

(i) The goods of the description mentioned in the contract must be produced or obtained.

(ii) The goods must come in deliverable state.

(iii) The Goods are unconditionally appropriated – (i) by the seller with the consent of the buyer or (ii) by the buyer with the consent of the seller.

(iv) The consent to the appropriation may be given either before or after the appropriation.

For Example: Twenty hogsheads of sugar out of a bulk were agreed to be sold. four hogsheads of sugar were filled up and taken away by the buyer. Subsequently, the seller filled up 16 hogsheads and informed the buyer. The buyer replied that he will take delivery as soon as possible. However, before the buyer could take their delivery, the goods were lost.

Held, the buyer was responsible as the ownership had passed to the buyer. —*Rhode* v *Thwaites* (1827)

2. Specific/Ascertained Goods [Sec. 19(1)]:

In this case, the property in the goods is transferred to the buyer, when the parties intend to transfer.

3. Where the Intention of the Parties are Not Clear (Secs. 20 -24):

(i) When goods are in a Deliverable State (Sec. 20): In this case, the property in the goods passes to the buyer, when the contract is made.

For Example: Mr. A selected a piece of jewellery from a jeweller's shop; A agrees to pay the price on the first day of the next month and asks the shopkeeper to send the jewellery at his (buyer's) home. Without any negligence, the jewellery is destroyed by Fire in the shop.

In this case, since the jewellery was in a deliverable state, so the ownership in the jewellery will be deemed to be transferred to the buyer at the time of forming the contract of sale, irrespective of the date of payment. Hence, the loss of jewellery due to fire shall be borne by the buyer.

(ii) When goods are not in a Deliverable State (Sec. 21): In this case, the property in the goods will pass only when—

(a) The goods are put in a deliverable state, and

(b) The buyer has a notice thereof.

For Example: A certain quantity of oil was purchased. The oil was to be filled in tins. B filled up some of the tins and informed A to take the delivery. In the meantime, a fire destroyed the entire quantity of oil.

Held, A will bear the loss of the oil which was filled in the tins and the seller must bear the loss of the balance.

(iii) When goods are in a Deliverable State, but the Seller is bound to do something (like, weight, measure, test, etc.) in order to ascertain price (Sec. 22):

(a) In this case, the property in goods will pass only when— (i) such act or thing is done and (ii) the buyer has notice thereof.

For Example: A stack of bark was sold. The bark was to be weighed. A part of the bark was weighed and carted away. The remainder of the bark was carried away by the flood.

Held, the ownership of the bark left with the seller did not pass to the buyer.

—*Simmons* v *Swift* (1826)

(b) Where the contract is for the sale of entire goods and nothing remains to be done to the goods by the seller to ascertain the price, then the *prima facie* ownership in them passes to the buyer, even if they have not been weighed by the buyer. In such a case, the weighing is to be done for the satisfaction of the buyer, but not as a part of the contract.

For Example: There was a sale of 975 quintals of rice lying in the godown. The buyer paid the entire price. However, the buyer agreed to remove the rice after weighing the same before a certain date. After only a part of the rice was delivered, the rest was destroyed by fire.

Held, the ownership in the entire quantity of rice had passed to the buyer irrespective of the weight not being done as the weighing was not a part of the contract, but was merely for the satisfaction of the buyer.

—*Soshi Mohan* v *Nobo Krishto* (1879)

(iv) 'Goods on Approval Basis' [Sec. 24]: In this case, the property in the goods shall be transferred to the buyer in the following cases:

(a) Express Acceptance: When the buyer signifies his acceptance to the seller,

(b) Implied Acceptance: When the buyer does any act for adopting the Goods, like subsequent sale of goods, consumption of goods, pledge of goods etc.

For Example: Certain jewellery was delivered to a buyer on sale or return basis. The buyer pledged the jewellery.

Held, the buyer had adopted the transaction and as such the property had passed and the seller could not recover the jewellery from the pawnee. —*Kirkham* v *Attenborough* (1897)

(c) Retention of Goods: Where he does not signify his approval or acceptance, but retains the goods beyond the time fixed for the return of the goods, or beyond a reasonable time, if no time is fixed.

Appropriation of goods by delivery of the goods to the carrier

Appropriation of goods may also be done by making delivery of the goods to the Carrier for transmission to the buyer. The delivery of goods may be of two types-

- **Unconditional Delivery:** In this case, the ownership passes from the seller to the buyer at the time when the goods are delivered to the carrier.
- **Conditional Delivery:** In this case, the ownership does not pass to the buyer, unless the condition is fulfilled, e.g. bill is accepted or payment is made. In such a situation, normally the seller reserves a right of disposal of goods.

  '*Right of disposal*' means 'the right not to transfer the possession of goods, until certain conditions are fulfilled'. For example –

(i) Where the seller takes out the **bill of lading or the railway receipt** in his own name, i.e. he himself becomes the consignee. In such a case, the ownership in the goods will not pass.

(ii) Where the **railway receipt or the bill of lading is in the name of the buyer**, but is sent through the bank with the instructions that the same is to be delivered against acceptance of the bill or payment of the price, the property in the goods shall not pass.

Deliverable State: Goods are said to be in a "deliverable state" when they are in such state that the buyer would under the contract be bound to take delivery of them. **— Sec. 2(3)**

PASSING OF RISK [Sec. 26]

- **Who is to bear the risk?**
  - ✓ Risk passes with ownership.
  - ✓ The fact that the goods have been delivered or not is irrelevant to decide the question of risk.
- **Exception:** However, the following are the exceptions to the rule that 'Risk passes with ownership':

(a) **Delayed delivery:** Where the delivery of goods has been delayed due to the fault of the buyer/seller, goods are at the risk of the party in fault as regards any loss, which might not have occurred, but for such fault.

(b) **Agreement between parties:** By agreement, the parties may decide that 'risk' will pass before or after the passing of property.

(c) **Customs:** Customs may put the ownership and risk separately on two parties.

TRANSFER OF TITLE BY NON-OWNERS [Sec. 27]

As a general rule, only an owner of the goods can transfer ownership in the goods. The general maxim is ***"Nemo Dat Quo Non Habet"***, i.e. "*no one can pass a better title than what he has*." The object of this rule is to protect the true owners.

For Example: If Mr. A steals an article and sells it to B, Mr. B does not become the owner of the article. It is only the owner of the goods, who can convey better title.

Exceptions to this Doctrine

1. Sale by Estoppel [Sec. 27]: Where the owner by his conduct or by his act leads the buyer to believe that the seller has the authority to sell and induces the buyer to buy the goods, he shall be estopped from denying the fact that the seller had no right to sell the goods.

For Example: A tells B within the hearing of C that he (A) is the owner of certain goods. In fact, C is the owner of these goods. Later on A sells these goods to B. B will get a good title to the goods, as C will be estopped from denying A's right to sell.

2. Sale by a Mercantile Agent [Sec. 27]: Where the goods are sold by a mercantile agent without proper authority, the buyer shall get better title, if the following conditions are satisfied:

(i) The agent must be mercantile. A mercantile agent is one, who in the customary course of business has the authority to sell or buy the goods or to raise money on the security of goods.

(ii) He must be in possession of the goods or documents of title to the goods with the consent of the owner

(iii) The sale is made by him in the ordinary course of business,

(iv) The buyer should have acted in good faith and had no notice at the time of sale, that the seller had no authority to sell.

For Example: A entrusted his car to a mercantile agent to receive offers and not to sell. A also delivered the signed documents to the agent. On the basis of these documents, the agent pretended to the buyer that he had the authority to sell the car and thus the car was sold.

Held, the owner was estopped from denying the buyer's title.—*Eastern Distributors Ltd.* v *Godring* (1957)

3. Sale by one of the Joint Owners [Sec. 28]: When the goods are sold by one of the several joint owners, the buyer shall get better title, if the following conditions are satisfied:

(i) The joint owner, who makes the sale, must be in the possession of the goods with the permission of the other joint owners,

(ii) The buyer should have acted in good faith and without notice that the seller had no authority to sell.

For Example: A and B jointly purchased a car. The car was in the possession of Mr. A with the consent of B. Later on A sold the car to an innocent purchaser. The purchaser will get a good title.

4. Sale by person in possession under voidable contract [Sec. 29]: When a person, who has obtained possession of goods under an avoidable contract, sells these goods, the buyer shall get a better title, if the following conditions are satisfied:

(i) The sale is made before the rescission of the contract,

(ii) The buyer should have acted in good faith and without notice that the seller had no authority to sell.

For Example: A purchased a watch from B by fraud. A sold the watch to C, who bought it in good faith. C gets good title.

5. Sale by seller in possession after sale [Sec. 30(1)]: The buyer, after purchasing the goods, may leave them with the seller. If the seller re-sells these goods to another buyer, that buyer shall get better title, if the buyer had acted in good faith.

For Example: A sells certain goods to B and promises to deliver the goods the next day. Before the delivery, A sells and delivers the goods to C, who buys them in good faith and without notice of the prior sale to B. C gets a good title to the goods, notwithstanding that the property had, before he purchased, passed to B.

6. Sale by buyer in possession after sale or agreement to sale [Sec. 30(2)]: Where a buyer sells the goods to a person, then such person (i.e. new buyer) shall get a better title, if the following conditions are satisfied:

(i) The original buyer must have bought or agreed to buy the goods.

(ii) The original buyer is in the possession of the goods or the documents of title to the goods with the consent of the seller,

(iii) The subsequent buyer is acting in good faith.

For Example: Mr. A bought some furniture on Instalment payment system. A sold the furniture to B before paying last instalment. B purchased the furniture *bona fide*.

In this case, B had obtained a good title to the furniture.

However, in the case of **Hire Purchase System**, the hire buyer is not a person who has bought or agreed to buy the goods. He has merely an option to buy, so he can never transfer the better title to the transferee.

7. Sale by an unpaid seller [Sec. 54(3)]: Where an unpaid seller, who has exercised his right of lien or stoppage in transit, re-sells the goods, the buyer acquires a good title to the goods as against the original buyer, even if no notice of resale is given.

8. Exceptions under other laws:

(a) Under the Contract Act: (i) Finder of lost goods can pass a better title in following cases (Sec. 169) -

(a) The true owner cannot be found with reasonable diligence; or

(b) The true owner found, but refuses to pay the lawful charges of the finder; or

(c) If the goods are in danger of perishing or of losing the greater part of their value; or

(d) If the lawful charges of the finder, in respect of the thing found, amount to two-third or more of their value.

(ii) A Pawnee, under certain circumstances, can pass a better title (Sec. 176)

(b) Under the insolvency Law: An official receiver or assignee can pass a better title.

(c) Under the Companies Act: A Liquidator of a company can pass a better title.

Performance of a Contract of Sale [Secs. 31-44]

Performance of a contract of sale implies—

(i) a duty of the seller to deliver the goods, and

(ii) a duty of the buyer to accept the delivery of the goods and make payment in accordance with the terms of the contract.

DELIVERY OF GOODS

☞ Meaning:

Delivery means a voluntary transfer of possession of goods from one person to another. — Sec. 2(2)

☞ Modes of delivery

1. Actual delivery: Actual delivery takes place, when the goods change hands physically. *For Example*, when Mr. X delivers goods to Mr. B, there will be actual delivery.

2. Constructive delivery: In this case, the goods do not change hands physically. This may happen in the following cases:

(a) Where the seller is in the possession of the goods and he agrees to hold it on behalf of the buyer,

(b) Where the buyer is in the possession of the goods on behalf of the seller before sale,

(c) Where a third person is in the possession of the goods and he agrees to hold it on behalf of the buyer.

For Example, A sells some goods to B. At the time of sale, the goods were in the possession of A's agent, i.e. Mr. C, who was also the agent of B. A directs C to deliver the goods to B. Mr. C does so and accordingly now possesses the goods as B's agent.

The delivery has been completed.

3. Symbolic delivery: Where the goods are bulky and incapable of actual delivery. *For example* handling over of the key of a warehouse to the buyer is symbolic delivery.

☞ Rules as to delivery:

1. Delivery by whom and to whom [Sec. 31]: Goods shall be delivered by the seller to the buyer.

2. Delivery and payment are concurrent conditions [Sec. 32].

3. Effect of part delivery [Sec. 34]:

- If the intention of parties behind the part delivery is the delivery of whole goods, then it shall be assumed that whole goods have been delivered.
- However, where the part delivery of the goods is made with an intention of severing it from the whole, then the part delivery does not operate as a delivery of the remainder.

4. Delivery to be made on request of the buyer [Sec. 35] : Apart from any express contract, a seller is not bound to deliver the goods unless and until requested by the buyer.

If the seller fails to deliver the goods on the application of the buyer, the seller is guilty of breach of contract.

5. Place of delivery [Sec. 36(1)]: In the absence of an express or implied agreement,

(i) *If the goods are sold* : At the place at which the goods are at the time of sale.

(ii) *If the goods agreed to be sold* : At the place at which goods are at the time of the agreement to sell,

(iii) *If not then in existence* : At the place at which they are manufactured or produced.

6. Time of Delivery [Sec. 36(1)]:

(i) If any time is specified by the parties, the goods must be delivered by that time.

(ii) If the seller is bound to send the goods to the buyer and no time has been fixed by the parties, the goods must be delivered within a reasonable time. What is a reasonable time is a question of fact in each case.

(iii) The demand for delivery should be made at a reasonable hour.

7. Delivery of goods in possession of third persons [Sec. 36(3)]: If at the time of sale, the goods are in possession of a third person, there is no delivery by the seller to the buyer, unless such third person acknowledges to the buyer that he holds the goods on his behalf.

It should be noted that this rule does not affect the transfer of goods by means of a document of title of goods, i.e. where goods have been sold by bill of lading and the consent of the third party is not necessary.

8. Expenses of putting goods in deliverable state [Sec. 36(5)]: Unless otherwise agreed, the expenses, incidental to putting the goods into a deliverable state, shall be borne by the seller. In case the buyer is compelled to pay these expenses, he can recover the same from the seller.

9. Effect of delivery of wrong quantity [Sec. 37]:

Options available to the buyer

Short delivery	**Excess Delivery**	**Mixed Delivery (with goods of different description)**
1st Option: Reject the whole delivery,	***1st Option:*** Accept the contracted goods and reject the rest	***1st Option:*** Accept the contracted goods and reject the rest,
2nd Option: Accept the short delivery and pay for them at the contract price.	***2nd Option:*** Accept the whole.	***2nd Option:*** Reject the whole.
	3rd Option: Reject the whole.	
	If the buyer accepts the whole of the goods so delivered, he shall pay for them at the contract rate.	

Negligible Variation: The right to reject the goods in excess of the contract does not apply where the variation is negligible. Further, the right to reject the goods is not equivalent to the right to cancel the contract. If the buyer rejects the goods (either because they are less than or in excess of the quantity contracted for), the seller has a right to tender again the contract quantity and the buyer is bound to accept the same [*Vilas Udyog Ltd.* v *Prag Vanaspati Products* (1975)].

10. Delivery by Instalment [Sec. 38]: Unless otherwise agreed, the buyer of the goods is not bound to accept delivery in instalments. He may, if he so desires, refuse the goods.

For Example: Tweive-five Tonnes of paper October/November shipment was sold. The seller shipped 20 tonnes in November and five tonnes in December. Held, the buyer was entitled to reject the whole.

—*Rener* v *Sala* (1879)

11. Default in Delivery of Instalments, which are to be paid for separately: In case, there is a contract for the sale of goods to be delivered by stated instalments, which are to be paid for separately and the buyer or seller commits a breach in respect of one or more instalments, in such a case, a question arises as to whether the buyer or the seller can treat it as a breach of the whole contract, or it is a severable breach giving rise to a claim for compensation, but not the right to repudiate the whole contract.

Deciding factor: The answer to this question would depend upon the facts and circumstances of each case. However, the following factors should be kept in mind:

(a) The quantum of breach, which it bears to the contract as a whole.

(b) The degree of probability that it will be repeated.

(c) The nature of breach whether it goes to the root of the transaction.

12. Delivery to carrier or wharfinger (Sec. 39):

(i) Unconditional delivery to carrier/wharfinger: Where in a contract of sale, the seller is required to send the goods to the buyer, the delivery of goods to a carrier for the purpose of transmission to the buyer/to a wharfinger for safe custody is *prima facie* deemed to be a delivery of the goods to the buyer.

(ii) Seller's duty to reasonably secure goods before delivery: The seller must enter into a reasonable contract with the carrier or wharfinger for the safe transmission of goods. If the seller fails to do so, he will be liable to make good the loss suffered by the buyer.

(iii) Seller's duty to inform the buyers to get the goods insured in case the goods involve a sea transit: Where the goods are sent by the seller to the buyer by a route involving sea transit, the seller shall give such notice to the buyer as may enable him to insure the goods during the sea transit. Failure to do so will mean that the goods are at the seller's risk during the transit and the seller will have to make good the loss suffered by the buyer.

– <u>Acceptance of delivery by the buyer</u>:

(i) Buyer's right to examine the goods [Sec. 41(1)]: Where the buyer has not previously examined the goods, he is not deemed to have accepted them unless and until he has had a reasonable opportunity of examining them.

(ii) When is a buyer deemed to have accepted the delivery of goods? (Sec. 42): A buyer is deemed to have accepted the goods under the following conditions:

✓ When the buyer ***expressly*** approves the goods.

✓ When the buyer ***impliedly*** approves the goods.

☑☑☑

MULTIPLE CHOICE QUESTIONS

☞ Transfer of Property and Risk

1. A agrees to purchase bales of paper from B at Madras. The goods are sent by railway, delivery to be against payment by A through bank. A paid the amount and obtained a delivery order. *But,* the goods had been destroyed by fire before he had paid the amount. Decide, who shall bear the loss?

(A) A

(B) B

(C) A and B equally

(D) A and B in some other agreed ratio

2. In case of a sale of goods by a person in possession of goods under a voidable contract, he can pass valid title to the Buyer –

(A) only if the contract has been rescinded.

(B) only if the contract has not been rescinded.

(C) only when fraud is proven to the new Buyer.

(D) only when misrepresentation is proven to the new Buyer.

3. Which of the following statement is/are correct?

(A) The general rule is "unless otherwise agreed, the goods remain at the seller's risk until the property therein is transferred to the buyer, but when the property therein is transferred to the buyer, the goods are at the buyer's risk whether delivery has been made or not".

(B) Where the delivery of the goods has been delayed through the fault of either the buyer or the seller, the goods are at the risk of the party in fault as regards any loss which might not have occurred but for such fault.

(C) In ordinary circumstances, risk is borne by the buyer only when the property in the goods passes over to him. However, the parties may by special agreement stipulate that risk will pass sometime after or before the property has passed.

(D) All of the above

4. In case of a sale the risk of loss resulting from the insolvency of the buyer is borne by –

(A) The seller.

(B) The buyer.

(C) Both of the above.

(D) General Insurance Company of India.

5. Selection of goods with the intention of using them in performance of the contract and with the mutual consent of the seller and the buyer is known as –

(A) Distribution.

(B) Appropriation.

(C) Amortisation.

(D) Storage.

6. In case the goods are destroyed or damaged or lost by accident the loss will fall on –

(A) The owner of the goods.

(B) The buyer.

(C) The owner and the buyer.

(D) The third party.

7. A contract of sale involves transfer of –

(A) Possession of goods.

(B) Ownership.

(C) Liability.

(D) None of these

8. In a concluded sale, if the goods are destroyed, the loss is to be borne by–

(A) The seller.

(B) The buyer.

(C) The party who is in possession of goods.

(D) Both seller and buyer in agreed proportions.

9. There was a contract to supply "waste coal and ash for the next six months, as and when the waste is generated by the Seller's Factory". The Buyer paid the lumpsum price for the next six months in advance. When does the property in the goods pass to the Buyer?

(A) After the lapse of six months period

(B) At the time of entering into the contract

(C) At the time of paying advance money

(D) As and when the Factory discharges the waste

10. In which of the following situations, the Buyer is NOT deemed to have accepted the Goods?

(A) When he intimates to the Seller that he has accepted them.

(B) When the Goods are delivered to him, he does some action which is inconsistent with the ownership of the Seller.

(C) When, after the lapse of a reasonable time, he retains the goods without intimating the Seller that he has rejected the Goods.

(D) When he does not return the goods after rejecting them.

11. 'The property in goods' means the–

(A) Possession of goods.

(B) Custody of goods.

(C) Ownership of goods.

(D) Both (A) and (B)

12. Where there is an unconditional contract for the sale of specific goods in a deliverable state, the property in goods passes to the Buyer, when the—

(A) parties intend.

(B) goods are delivered.

(C) price is paid.

(D) contract is made.

13. The goods are at the risk of a party, who has the–

(A) Ownership of goods.

(B) Possession of goods.

(C) Custody of goods.

(D) Both (B) and (C)

14. In case of unconditional contract of sale, the property passes to the buyer at the time of making the contract. For this rule to apply, the goods must be –

(A) Specific.

(B) In a deliverable state.

(C) Physically transferred to buyer.

(D) Both (A) and (B)

15. In case of sale on approval, the ownership is transferred to the buyer, when he –

(A) Accepts the goods.

(B) Adopts the transaction.

(C) Fails to return the goods.

(D) In all the above cases.

16. In case of sale of standing trees, the property passes to the buyer, when the trees are –

(A) felled and ascertained.

(B) not felled but earmarked.

(C) counted and ascertained.

(D) both (A) and (B)

17. In case, the delivery of goods is delayed due to the fault of party, the goods shall be at the risk of the defaulting party, even though the ownership is with the other party.

(A) True, as there is a provision to this effect.

(B) False, as it is against the general rule.

18. In pursuance of a contract to fill 20 bags of sugar out of a large quantity, the seller filled four bags, which the buyer takes away. Subsequently, the seller filled 16 more bags, informed the buyer of this and requested him to take them away. Before the buyer could take the delivery, the 16 bags caught fire and damaged. Decide, who shall bear the loss.

(A) Seller

(B) Buyer

(C) Seller and Buyer equally

(D) Seller and Buyer in some other agreed ratio

19. In case of sale of unascertained goods, the ownership is transferred to the buyer when the goods are –

(A) ascertained.

(B) appropriated to the contract.

(C) weighed and measured.

(D) both (A) and (B)

20. Essentials involved in appropriation of the goods are –

(A) The goods should conform to the description and the quality stated in the contract.

(B) The goods must be in a deliverable state.

(C) The goods must be unconditionally appropriated to the contract either by delivery to the buyer or to is agent or the carrier.

(D) All of the above

21. One Blenkarn, knowing that Blenkiron & Co were reputed customers of Lindsay & Co, placed an order with Lindsay & Co. by imitating signatures of Blenkiron. Goods were then sold to Cundy, an innocent buyer. Lindsay & Co. Sued Cundy for recovery of goods. In this case—

(A) Cundy has good title to goods and can retain them.

(B) Sale made by Blenkarn to Cundy is valid.

(C) Both (A) and (B)

(D) Lindsay never intended to contract with Blenkarn, there was no contract. So, Cundy's title is defective.

22. X offers Y his buffalo for Rs. 12,000, the same to be delivered to Y on a stipulated day and price to be paid on another stated day. Y accepts the offer. Decide– Does the property in the buffalo pass to Y?

(A) The property in the buffalo passes to Y.

(B) The property in the buffalo does not pass to Y, as the price is not decided.

(C) The property in the buffalo does not pass to Y, as the buffalo is not in a deliverable situation.

(D) Both (B) and (C)

23. The defedendant purchased 975 bags of rice being the whole contents of a "Gola", paid earnest money and took part delivery of rice. The rest was afterwards destroyed by fire. Decide–

(A) Defendant is liable to pay the balance of the price.

(B) Defendant is not liable to pay the balance of the price, as the balance of the rice was not delivered.

(C) Defendant is not liable to pay the balance of the price, as the ownership in the balance of the rice was not transferred to him.

(D) Both (B) and (C)

24. A, B, and C own certain cattle in common. A is left by B and C in possession of a cow which he sells to D. D purchases it *bona fide*. Decide–

(A) The property in the cow transferred to D.

(B) The property in the cow is not transferred to D, as consent of B and C was not taken in the Sale.

(C) The property in the cow is not transferred to D, the cow was sold by A, who is not the sole owner of the cow.

(D) None of the above

25. A delivers bags of cements to B on `Sale on approval basis for 10 days. The cement became stone due to heavy rainfall (without any fault of B) on the fifth day itself.

The loss is to be borne by –

(A) A, because the ownership has not passed to B.

(B) A, if B refuses to bear the loss.

(C) B, if A refuses to bear the loss.

(D) B, because the ownership has passed to B.

26. In *Q. 25* above, if the cement became stone, after being accepted by B, the loss is to be borne by–

(A) A, if B refuses to bear the loss.

(B) B ,if A refuses to bear the loss.

(C) A, because the ownership has not passed to B.

(D) B, because the ownership has passed to B.

27. In *Q. 25* above, if B retains the good and gives notice of rejection on the fourth day, the loss is to be borne by–

(A) A, because the ownership has not passed to B.

(B) B, because the bags were in custody of B, at the time of damage.

(C) B, because B has retained the bags for more than three days.

(D) B, because the ownership has passed to B.

28. In *Q. 25* above, if B neither returns nor rejects the bags till the tenth day and eventually the damage occurs on the eleventh day, the loss shall be borne by–

(A) A, because the ownership has not passed to B.

(B) A, because ten days has elapsed.

(C) A, because the agreement has become void.

(D) B, because the ownership has passed to B.

29. Where the Seller agrees to deliver the Goods at his own risk at a place other than at which they are sold, the __________ shall bear the risk of deterioration necessarily incident in the course of transit, unless otherwise agreed.

(A) Buyer

(B) Seller

(C) Carrier

(D) Railway administration

30. Section ______ of the Sale of Goods Act, provides for passing of property in goods where there is an unconditional contract for the sale of specific goods in a deliverable state.

(A) 18

(B) 19

(C) 20

(D) 21

31. The rule as to passing of property as laid down in Sec. 20 of the Sale of Goods Act, shall apply when—

(A) the time of payment of price is postponed.

(B) the time of delivery of the goods is postponed.

(C) even the time of payment of price and the time of delivery of the goods are both postponed.

(D) neither the time of payment of price nor the time of delivery of the goods is postponed.

32. In case of an unconditional contract for sale of specific goods in a deliverable state, the property passes to the Buyer—

(A) upon delivery of goods.

(B) upon payment of price.

(C) at such time as the parties intend it to be transferred.

(D) at the time when contract is made.

33. In a sale of specific or ascertained goods, the property therein is transferred to the Buyer—

(A) upon delivery of goods.

(B) upon payment of price.

(C) at such time as the parties intend it to be transferred.

(D) at such time as decided by the Court.

34. The property in goods in a contract for sale of specific or ascertained goods, passes to the Buyer—

(A) when the price is paid.

(B) when the contract is made.

(C) when the parties intend the property in goods to pass.

(D) all of the above

35. Which of the following is relevant for determining the passing of property in ascertained goods?

(A) Intention of Parties

(B) Delivery of Goods

(C) Payment of Price

(D) All of the above

36. Goods delivered on sale or return basis were pledged by the delivery. Decide–

(A) The original owner can recover the goods from the pledgee, as goods are not expressly approved by the buyer.

(B) The original owner can recover the goods from the pledgee, as Pledgee is not the owner of the goods.

(C) The original owner cannot recover the goods from the pledgee, as goods are impliedly approved by the buyer.

(D) Both (A) and (B)

37. In a sale on "approval" basis, any act of the Buyer exercising domination over the goods, showing an unequivocal intention to buy is called—

(A) adopting the transaction.

(B) adapting the transaction.

(C) revoking the transaction.

(D) rejecting the transaction.

38. In a sale on "approval" basis, where a time has been fixed for return of goods, property passes to the Buyer when the Buyer, without giving notice of rejection retains the goods beyond—

(A) contract-specified time.

(B) reasonable time.

(C) natural time.

(D) questionable time.

39. In case of sale on "sale or return" or "approval" basis, property passes to the Buyer when—

(A) Buyer retains the goods for more than the contract-stipulated time.

(B) Buyer retains the goods for more than a reasonable time.

(C) neither (A) nor (B)

(D) either (A) or (B)

40. A Buyer from one of the Joint Owners of the goods get a good title if he buys the goods—

(A) in good faith.

(B) without having notice of any want of authority in the seller.

(C) either (A) or (B)

(D) both (A) and (B)

41. When the property in Goods in transferred to Buyer, Goods are at the _____ risk, irrespective of whether delivery has been made or not.

(A) Buyer's

(B) Seller's

(C) Carrier's

(D) All of the above

42. Section 27 of the Sale of Goods Act, 1930 provides for transfer—

(A) of authority in goods.

(B) of risk in goods.

(C) of title in goods.

(D) of interest in goods.

43. Ordinarily, if any person who does not possess a good title to the goods makes a sale, the Buyer _____ even though he has acquired it *bona fide* and for value.

(A) would acquire title

(B) would acquire possession

(C) would not acquire title

(D) would not acquire possession

44. In case of sale on "sale or return" or "approval" basis, property passes to the Buyer, when—

(A) Buyer approves or accepts the goods.

(B) Buyer does any act adopting the transaction.

(C) Buyer retains the goods for more than the contract-stipulated time or reasonable time, without giving notice of rejection.

(D) All of the above

45. In case of sale on "sale or return" or "approval" basis, the term "Buyer" signifies a Bailee in possession with option to purchase the goods.

(A) True

(B) Partly True

(C) False

(D) None of the above

46. In case of sale of unascertained goods, the property in goods passes—

(A) when the contract provides that the property in goods shall pass.

(B) when the goods are ascertained.

(C) when the contract is made.

(D) all of the above

47. For passing of property in respect of specific or ascertained goods, the intention of the parties can be ascertained from—

(A) Terms of the contract.

(B) Conduct of the parties.

(C) Circumstances of the case.

(D) All of the above

48. Section 26 of the Sale of Goods Act, lays down the rule that Risk follows—

(A) the property.

(B) the delivery.

(C) the defaulter.

(D) the Seller.

49. Risk *prima facie* passes with—

(A) property or ownership.

(B) completed agreement.

(C) verification and delivery of goods.

(D) payment of price.

50. By an agreement between the parties—

(A) risk can be separated from ownership in particular.

(B) risk cannot be separated from ownership.

(C) either (A) or (B)

(D) neither (A) nor (B)

☞ Transfer by Non-owner

51. Mercantile Agent is having an authority to–

(A) sell or consign goods.

(B) raise money on the security of goods.

(C) sell or buy goods.

(D) any of the above

52. Where goods are sold by a person, who is not the owner thereof, the buyer –

(A) Acquires no better title to the goods than the seller had.

(B) Acquires same title of the goods as the owner had.

(C) Acquires no title of goods.

(D) None of these

53. 'A' acquired certain goods from 'C' by falsely representing that he was acting on behalf of 'B' and was authorized to collect the goods. 'A' later sold the goods to 'D'. Is the sale valid?

(A) The sale is valid as 'D' is not supposed to inquire the status of, 'A' as a seller.

(B) The sale is valid because 'D' has purchased the goods in goods faith.

(C) The sale is valid as 'A' has acquired the goods by way of fraud.

(D) The sale is not valid as because it a sale by non-owner and therefore, 'D', the buyer, will not acquire Good Title of the goods.

54. In case of hire purchase, the hirer can pass title to a *bona fide* purchaser.

(A) True, as it would be sale by buyer in possession after agreement to sale.

(B) false, as the rule *'Nemo dat quo non Habet'* will apply.

(C) None of these

55. In case of hire purchase, the hirer can pass the title to a *bona fide* purchaser.

(A) True

(B) Partly True

(C) False

(D) None of the above

56. In case of a sale the buyer –

(A) Can pass a good title to a *bona fide* purchaser.

(B) Cannot pass a good title to a *bona fide* purchaser.

(C) Both of the above

(D) None of the above

☞ Delivery

57. Which of the following is not a form of delivery?

(A) Constructive delivery

(B) Structured delivery

(C) Actual delivery

(D) Symbolic delivery

58. If a seller handed over the keys of a warehouse containing the goods to the buyer results in–

(A) Constructive delivery.

(B) Actual delivery.

(C) Symbolic delivery.

(D) None of the above.

59. Which of the following modes of delivery of goods is considered effective for a valid contract of sale?

(A) Actual delivery

(B) Symbolic delivery

(C) Constructive delivery

(D) All of these.

60. X of Cochin agreed to sell 400 tons of rice to Y of Calcutta to be shipped in November or December 2007. X puts the rice on ship in October 2007. Is the buyer bound to accept the consignment?

(A) Yes

(B) No

61. If Goods are sent by sea-route, the Seller _____ give notice to Buyer so as to enable him to insure the Goods during transit.

(A) must

(B) may

(C) shall

(D) any of the above

62. Section _______ of the Sale of Goods Act, 1930 defines the term "Delivery".

(A) 2(1)

(B) 2(2)

(C) 2(3)

(D) 2(4)

63. Acceptance of delivery of goods is deemed to take place, when the buyer –

(A) intimates to the seller that he had accepted the goods.

(B) does any act to the goods, which is inconsistent with the ownership of the seller.

(C) retains the goods after the lapse of a reasonable time without intimating the seller that he has rejected them.

(D) any of the above.

64. If the buyer rejects the whole quantity of goods due to short delivery or excess delivery, the contract is treated as—

(A) subsisting.

(B) cancelled.

(C) void.

(D) invalid.

65. A owes B Rs. 2,000. B accepts some of A's goods in deduction of the debt. Does the delivery of the goods operate as a part payment ?

(A) Yes

(B) No

66. Voluntary transfer of possession by one person to another is popularly known as–

(A) Transfer.

(B) Possession.

(C) Delivery.

(D) None of the above

67. Where the seller wrongfully neglects to deliver the goods to the buyer, then the buyer –

(A) cannot sue the seller for damages for non-delivery.

(B) may sue the seller for damages for non-delivery.

(C) either (A) or (B)

(D) none of the above

68. Delivery of a thing in token of a transfer of something else is known as—

(A) Actual Delivery.

(B) Constructive Delivery.

(C) Delivery by acknowledgment.

(D) None of the above

69. The action of goods being physically delivered to the buyer is known as–

(A) Actual Delivery.

(B) Constructive Delivery.

(C) Symbolic Delivery.

(D) All of the above.

70. Delivery which is effected without any change in the custody or actual possession of the thing is known as—

(A) Actual Delivery.

(B) Symbolic Delivery.

(C) Constructive Delivery.

(D) None of the above

71. Delivered by acknowledgement is—

(A) Actual Delivery.

(B) Constructive Delivery.

(C) Symbolic Delivery.

(D) None of the above

72. The delivery of goods and payment of price are–

(A) Concurrent conditions.

(B) Principal conditions.

(C) Mutual conditions.

(D) All of these

73. Which of the following is true, delivery means –

(A) Compulsory transfer of possession by one person to another person.

(B) Voluntary transfer of possession by one person to another.

(C) Mere transfer of possession by one person to another person.

(D) All of these

74. Which of the following sentence is true?

(A) There should be immediate delivery of goods.

(B) There should be immediate payment of price.

(C) There may be delivery of goods and payment of price on to be made at some future date.

(D) All of these

75. A buys from B bales of Branch Cotton, December, 1991 delivery, at Rs. 1,250 per bale. On the date of delivery, the price is Rs. 1,000 per bale. A wants to avoid contract. Can he do so with impunity?

(A) Yes

(B) No

76. A promises to deliver goods to B's warehouse, on the 1st January. On that day A brings the goods to B's warehouse, but after the usual hour for closing the warehouse and they are not received. Has A performed his promise?

(A) Yes

(B) No

77. Where the goods are delivered to a carrier or wharfinger for the purpose of transmission to the buyer, the delivery is –

(A) Invalid and ineffective.

(B) Valid and effective.

(C) Conditional.

(D) None of these

78. P agrees to sell and deliver to Y 300 quintals of rice, but only 200 quintals are delivered. Y has the rice weighed and accepts the quintals sent. Y afterwards objects that the whole of the 300 quintals was not delivered and he refuses to pay for 200 quintals. Is Y liable to pay for what he has accepted?

(A) Yes

(B) No

79. There was a sale of 25 tonnes of cloves for October/ November shipment. The seller shipped 20 tonnes in November and 5 tonnes in December. Would the buyer be entitled to reject the whole 25 tonnes?

(A) Yes

(B) No

80. A agrees to sell 50 Refrigerators to B, at a price to be determined by C. 30 of 50 Refrigerators are delivered to B B agreed to the above agreement, without asking the dealer whether the refrigerators are fit to make ice and paid the determined consideration. The refrigerators failed to make ice.

(A) A must refund the price, because refrigerators are mean to make ice.

(B) A will refund the price, only if buyer would have disclosed this particular purpose.

(C) A will refund the price at his option.

(D) A need not refund the price.

81. In *Q. 80* above, what would be the legal position, if C denies to determine the price?

(A) C can be compelled to determine the price.

(B) The contract becomes voidable at the option of parties.

(C) The contract becomes void and B must return those 30 refrigerators.

(D) The contract becomes void and B must pay reasonable price for 30 refrigerators.

82. In *Q. 80* above, what would be the legal position, if B prevents C from determining the price?

(A) C can be compelled to determine the price.

(B) The contract becomes voidable at the option of A.

(C) The contract become void, and B must pay reasonable price for 30 refrigerators.

(D) B has to return the refrigerators.

83. In *Q. 80* above, If 20 refrigerators are stolen at time of making contract, the aforesaid contract becomes

(A) Void, because the goods have perished.

(B) Void, because the contract was indivisible.

(C) Voidable at the option of B.

(D) Party Void and partly valid.

84. A sells 50 quintals of wheat to B. The wheat remains in A's warehouse after the sale. B sells to C 10 quintals of wheat, and A at B's desire sends those 10 quintals of wheat to C. In the circumstances can it be regarded as the delivery of the whole quantity?

(A) Yes

(B) No

(C) Partly Yes

(D) None of the above

85. Where the Seller repudiates a contract before the date of delivery, the Buyer may treat the contract–

(A) as subsisting and wait till the date of delivery.

(B) as rescinded and sue the Buyer for damages for the breach on his part.

(C) neither (A) nor (B)

(D) either (A) or (B)

86. Section 60 of the Sale of Goods Act, is applicable where the contract of sale is repudiated by either party before the date of –

(A) payment of price.

(B) delivery.

(C) both (A) and (B)

(D) either (A) or (B)

87. Delivery of Goods sold may be made by doing—

(A) anything which the parties agree shall be treated as delivery.

(B) anything which has the effect of putting the Goods in the possession of the Buyer or of any person authorized to hold them on his behalf.

(C) Both (A) and (B)

(D) Either (A) or (B)

88. In case of repudiation of contract of sale before the date of delivery, where the delivery was to be made by installments, the measure of damages is the difference between the Contract Price and Market price on—

(A) date of making the contract.

(B) date of last intended delivery under the contact.

(C) several dates when the goods ought to have been accepted/delivered.

(D) date of Court's Order.

ANSWERS TO MULTIPLE CHOICE QUESTIONS

1. B	**19.** D	**37.** A	**55.** C	**73.** B
2. B	**20.** D	**38.** A	**56.** A	**74.** C
3. D	**21.** D	**39.** D	**57.** B	**75.** B
4. A	**22.** A	**40.** D	**58.** C	**76.** B
5. B	**23.** A	**41.** A	**59.** D	**77.** B
6. A	**24.** A	**42.** C	**60.** B	**78.** A
7. B	**25.** A	**43.** C	**61.** C	**79.** A
8. B	**26.** D	**44.** D	**62.** D	**80.** A
9. D	**27.** A	**45.** A	**63.** A	**81.** B
10. D	**28.** D	**46.** B	**64.** D	**82.** C
11. C	**29.** B	**47.** D	**65.** A	**83.** B
12. D	**30.** C	**48.** A	**66.** C	**84.** D
13. A	**31.** C	**49.** A	**67.** B	**85.** B
14. D	**32.** D	**50.** A	**68.** B	**86.** B
15. D	**33.** C	**51.** D	**69.** A	**87.** D
16. A	**34.** C	**52.** A	**70.** C	**88.** C
17. A	**35.** A	**53.** D	**71.** B	
18. B	**36.** C	**54.** B	**72.** A	

Chapter 3

Unpaid Seller And Auction Sale

WHO IS AN UNPAID SELLER?

A seller of goods is deemed to be unpaid in the following cases:

1. The price must be due, but not paid.
2. He must have an immediate right of action for the price.
3. A negotiable instrument, like cheque, bill of exchange, etc. was received, but the same has been dishonoured.
4. Further, a seller who has obtained a decree for the price of the goods will also be an unpaid seller, if the decree has not been satisfied.

Seller includes agent: It is to be noted that here the term 'seller' is used in a very elastic sense. It includes any person, who is in the position of a seller, such as an agent of the seller, to whom a bill of lading has been endorsed or an agent, who has himself paid or is directly responsible for the price.

RIGHTS OF AN UNPAID SELLER

Rights against Goods

1. Right of Lien
2. Right of Stoppage in Transit
3. Right of Re-sale.

Rights against Buyer personally

1. Sue for Price
2. Sue for damages for non-acceptance
3. Right to repudiate the contract
4. Sue for Interest

I. RIGHT AGAINST GOODS

1. Right of Lien [Secs. 47 to 49]

The right of lien means a right to retain possession of goods, until the buyer pays the price. The unpaid seller can retain the goods in his possession, if all the following conditions are satisfied:

(i) The goods have not been sold on credit or the credit period has been expired, or

(ii) The buyer has become insolvent.

☞ ***Rules Regarding the Right of Lien:***

1. **Right of lien is a possessory right**. As such, it can be exercised only when the goods are in possession. Once the possession of goods is lost, this right of lien is also lost.
2. It should be noted that here the word **'insolvent'** means a person who is commercially insolvent, not necessarily he has been adjudged insolvent.
3. Further, in case the buyer becomes insolvent, the unpaid seller can exercise his right of lien, even if the period of credit has not expired, if the buyer becomes insolvent before the period of credit has expired.
4. Lien right can be exercised **only for price**, not for other charges like, godown rent, interest, etc.
5. Lien right can be exercised, even if the goods are in the seller's possession in any other capacity, like that of a bailee or agent.
6. Finally, even if the seller has made part delivery, the lien may be exercised on the goods remaining in his possession.

☞ ***Loss of the Lien Right:***

1. When the unpaid seller delivers the goods to a carrier or other bailee for the purpose of transmission to the buyer without reserving the right of disposal of the goods;
2. When the buyer or his agent lawfully obtains possession of the goods;
3. The right of lien cannot be exercised, where the right lien has been expressly excluded.

2. Right of Stoppage in Transit [Secs. 50 to 52]

The right of stoppage in transit is an extension of the right of lien. The right of lien is a right to retain possession, whereas the right of stoppage in transit is a right to regain possession.

The right of stoppage in transit can be exercised, if—

(i) the goods are in transit, and

(ii) the buyer has become insolvent in the meantime.

☞ ***Duration of Transit** [Sec. 51]:*

1. First of all, it is to be noted that the carrier may hold goods in three capacities:—
   (i) **As Seller's Agent:** In this case, the seller has a lien on the goods, so the question of right of stoppage in transit does not arise.
   (ii) **As Buyer's Agent:** In this case, the seller cannot exercise the right of stoppage in transit.
   (iii) **In an Independent Capacity:** In this case, the seller can exercise the right of stoppage in transit.
2. Goods are deemed to be in course of transit from the time they are delivered to a carrier or other bailee for the purpose of transmission to the buyer, until the buyer or his agent takes their delivery from such carrier or other bailee.
3. The goods are in transit, even if the buyer asks the carrier to take them to some other destination until they are delivered to the buyer.
4. If the goods are rejected by the buyer and the goods are in the possession of the carrier, the transit is not at an end, even if the seller has also refused to take them back.

☞ ***How to exercise the Right of Stoppage of Goods in Transit:***

(i) by taking actual possession of the goods, or

(ii) by giving notice of his claim to the carrier, who holds the goods.

3. Right of Re-Sale [Sec. 54]

An unpaid seller has a right to resell the goods in the following cases:

(i) When the goods are of a perishable nature, or

(ii) When he gives notice to the buyer showing his intention to re-sell the goods and the buyer does not within a reasonable time, pay or tender the price, or

(iii) When the seller expressly reserves a right of re-sale in case the buyer makes a default.

☞ ***When the Notice of Re-sale is not required?***

- When the goods are of a perishable nature, or
- When the seller expressly reserves a right of re-sale in case the buyer defaults

☞ ***Effect of the Notice of Re-sale:***

(1) Where on re-sale there is a profit, the seller is entitled to retain it.

(2) On the other hand, if there is a loss, the seller can recover his loss from the buyer.

When notice is necessary and seller does not give notice to buyer, then the buyer will not be liable for the loss caused to seller due to re-sale, but will be entitled to take the profit of re-sale.

(3) The second buyer will get good title to the goods irrespective of the fact, whether notice of re-sale was given or not.

(4) By re-sale, the original contract is not rescinded.

(5) Right of re-sale does not bar other remedies.

II. RIGHT AGAINST THE BUYER PERSONALLY [Secs. 55 to 61]

1. **Suit for price:**

(a) **Where Property has passed [Sec. 55(1)]:** In this case, the seller may sue him for the price of the goods.

(b) **Where Property in the Goods has not passed [Sec. 55(1)]:** In this case, the seller cannot file a suit for price. His remedy is to claim for damages.

However, where under the contract of sale, price is payable on a certain day irrespective of delivery and the buyer wrongfully neglects or refuses to pay such price, the seller may sue him for the price, although the property in the goods has not passed and the goods have not been appropriated to the contract.

2. **Suit for Damages for Non-Acceptance (Sec. 56):** Where the buyer wrongfully neglects or refuses to accept and pay for the goods, the seller may sue him for damages for non-acceptance. Sec. 73 of the Indian Contract Act deals with measure of damages.

3. **Right to repudiate contract before the due date (Sec. 60):** Where either party to a contract repudiates the contract before the date of delivery, the other party to a contract has two options:

   (i) either treat the contract as subsisting and wait till the date of delivery, or

   (ii) treat the contract as rescinded and sue for damages for the breach.

4. **Suit for Interest:** In the absence of any contract to the contrary, no interest shall be payable by the buyer on the delayed payment. As such interest may be recovered only when there is a specific agreement in this respect. If there is no such agreement, the seller may give notice to the buyer of his intention to charge interest on delayed payment.

EFFECT OF SUB-SALE OR PLEDGE BY THE BUYER

According to Sec. 53(1), the seller's right of lien or stoppage in transit is not affected by any sale, pledge or other disposition of the goods by the buyer, unless the seller has assented to it.

– Exceptions:

If a document of title to goods, e.g., bill of lading has been issued or lawfully transferred to the buyer and the buyer transfers the document to a purchaser, who takes it in good faith and for consideration, then—

(i) If such transfer by the buyer is a sale, the seller's rights against goods are completely defeated, i.e. better title will be transferred to the second buyer.

(ii) If such transfer is a pledge, the seller's rights against goods are not completely defeated, but are only subject to such right.

For Example: (a) A sold goods to B and sent the bill of lading to B. B before making payment for the goods, transferred the bill of lading to C for consideration. Thereafter, B became insolvent. A's right to stop goods is defeated and C has a good title on the goods.

(b) A sold certain goods to B and transferred a bill of lading to him. B without paying for goods, pledge the bill with C for Rs. 4,000. Thereafter, B became insolvent. A can get the bill of lading subject to paying a sum of Rs. 4,000 to C.

RIGHTS OF THE BUYER

The buyer has the following rights:–

1. Suit for damages for non-delivery of the goods [Sec. 57],
2. Suit for specific performance [Sec. 58]– Where damages are not an adequate remedy, the court may at its discretion order specific performance of the contract.
3. Suit for breach of warranty [Sec. 59],
4. Suit for repudiation of contract before the date of contract [Sec. 60],
5. Right to claim interest.

AUCTION SALE [Sec. 64]

– Meaning:

First of all, it is to be noted that the law has not defined an auction sale. A sale by auction is a public sale where different buyers try to outbid each other. The goods are ultimately sold to the highest bidder. The auctioneer, who sells the goods by auction, is an agent of the seller. His relationship with the seller is governed by the law of agency.

– Rules Regarding Auction Sale:

1. Bid: When a person bids, it is only an offer and his bid (i.e. offer) is deemed to be accepted by the fall of the hammer or by say, calling 'one', 'two', and 'three'. Before its acceptance, it can be withdrawn.

2. Acceptance: The sale is complete, when the auctioneer announces its completion by the fall of the hammer or in some other customary manner. For example, saying 'one', 'two' and 'three' or 'going', 'going' and 'gone'.

Any rule, which does not permit a bidder to withdraw his bid before it is accepted is invalid. It is against the provision of law which provides that an offer can be revoked before it is accepted.

For Example: In an auction sale, it was notified that, a "bid once made shall not be withdrawn." One of the bidders, who made a bid wanted to withdraw it before the fall of the hammer. Held, he was entitled to withdraw his bid before it was accepted.

3. An Auction sale is complete when the bid has been accepted. As such if the goods are damaged before the completion of sale, the loss will fall on the seller.

4. Where goods are put up for sale in lots, each lot is *prima facie* deemed to be subject of a separate contract of sale. The rule can be excluded by an agreement.

– Reserve Price:

It is usual for the auctioneer to notify a reserve price. Reserve price is the lowest price below which the auctioneer will not sell. This reserve price is fixed by the auctioneer to protect himself from the goods selling at an extremely low price. Where the sale is notified subject to a reserve price, the buyer is bound by the reserve price even if the auctioneer by mistake accepted a bid lower than the reserve price.

For Example: An auctioneer by mistake accepted a bid for less than the reserve price. On discovering the mistake, the auctioneer refused to complete the sale. Held, the buyer was bound by the reserve price.

—*Rainbow* v *Hawkins* (1904)

☞ **Whether an auctioneer is bound to sell to the highest bidder:**

Unless a reserve price has been notified, the auctioneer is bound to sell to the highest bidder.

☞ **Whether an auctioneer can refuse to auction on the day advertised:**

Yes, he can. This is because, advertisement is only an invitation to offer.

☞ **Whether knockout agreement is valid:**

In the case of a knockout agreement, the buyers join their hands to eliminate competition among themselves at an auction sale. They agree that they will not raise the bid against each other and only one of them will bid at the auction. When the goods have been purchased, they will share the profit.

Prima facie, a knock-out agreement is not illegal. However, if the intention of the parties to the agreement is to defraud a third party, this will be illegal.

☞ **Damping:**

Damping is an illegal act, dissuading the intending buyer from bidding. It includes—

1. Pointing out defects in the goods, or
2. Misleading the purchaser or doing any other act so that he may not participate in the auction.

Damping is illegal. It empowers the auctioneer to withdraw the property from the auction.

☞ **Bidding by Seller (i.e. Pretended Bidding):**

If the right to bid is expressly reserved by the seller, the seller or any one person on his behalf may bid at the auction. In this regard, the rules are as follows:

1. A seller is not allowed to bid at an auction unless he had expressly reserved this right.

2. Where the sale is not notified to be subject to a right to bid on behalf of the sellers, it shall not be lawful for the seller to bid himself or employ any person to bid at such sale, or for the auctioneer knowingly to take any bid from the seller or any such person. Any sale contravening this rule may be treated as fraudulent by the buyer.

3. If the seller makes use of pretended bidding to raise the price, the sale is voidable at the option of the buyer. The bid is said to be pretended when it is made by the seller or some one on his behalf.

MULTIPLE CHOICE QUESTIONS

☞ Rights of Unpaid Seller

1. X of Delhi orders Y of Chennai, to deliver certain goods to him at Delhi. White the Goods are lying at Delhi Railway Station, the Station Master informs X that Goods are held at the Station at X's risk. But X has become insolvent. In this case—

(A) Y has the right of stoppage in transit.
(B) Y has lost his right of stoppage in transit.
(C) Station Master has the right of stoppage in transit.
(D) Station Master has lost the right of stoppage in transit.

2. An unpaid seller is having rights against –

(A) Goods only.
(B) The buyer only.
(C) Both goods and buyer.
(D) None of the above.

3. When the unpaid seller has parted with the goods to a carrier and the buyer has become insolvent he can exercise–

(A) Right of lien.
(B) Right of stoppage in transit.
(C) Right of resale.
(D) None of the above.

4. The essence of a right of lien is to–

(A) Deliver the goods.
(B) Retain the possession.
(C) Regain the possession.
(D) None of the above.

5. Seller has the right of resale, where–

(A) goods are perishable.
(B) seller has reserved such right.
(C) seller gives notice.
(D) all of these

6. Under which circumstances the unpaid seller can exercise his right of re-sale.

(A) when the goods are of perishable nature.
(B) when he gives notice to the buyer.
(C) when he gives notice to the buyer of his intention to re-sale and the buyer does not within a reasonable time pay the price.
(D) both (A) and (C)

7. Under which circumstances, the right of stoppage can be exercised by an unpaid seller.

(A) the buyer has become insolvent.

(B) the goods are in transit.

(C) the seller must be unpaid.

(D) all of the above

8. An unpaid seller loses the right of lien under the following circumstances–

(A) Where the seller so conducts himself that he leads third parties to believe that the lien does not exist i.e. estopple.

(B) Where the seller has waived the right of lien.

(C) Where the buyer or his agent lawfully obtains possession of the goods.

(D) All of the above

9. In case of interest by way of damages and special damages in a suit by the Seller u/s 61, the interest may be calculated from—

(A) date of tender of goods.

(B) date on which the price was payable.

(C) either (A) or (B)

(D) both (A) and (B)

10. The right of lien means –

(A) To refuse to deliver the goods

(B) To take back delivery of goods

(C) To hold goods until payment is made

(D) None of these

11. The right of lien can be exercised –

(A) Only for the price

(B) Only for the expenses

(C) Either for the price or expenses

(D) All of these

12. In case of perishable goods the unpaid seller can–

(A) Resell goods.

(B) Not resell goods.

(C) Resell after giving notice to the buyer.

(D) Resell goods without giving notice to the buyer.

13. Which of the following is Unpaid Seller?

(1) Right to re-sale

(2) Right to stop the goods in transit

(3) Right of lien

(4) Right to demand back the goods

(A) 2, 3, 4

(B) 1, 2, 3

(C) 1, 3, 4

(D) 1, 2, 3, 4

14. The right of stoppage can be exercised by an unpaid seller, if –

(A) The buyer has become insolvent.

(B) The goods are in transit.

(C) The seller must be unpaid.

(D) All of these

15. In which of the following cases, the unpaid seller loses his right of lien?

(A) Delivery of goods to buyer

(B) Delivery of goods to carrier

(C) Tender of price by buyer

(D) All of these.

16. The transit comes to an end –

(A) When buyer takes the delivery

(B) When delivery is made unconditionally to a ship

(C) When there is part delivery of goods with the intention to deliver whole goods.

(D) All of these

17. J sells and consigns certain Goods to S for cash and sends the Railway Receipt to him. S becomes insolvent and while the Goods are in transit, he assigns the Railway Receipt to N, who does not know that S is insolvent. In this case, J—

(A) cannot exercise the right of stoppage of Goods in transit.

(B) can exercise the right of stoppage of Goods in transit.

(C) cannot exercise the right of lien on goods.

(D) can exercise the right of lien on goods.

18. The unpaid seller has right of stoppage of goods in transit only where the buyer –

(A) Become insolvent.

(B) refuses to pay price.

(C) Acts fraudulently.

(D) All of these

19. Even if a substantial portion of the price is paid and only a small balance is pending, the Seller is still regarded as an Unpaid Seller.

(A) True

(B) Partly True

(C) False

(D) None of the above

20. The Seller of Goods is deemed to be an Unpaid Seller when the _______ of the price has not been paid or tendered.

(A) Whole

(B) Part

(C) Substantial portion

(D) Minimal portion

21. In the context of Rights of an Unpaid Seller, Quasi Lien means—

(A) Right of Lien
(B) Right of Stoppage of goods in transit
(C) Right of withholding delivery of goods
(D) Right of Re-sale

22. Goods-in-transit can be stopped for—

(A) Price.
(B) Any other expenses, *e.g.* Godown Charges, Interest, etc.
(C) Both (A) and (B)
(D) Either (A) or (B)

23. The right of lien exercised by an Unpaid Seller is to—

(A) retain possession.
(B) regain possession.
(C) recover price and other charges.
(D) recover damages.

24. In case of re-sale by an Unpaid Seller, the subsequent Buyer acquires good title thereof as against the original Buyer, despite the fact that no notice of resale has been given by the Seller to the original Buyer.

(A) True
(B) Partly True
(C) False
(D) None of the above

25. The term "Unpaid Seller" includes—

(A) Buyer's agent to whom the Bill of Lading is endorsed.
(B) Buyer's agent to whom the goods have been delivered.
(C) Seller's agent to whom the Bill of Lading is endorsed.
(D) Seller's agent to whom the goods have been delivered.

26. The lien of a Unpaid Seller depends on —

(A) Possession .
(B) Title.
(C) Ownership.
(D) Whether the Buyer has paid the price or not.

27. The Seller of Goods is deemed to be an Unpaid Seller—

(A) when the whole of the price has not been paid or tendered.
(B) when a bill of Exchange or other Negotiable Instrument has been received as conditional payment and the condition has not been fulfilled by reason of the dishonour of the instrument or otherwise.
(C) both (A) and (B)
(D) either (A) or (B)

28. The Unpaid Seller's right of stoppage in transit is to—

(A) re-organize possession of goods.
(B) re-sell the goods lying with the Carrier.
(C) regain possession of goods which were handed over to the Carrier.
(D) retain possession of goods already available with him.

29. To exercise the Unpaid Seller's right of lien, the Buyer should be compulsorily insolvent.

(A) True
(B) Partly True
(C) False
(D) None of the above

30. Generally, where an Unpaid Seller has made part delivery of the Goods, he—

(A) may exercise his right of stoppage in transit on the remainder.
(B) has to honour the entire contract.
(C) loses his right of stoppage in transit on the remainder of the goods.
(D) can supply defective goods in respect of the remainder.

31. Which of the following right can be exercised by an unpaid seller against the buyer, who is not insolvent?

(A) Right of lien
(B) Right of stoppage in transit
(C) Both (A) and (B)
(D) None of the above

32. Where under a contract of sale the property in Goods has passed to Buyer, and Buyer wrongfully neglects or refuses to pay the price, Seller can sue the Buyer for—

(A) payment of price of goods.
(B) damages for non-acceptance of goods.
(C) payment of other charges like insurance, forwarding etc.
(D) all of the above

☞ Rights of Buyer

33. Which of the following is a buyers right against the seller in case of breach of contract?

(A) Suit for non-delivery
(B) Suit for specific performance
(C) Suit for damages for breach of warranty
(D) All of the above

34. Where the buyer wrongfully neglects or refuses to accept and pay for the goods –

(A) the seller may sue buyer for damages for non-acceptance.

(B) the seller cannot sue buyer for damages for non-acceptance.

(C) the seller can sue buyers' banker for damages.

(D) none of the above

35. Where the seller wrongfully neglects to deliver the goods to the buyer, then the buyer –

(A) Cannot sue the seller for damages for non-delivery.

(B) May sue the seller for damages for non-delivery.

(C) Either (A) or (B)

(D) None of the above

36. Under section 61 of the Sale of Goods Act, in a suit for the refund of the price where there is a breach of contract on the part of the Seller, the Court can award interest to the Buyer, from the date on which—

(A) the contract was to be performed.

(B) the payment was committed.

(C) the breach was committed.

(D) all of the above

37. Where delivery has been delayed though the fault of either Buyer or Seller, as regards any loss which might not have occurred but for such fault, goods are at the risk of—

(A) Buyer.

(B) Seller.

(C) Party in fault.

(D) Party not in fault.

38. Which of the following is a Buyer's right against the Seller in case of breach of contract?

(A) Suit for non-delivery

(B) Suit for specific performance

(C) Suit for damages for breach of warranty

(D) All of the above

☞ Effect of Sub-Sale/Pledge

39. A purchased a refrigerator on hire purchase from B and pledged with C. D purchased the refrigerator from C in good faith. On knowing the facts, B wants to recover the refrigerator from D. which of the following statement(s) is/are correct?

(A) B can recover the refrigerator from D.

(B) B can recover the refrigerator from A only.

(C) B cannot recover the refrigerator from D.

(D) D will get good title for the refrigerator as he bought it in good faith.

40. Raman sold 100 quintals of rice to Suman, who paid by cheque. The Cheque was dishonoured upon presentation. Raman gave delivery orders to Suman. Suman resold-it to Gagan, a Buyer, in good faith for consideration, endorsing the delivery order to him Raman refuses to deliver the goods to Gagan, on the plea of non-payment. In this case –

(A) Gagan gets good title to goods.

(B) Suman gets good title to goods.

(C) Raman gets good title to goods.

(D) Raman retains the title to goods.

☞ Auction Sale

41. In an auction sale, if the seller makes use of pretended bidding to raise the price, then the sale is –

(A) valid.

(B) void.

(C) voidable.

(D) illegal.

42. Where in an auction sale, the seller appoints more than one bidder, the sale is –

(A) void.

(B) illegal.

(C) conditional.

(D) voidable.

43. In an Auction Sale, the property shall be sold to the—

(A) Lowest Bidder.

(B) Highest Bidder.

(C) All Bidders.

(D) Seller's Relative.

44. In the case of sale by auction, the Seller of goods has right to bid at the auction—

(A) with the permission of the auctioneer.

(B) only when the right to bid has been expressly reserved.

(C) even when the right to bid has been impliedly reserved.

(D) with the permission of the bidder.

45. In the case of ________, the sale may be notified to be subject to a reserve or upset price.

(A) sale by description

(B) sale by auction

(C) sale by sample

(D) sale by estoppels

46. Where in an Auction Sale notified with Reserve Price, the Auctioneer mistakenly knocks down the goods for less than the Reserve Price, then the auctioneer is—

(A) bound by auction

(B) not bound by auction

(C) liable for damages

(D) both (A) and (C)

47. K made a bid for an old and rare stamp at an auction sale but withdrew it before the fall of hammer. One of the conditions of sale was "bid once made shall not be withdrawn", which K knew. K. cannot withdraw the bid before the fall of hammer.

(A) True

(B) Partly True

(C) False

(D) None of the above

ANSWERS TO MULTIPLE CHOICE QUESTIONS

1. B	**11.** A	**21.** C	**31.** A	**41.** C
2. C	**12.** D	**22.** A	**32.** A	**42.** D
3. B	**13.** B	**23.** A	**33.** D	**43.** B
4. B	**14.** D	**24.** A	**34.** A	**44.** B
5. D	**15.** D	**25.** C	**35.** B	**45.** B
6. D	**16.** D	**26.** A	**36.** B	**46.** B
7. D	**17.** A	**27.** D	**37.** C	**47.** C
8. D	**18.** A	**28.** C	**38.** D	
9. C	**19.** A	**29.** C	**39.** A	
10. C	**20.** A	**30.** C	**40.** A	

DIVISION III
THE INDIAN PARTNERSHIP ACT, 1932

Chapter 1
General Nature, Rights And Duties Of a Partner

☞ **General Introduction:**

- **Extent:** This Act extends to the whole of India, except the State of Jammu and Kashmir.
- **Effective date:** This Act came into force w.e.f. 1-10-1932 and section 69 came into force w.e.f. 1-10-1933
- **Chapters:** The Partnership Act, 1932 has 8 chapters.
- **The Objective** of the Partnership Act, 1932 is to define and amend the law relating to Partnerships.
- A word will take its colour from the Indian Contract Act, 1872, if it is not defined in the Indian Partnership Act, 1932.

☞ **Definitions**

Sec. 2(a) : **"Act of a firm"** *means* any act or omission –

– by all the partners, or

– by any partner or

– agent of the firm,

which gives rise to a right enforceable by or against the firm.

Sec. 2(b) : **"Business"** includes every trade, occupation and profession.

Sec. 2(d) : **"Third party"** used in relation to a firm or to a partner therein means any person, who is not a partner in the firm.

☞ **What is Partnership?**

"Partnership is –

– a relation

– between two or more persons

– who have agreed to share the profits of a business,

– carried on by all or any of them acting for all."

– – – Sec. 4

☞ **Essential characteristics of a partnership:**

1. Relation/partnership agreement : The relation between partners is created by an Agreement, i.e. the Partnership Deed. It may be express (i.e. oral or written) or implied.

2. Relation of two or more persons:

a. Minimum Numbers:	There should be at least two persons to form a partnership.
b. Maximum Numbers: (Sec. 11 Companies Act)	*In case of a banking business*, the maximum number of partners is 10 *In case of other business*, the maximum number of partners is 20 If the number of partners exceeds this limit, the partnership will become an illegal association.

3. Partnership can be formed to carry on business., not for social welfare activity.

4. There must be sharing of profits.

5. Mutual agency– Cardinal Principle: The business of partnership may be carried on by all the partners or any of them acting for all. In the case of *Cox* v *Hickman*, the honourable court observed that a partner assumes a **two-fold character**:

1. He is the agent of the firm, so he can bind the firm by his act, provided—
   (a) the act is within the scope of his authority,
   (b) the act is done in the firm's name, and
   (c) the act is done for the purpose of the firm.
2. He is the principal for the acts of other partners.

WHO MAY BE A PARTNER?

- A person, who is competent to enter into a contract, can be a partner [Sec. 11 of the Indian Contract Act, 1872].
- Company : Yes
- Foreigner : Yes, if alien friend.
- Minor : A minor can be ADMITTED for the benefit of a partnership firm.

The following persons are not deemed to be partners:
1. Members of HUF, carrying on family business
2. A Burmese Buddhist husband and wife carrying on a business

TRUE TEST OF PARTNERSHIP

☞ Sec. 4 contains five basic conditions. These conditions are a True Test of partnership.

☞ **Intention cannot change the character.** No single factor can determine the existence of partnership. Further, the intention of the parties cannot change the character. *For example*, in one case, the parties may state that they are partners; however they may not be partners in the eyes of law. Similarly, they may expressly agree that they are not partners, yet the law may hold them as partners.

— *Hadley* v *Baxendle*

☞CASES WHERE NO PARTNERSHIP EXISTS [Sec. 6]

1. Joint owners, sharing gross returns [Explanation-I of Sec. 6]:

Joint owners of a property, sharing profits or gross returns arising from the property do not become partners.

2. Sharing of Profits [Explanation-II of Sec. 6]:

The sharing of profits is *prima facie* a strong evidence of partnership, but it is not a conclusive evidence. Therefore, if a person shares profits, it does not necessarily mean that he is a partner as laid down in the following cases:

(a) Where a loan provider receives a share in profit.
(b) Where a servant/agent is engaged in a business and receives his remuneration as a share of profit.
(c) Where the widow or child of a deceased partner receives a portion of the profits.

(d) Where a person has sold his business along with its goodwill and receives a portion of the profits in consideration of the sale.

State whether X and Y are partners in the following cases:

(1) X agrees with Y to carry passengers by taxi from Delhi to Gurgaon on the following terms— Y is to pay X Rs. 100 per mile. X and Y are to share costs of repairing and replacement of cars and divide equally between them proceeds of fares received from passengers.	:	Yes
(2) X and Y are co-owners of a house let out to a tenant. X and Y divide the net rents (after deduction of incidental taxes, etc.) between themselves.	:	No
(3) X and Y, the co-owners of a house, use the house as a hotel managed either by themselves or by a duly appointed manager for their common profit.	:	Yes
(4) X and Y buy 200 bales of cotton, agreeing to share the profit between them.	:	No
(5) X agrees with Y, a goldsmith, to buy and furnish gold to Y to be worked up by him and sold and that they shall share in the resulting profit or loss.	:	Yes
(6) X and Y agree to work together as carpenters, but X shall receive all profit and shall pay wages to Y.	:	No
(7) X and Y are joint owners of a ship.	:	No
(8) X, a publisher, agrees to publish at his own expense a book written by Y and to pay Y half of the net profit.	:	No

PARTNERSHIP AT WILL
[Sec. 7]

1. Meaning [Sec. 7] : *A Partnership is said to be at will*, when no provision is made in the Deed–

(i) for the duration of their partnership, or

(ii) for the determination of their partnership.

2. Retirement [32(1)] : Where the partnership is at will, by giving notice to all the other partners of one's intention to retire.

☞ *Examples of 'Partnership at will'*:

(a) When the partners of a particular Partnership decide to continue the Partnership after completion of the adventure

(b) When a Partnership is entered into for a fixed term, but the Partners carry on business even after such period

(c) When the duration of Partnership is not fixed

PARTICULAR PARTNERSHIP
[Sec. 8]

This partnership is formed for a specific venture and is dissolved automatically on the completion of that venture.

ILLEGAL PARTNERSHIP

When the rules of Partnership Act are violated, then the partnership is called illegal partnership. *For example* –

(1) Less than two partners

(2) More than maximum permissible partners (*i.e.* 10 or 20, as the case may be)

(3) Object becoming illegal

(4) Business against government policies

(5) Any partner is alien enemy

(6) Carrying over the business even after the order of dissolution by court.

Effect: Illegal Partnership cannot sue against the third party, but the third party can sue against the illegal association or any of its members.

RELATIONS OF A PARTNER

The mutual rights and duties of the partners shall be governed by the agreement among the partners. Such agreement may be express or implied. However, where the agreement is silent, the following provisions of the Act shall apply:

RIGHTS OF PARTNERS

1. Right to take part in business [Sec. 12(a)]: In the absence of any agreement between the partners, every partner has a right to take part in the conduct of the business. But where a partner neglects or refuses to perform his duties and the burden of performing such duties for the conduct of the business falls on other partners, the other partners have a right to compensation.

2. Right to share profit equally [Sec. 12(b)].

3. Right to be consulted [Sec. 12(c)]: The ordinary matters of business may be decided by the majority of the partners, and every partner shall have a right to express his views before the matter is decided.

But, no change can be made in the nature of the business without the consent of all the partners. For example, a partner cannot be admitted, unless all the partners agree to it.

4. Right to access the books of account [Sec. 12(d)]: Every partner has a right to access and inspect and take copy of the books of the firm. It is to be noted that a minor partner has a right to inspect and copy the accounts of the firm, but not the books.

5. Right to interest on capital [Sec. 13(c)]: In the absence of any agreement, no partner is entitled to interest on capital. Such Interest, subject to a contract between the partners, is payable only out of the profits of the firm.

6. Right to interest on loans/advances [Sec. 13(d)]: @ 6% p.a.

7. Right to be indemnified [Secs. 13(e) & 21]: Every partner has a right to be indemnified in respect of payments made and liabilities incurred by him—

(i) in the ordinary course of business [Sec. 13(e)], and

(ii) in doing such act in an emergency, for the purpose of protecting the firm from losses, as would be done by a person of ordinary prudence, in his own case, under similar circumstances [Sec. 21].

8. Right to use the firm's Property for the firm's business [Sec. 15]:

Property of the firm includes—

(i) All property and rights/interests in property originally brought into the stock of the firm, or

(ii) All property and rights/interests in property purchased by the firm, or for the purposes and in the course of business of the firm,

(iii) Goodwill of the business.

In the absence of any agreement, the property of the firm must be held and used by the partners only for the purposes of the business of the firm. No partner has a right to treat it as his individual property.

9. Right of outgoing partner [Sec. 37]: Where the other partners carries on the firm's business without making a final settlement of outgoing partners, then in the absence of any agreement, the outgoing partner or his legal representative shall be entitled to, **at his option**, to—

(i) such share of the profits as is proportionate to his share in the property of the firm, or

(ii) interest @ 6% p.a. on the amount of his share in the property of the firm.

DUTIES OF PARTNERS

1. General Duties [Sec. 9]:

(a) to carry on the business of the firm to the greatest common advantage,

(b) to be just and faithful to each other, and

(c) to render the true accounts and full information of all things relating to the firm to any partner or his legal representative.

2. To Indemnify for fraud [Sec. 10]: This duty cannot be changed by contract.

3. To attend his duties Diligently [Secs. 12(b) & 13(f)]: Loss, arising to the firm due to willful negligence of any partner, shall be compensated by the partner.

4. To share losses equally [Sec. 13(b)].

5. To hold and use the property of the firm only for the firm [Sec. 15].

6. To account for personal profits [Sec. 16(a)]: If any personal profit is made by any partner from the partnership transactions or from any use of the partnership property, name or business connection, he must account for it and pay it to the firm.

7. To account for profits in competing business [Sec. 16(b)]: In the absence of any agreement, a partner cannot carry on competing business. If he does, he is bound to account for and pay to the firm all profits made by him in that business.

For Example: A and B are partners in a business which consists of supplying meat to the government. Subsequently. it is found out that A is engaged with C in the supplying of meat to the same government.

Held, A is bound to account to the firm for the profits so made by him. — *Loch* v *Lynam* (1854)

8. To act within authority [Sec. 19] Where he exceeds the authority conferred on him and the firm suffers a loss, he shall have to compensate the firm such loss.

9. To be Liable *Jointly and Severally* [Sec. 25].

MULTIPLE CHOICE QUESTIONS

☞ Meaning & True Test

1. A firm is the name of –

(A) The partners.

(B) The minors in the firm.

(C) Majority shareholders.

(D) The collective name under which it caries on business.

2. The term "Act of a Firm", means an act or omission by__________, which gives rise to a right enforceable by or against the Firm.

(A) all the Partners

(B) any partner

(C) agent of the Firm

(D) any of the above

3. The term "Act of a Firm", means______by all the Partners, or by any Partner or agent of the Firm, which gives rise to a right enforceable by or against the Firm.

(A) act

(B) omission

(C) both (A) and (B)

(D) either (A) or (B)

4. X and Y are co-owners of a house let to a tenant. X and Y divide the net rents (after deduction of the incidental taxes; etc.) between themselves. Decide–

(A) There is partnership between X and Y.

(B) There is no partnership between X and Y. They are simply treated as joint owners of property.

(C) There is no partnership between X and Y. As there is no sharing of profits.

(D) Both (B) and (C)

5. Where the number of Partners exceeds the maximum limit (10 or 20 as the case may be), the illegal association cannot be sued by third party.

(A) True

(B) Partly True

(C) False

(D) None of the above

6. Where the Firm carries on an illegal business, e.g. dealing in illicit liquor, it cannot be sued.

(A) True

(B) Partly True

(C) False

(D) None of the above

7. Where the number of Partners exceeds the maximum limit (10 or 20 as the case may be), a suit may be brought against —

(A) The association itself.

(B) Members or the association.

(C) Either (A) or (B)

(D) Both (A) and (B)

8. X and Y buy 200 bales of cotton, agreeing to share the same between them. Decide –

(A) There is partnership between X and Y.

(B) There is no partnership between X and Y. as there is no intention to carry on business. They are simply treated as joint owners of cotton.

(C) There is no partnership between X and Y. As there is no sharing of profits.

(D) Both (B) and (C)

9. X and Y are joint owners of a ship. Decide –

(A) There is partnership between X and Y.

(B) There is no partnership between X and Y. They are simply treated as joint owners of ship.

(C) There is no partnership between X and Y as there is no sharing of profits.

(D) Both (B) and (C)

10. X agrees with Y to carry passengers by taxi from Delhi to Gurgaon on the following terms, namely, Y is to pay X Rs. 50 per mile per annum, and X and Y are to share the costs of repairing and replacement of the cars, and to divide equally between them the proceeds of fares received from passengers.

Choose the correct alternative–

(A) X and Y are partners

(B) X and Y are cab owners

(C) X and Y are co-owners

(D) Can't be decided.

11. In the case of a firm carrying on the business of banking—

(A) There should be at least 7 members and the maximum number of members should not exceed 50.

(B) There should be at least 2 members and the maximum number of members should not exceed 10.

(C) There should be at least 10 members and the maximum number of members should not exceed 20.

(D) There should be at least 2 members and the maximum number of members should not exceed 50.

12. In case of a firm carrying on business other than banking—

(A) There should be at least 7 members and the maximum number of members should not exceed 50.

(B) There should be at least 2 members and maximum number of members should not exceed 10.

(C) There should be at least 2 members and the maximum number of members should not exceed 20.

(D) There should be at least 2 members and the maximum number of members should not exceed 50.

13. The law dealing with the partnerships is contained in—

(A) The Indian Partnership Act, 1932.

(B) The Indian Partnership Act, 1930.

(C) The Indian Partnership Act, 1872.

(D) The Indian Partnership Act, 2008.

14. Each partner is a principal as well as an agent of other partners.

(A) The above statement is correct.

(B) The above statement is not correct in case of unregistered partnerships.

(C) The above statement is incorrect.

(D) The above statement is correct only in case of registered partnerships.

15. True test of partnership is—

(A) Sharing of profits.

(B) Sharing of profits and losses.

(C) Mutual agency.

(D) Existence of an agreement to share profits of the business.

16. A and B were partners with 70 P and 30 P shares respectively. On the death of A, his son stepped into his shoes and without any express agreement carried on the business. Is it a partnership?

(A) Yes

(B) No

17. A valid partnership can be formed with one major partner and other minors, admitted only to the benefits of the firm.

(A) True, as minors are to share in profits only.

(B) False, as no partnership can be formed with minor partner. He can only be admitted to the existing firm.

(C) True, as a valid partnership can be formed with minor partner as well as He can also be admitted to the existing firm.

(D) Both (A) and (C)

18. Which of the following is not correct –

(A) A Partner of a firm cannot enter into a contract with the partnership firm.

(B) A member of a company can enter into a contract with the company.

(C) The Partner of a firm can enter into a contract with the partnership firm.

(D) All of the above.

19. The cardinal principle of a partnership law implies that –

(A) The business must be carried on by all the partners or by anyone or more of the partners acting for all.

(B) The business may be carried on by all the partners acting for all.

(C) The business may be carried on by anyone or more of the partners acting for all.

(D) The business must be carried on in accordance with the decided profit (loss) sharing ratio.

20. Partnership –

(A) Arises by operation of law.

(B) Comes into existence only after registration.

(C) Can arise by agreement or otherwise.

(D) Arise by way of an agreement only.

21. The maximum number of partners is mentioned in—

(A) The Partnership Act.

(B) The General Clauses Act.

(C) The Companies Act.

(D) The Societies Registration Act

22. The Law of Partnership was earlier contained in–

(A) Chapter XI of the Indian Contract Act

(B) Indian Partnership Act, 1930

(C) Indian Partnership Act, 1932

(D) Companies Act, 1956

23. In any partnership business, the number of partners should not exceed -

(A) 10

(B) 20

(C) 15

(D) 25

24. The partnership agreement may be—

(A) Express or implied.

(B) Only written.

(C) Only oral.

(D) Only Implied.

25. Which is not appropriate regarding the kind of partner -

(A) Actual partner.

(B) Sleeping partner.

(C) Active partner.

(D) Dummy partner

26. Partnership is the relation -

(A) Between persons.

(B) Between firms.

(C) Between companies.

(D) Among numberless persons.

27. X and Y, who are the co-owners of the house use the house as a hotel managed either by themselves or by a duly appointed manager for their common profit. Is it a partnership?

(A) There is partnership between X and Y.

(B) There is no partnership between X and Y. They are simply treated as joint owners of property.

(C) There is no partnership between X and Y. As there is no sharing of profits.

(D) Both (B) and (C)

28. X and Y agree to work together as carpenters, but X shall receive all profit and shall pay wages to Y.

(A) There is partnership between X and Y.

(B) There is no partnership between X and Y. They are simply treated as joint owners of the property.

(C) There is no partnership between X and Y as there is no sharing of profits.

(D) Both (B) and (C)

29. X, a publisher, agrees to publish at his own expense a book written by Y and to pay Y half the net profit. Decide –

(A) There is partnership between X and Y.

(B) There is no partnership between X and Y, as there is absence of mutual agency.

(C) There is no partnership between X and Y. As there is no sharing of profits.

(D) Both (B) and (C)

30. X and Y purchase 1,000 bags of cement, which they agree to sell for their joint account. Decide–

(A) There is partnership between X and Y.

(B) There is no partnership between X and Y. They are simply treated as joint owners of cement.

(C) There is no partnership between X and Y. As there is no sharing of profits.

(D) Both (B) and (C)

31. A, B, C, D and E, all adult members of a Joint Hindu Family, convert their family business into a partnership. Is the partnership valid?"

(A) Yes

(B) No

32. Each of the partners is –

(A) Principals as well as agents.

(B) Only Agent of the firm.

(C) Only Representative of the firm.

(D) Only Co-partner of the firm.

33. X and Y are joint owners of a ship. There is a valid partnership between X and Y.

(A) Yes
(B) No
(C) Partly Yes
(D) None of the above

34. K, a money-lender, advances Rs. 30 Lakh to ABC Co., a partnership firm. K is entitled to 6% interest on the amount lent by him plus 3% on the Profits of the Firm, if profits exceed Rs.20 Lakh. Here—
(A) K is deemed as a partner in the firm.
(B) K is not deemed as a partner in the firm.
(C) The agreement to lend money is invalid.
(D) K can claim only interest but not a share.

35. X, Y and Z took over the running proprietary concern of Mr. A and continued in partnership. Under the business takeover agreement, A was to be paid 8% share of the profits, for a period of five years from the date of takeover. Here—
(A) A is deemed as a partner in the firm.
(B) A is not deemed as a partner in the firm.
(C) The payment of a share of profits to A is invalid.
(D) The payment of share of profits to A is valid only for three years.

36. Sharing of profits is ____ evidence of existence of partnership.
(A) Collaborative
(B) Confirmative
(C) Conclusive
(D) Not a conclusive

37. According to the Partnership Act, "Business" includes—
(A) Trade.
(B) Occupation.
(C) Profession.
(D) All of the above

38. If an expression is not defined in the Partnership Act, reference shall be had to—
(A) Indian Contract Act.
(B) Negotiable Instruments Act.
(C) Sale of Goods Act.
(D) Evidence Act.

39. The unrepealed provisions of the ________ Act shall continue to apply to firms, save in so far as they are inconsistent with the express provisions of the Partnership Act.
(A) Transfer of Property Act
(B) Indian Evidence Act
(C) Indian Contract Act
(D) Sale of Goods Act

40. The Partnership Act, 1932 has _______ chapters.
(A) Four
(B) Seven
(C) Eight
(D) Five

41. The objective of the Partnership Act, 1932 is to define and amend the law relating to—
(A) Partnerships.
(B) Joint ventures.
(C) Business collaborations.
(D) All of the above

42. The Partnership Act, 1932 came into force on —
(A) 1st day of April, 1932
(B) 1st day of October, 1932
(C) 1st day of January, 1932
(D) 31st day of December, 1932

43. The Partnership Act, 1932 deals with—
(A) Business collaborations.
(B) Joint venture.
(C) Partnerships between individuals.
(D) Partnership in general.

44. Which of these statements does not reflect the mutual agency principle in partnership?
(A) The partner is both an agent and principal
(B) A partner can, by his act bind other partners and is in turn bound by acts of the other partners.
(C) All partners should actively participate in the business.
(D) Business may be managed by one or more partners.

45. Subject to the provisions of the Act, a partner is an agent of a firm, for —
(A) The purpose of the management of the Firm.
(B) The purpose of other partners.
(C) The purpose of liability to third parties.
(D) The purpose of business of the firm.

46. Which of these gives the correct definition of Partnership?
(A) It is a written agreement between persons for sharing the profits of the business mutually.
(B) It is an oral arrangement between parties for sharing profits of the business mutually.
(C) It is a relation between persons who have agreed to share the profits of the business carried on by all or any of them acting for all.
(D) It is an unregistered form of a Private Limited Company.

47. Section ________ of the Partnership Act, 1932 defines the term "Third Party".

(A) 2(a)

(B) 2(b)

(C) 2(c)

(D) 2(d)

48. Are the members of a Hindu Undivided Family, carrying on a family business as such, the Partners in such business?

(A) Yes

(B) No

(C) Partly Yes

(D) None of the above

☞ Partnership-at-will

49. A partnership-at-will is one—

(1) Duration not fixed.

(2) Duration fixed.

(3) Dissolved at any time.

(4) Can be dissolved only on the happening of an event.

(A) 1 & 2

(B) 2 & 3

(C) 3 & 4

(D) 1 & 3

50. Where a Partnership agreement provides neither for the duration nor for the determination of the Partnership, it is called –

(A) Partnership for a fixed term

(B) Partnership at will

(C) Either (A) or (B)

(D) Neither (A) nor (B)

51. Which of this is not a Partnership at will?

(A) When the parties of a particular Partnership decide to continue the Partnership after completion of the adventure.

(B) When a Partnership is entered into for a fixed term, but the Partners carry on business even after such period.

(C) When the duration of Partnership is not fixed.

(D) When the duration of Partnership can be implied from the Partner's conduct.

52. A Partnership at Will is one —

(A) Which does not have any Deed.

(B) Which does not have any Partner.

(C) Which can be terminated at any time.

(D) Which cannot be dissolved.

53. In case of partnership-at-will, notice of intention to dissolve the Firm may be served by –

(A) Sleeping Partners only.

(B) Any of the working partners.

(C) Any of the partners.

(D) Majority of the Partners.

54. In case of a notice of dissolution in partnership at will, where no date has been mentioned in the notice.

(A) The date decide by the Registrar of Firms.

(B) The date as decided by the Partners.

(C) The date when the notice is communicated.

(D) The date mentioned in the notice of dissolution.

☞ Particular Partnership

55. A person may become a Partner with another person for particular adventures or undertakings. This arrangement is called —

(A) Partnership at Will.

(B) Particular Partnership.

(C) Undisclosed Partnership.

(D) Joint Venture.

☞ Rights of Partner

56. Which of the following is not the right of a partner?

(A) Right to take part in business.

(B) Right to have access to account books.

(C) Right to receive remuneration.

(D) Right to share profits.

57. In the absence of an agreement to the contrary, all partners are –

(A) Not entitled to share profits.

(B) Entitled to share profits in their capital ratio.

(C) Entitled to share profits in the Current account ratio.

(D) Entitled to share the profits equally.

58. When a partner makes advances to the firm over and above the amount of capital to be contributed by him, can he claim interest thereon?

(A) Yes @ 5% p.a.

(B) Yes @ 6% p.a.

(C) Yes @ 7% p.a.

(D) No

59. Every partner has the right to –

(A) Take part in the business of the firm.

(B) To share exclusive profits.

(C) Receive remuneration.

(D) Pay taxes.

60. A and B are Partners A, without the authority of B, buys shares in ABC Ltd, in his own name with the moneys and on account of the Firm. Are the shares thus purchased, Partnership property?

(A) Yes
(B) No
(C) Partly Yes
(D) None of the above

61. Every partner cannot participate in the conduct of the business.

(A) True
(B) False

62. Every Partner need not participate in the conduct of the business.

(A) True
(B) Partly True
(C) False
(D) None of the above

63. In the absence of any contract between the partners, a partner is entitled to receive remuneration for taking part in the conduct of the business.

(A) True
(B) False

64. Where the continuing partners carry on the business of the firm, the outgoing partner is entitled to a share of profits or interest. For this purpose, the condition is that —

(A) The partner must not have been expelled.
(B) No new partner must not have been admitted.
(C) Final settlement of accounts has not been done between the firm and outgoing partner.
(D) There is a change in the nature of the firm's business.

65. Unless agreed otherwise, every Partner can have access to, inspect and take a copy of any of the books of accounts of the Firm.

(A) True
(B) Partly true
(C) False
(D) None of the above

66. In case of an emergency, a Partner has the authority to do all such acts so as to protect the Firm from loss, as would be done by______ under similar conditions.

(A) Any of the Working Partners
(B) Any of the Sleeping Partners
(C) Any agent of the Firm
(D) Any man of ordinary prudence.

67. L, M, and N are partners in trade. N without the knowledge of L and M, obtains for his own sole benefit a lease of the house in which the partnership business is carried on. Are L and M entitled to participate in the benefit of the lease?

(A) Yes
(B) No

68. R and K were Partners in a business as suppliers of leather goods and were regular contractors to Government. K, without knowledge of R, supplied to Government certain leather goods in which the Firm was also dealing and made substantial profits.

(A) R is entitled to claim profit from K.
(B) R is not entitled to claim profit from K.
(C) K is entitled to claim profit from R.
(D) K is not entitled to claim profit from R.

69. A Partner, who receives certain remuneration from the Firm as per the express agreement, become an employee of the Firm.

(A) True
(B) Partly True
(C) False
(D) None of the above

☞ Duties of Partner

70. Relations of partners to one another is dealt is governed by the following Section of The Indian Partnership Act, 1932

(A) 1-8
(B) 9-17
(C) 18-27
(D) 28-36.

71. It is the duty of every partner to share in equal proportions the losses suffered by the firm–

(A) True, as losses are always shared equally.
(B) False, as losses should be shared in the capital ratio.
(C) False, as partners may agree to share losses in different proportions.
(D) None of these

72. In which of the following cases, a Partner is not required to pay over the profits to the Firm—

(A) Personal Profit derived from any transaction of the Firm.
(B) Personal Profit derived from the use of Firm's property or business name of the Firm.
(C) Personal Profit derived from the use of business name of the Firm.
(D) Personal Profit derived from a non-competing business.

73. Every Partner is bound to attend ______ to his duties, in the conduct of the business.

(A) Systematically

(B) Diligently

(C) Sincerely

(D) Effectively

74. Unless agreed otherwise, every Partner is bound to attend diligently to his duties in the conduct of the business.

(A) True

(B) Partly True

(C) False

(D) None of the above

75. Partners are bound to carry on the business of the Firm —

(A) To the advantage of the working Partner

(B) For reasonable advantage

(C) For the advantage of minor Partners

(D) To the greatest common advantage.

76. Which of the following is not one of the general duties of Partners?

(A) To claim remuneration for the services rendered to the Firm

(B) To render true accounts and full information of all things affecting the Firm to any Partner or his legal representative

(C) To carry on the business of the Firm to the greatest common advantage

(D) To be just and faithful to each other.

77. For loss caused to the Firm by his fraud in the conduct of the business, that Partner shall —

(A) Indemnify the Firm.

(B) Indemnify the other Partners.

(C) Indemnify all the retiring Partners.

(D) Indemnify only the working Partners.

ANSWERS TO MULTIPLE CHOICE QUESTIONS

1. D	**17.** B	**33.** B	**49.** D	**65.** A
2. D	**18.** C	**34.** B	**50.** B	**66.** D
3. D	**19.** A	**35.** B	**51.** D	**67.** A
4. B	**20.** D	**36.** D	**52.** C	**68.** A
5. C	**21.** C	**37.** D	**53.** C	**69.** C
6. C	**22.** A	**38.** A	**54.** C	**70.** B
7. D	**23.** B	**39.** C	**55.** B	**71.** C
8. B	**24.** A	**40.** C	**56.** C	**72.** D
9. B	**25.** D	**41.** A	**57.** D	**73.** B
10. A	**26.** A	**42.** B	**58.** B	**74.** A
11. B	**27.** A	**43.** D	**59.** A	**75.** D
12. C	**28.** C	**44.** C	**60.** B	**76.** A
13. A	**29.** B	**45.** D	**61.** B	**77.** A
14. A	**30.** B	**46.** C	**62.** A	
15. C	**31.** A	**47.** D	**63.** B	
16. B	**32.** A	**48.** B	**64.** C	

Chapter 2

Registration Of Firm

Chapter VII of Partnership Act, 1932

State government is empowered to grant exemption from the application of Chapter VII of the Partnership Act.

(Secs. 56-71)

The registration of partnership firm is *not compulsory*. It is optional. The rules regarding the registration are as below:

PROCEDURE FOR REGISTRATION [Secs. 58 & 59]

1. Application for Registration (Sec. 58):

☞ **Contents of : Application** First of all, an application for registration is required to be made in the prescribed format. The application is to be made to the Registrar of Firms. The application shall be accompanied by the prescribed fees and shall contain the following particulars:

(a) The firm name,

(b) The place or principal place of business of the firm,

(c) The names of any other places where the firm carries on business,

(d) The date when each partner joined the firm,

(e) The names in full and permanent addresses of the partners, and

(f) The duration of the firm, if any.

☞ **Care in : Selection of Name of Firm**

1. Name should not be familiar with the name of any existing firm.
2. A firm name shall not contain any of the following words without the consent of the State Government, namely—

   Crown, Emperor, Empress, Empire, Imperial, King, Queen, Royal, or words implying the patronage of Government.
3. Further the requirements of 'Name and Emblems Act, 1950' should also be satisfied.

☞ **Signing & : Verification** The Application shall be signed by all the partners, or by their agents authorised in this behalf.

2. Certificate of Registration (Sec. 59):

When the Registrar is satisfied that the above provisions have been duly complied with, he shall make an entry in the Register of Firms, he shall then issue under his hands a certificate of registration.

Registration is effective from the date when the Registrar files the statement and makes entries in the register.

3. Time for Registration:

The law has not laid known any particular time for registration. So, it is open to the partners to get the registration at any time.

Section 69(2), however, lays down that no suit can be instituted in any Court by or on behalf of a firm against any third party, unless the firm is registered.

This means before any suit is filed in a Court, registration must be effected. Subsequent registration does not cure the initial defect at the time of the institution of the suit. The right course in such a case is to –

- withdraw the suit from the Court,
- get the firm registered, and
- then file a fresh suit.

Effects of Non-Registration [Sec. 69]

1. **No suit against other partners and firm:** An unregistered firm or its partners cannot file a suit against other partners or the firm to enforce a right arising out of a contract or conferred by this Act.
2. **No suit against third party:** An unregistered firm or its partners cannot file a suit against third parties to enforce a right arising out of a contract or conferred by the Act.
3. **No claim of Set-off:** An unregistered firm or its partners cannot claim set-off in a suit filed against the firm by a third party except for a sum not exceeding Rs. 100.
4. **Non-registration, however, does not affect the following:**
   (i) The right of third parties to sue the firm for its partners.
   (ii) The right of partner—
      (a) to sue for the dissolution of firm, or
      (b) to sue for accounts of a dissolved firm, or
      (c) to enforce any right or power to realize the property of a dissolved firm.
   (iii) The power of an Official Assignee or Receiver to realize the property of an insolvent partner.
   (iv) The rights of firms or partners of firms having no place of business in India.
   (v) Right to set off, where the claim does not exceed Rs. 100.
   (vi) The right of an Unregistered firm to enforce a right other than a right arising out of a contract or conferred by this Act.

Registration of Alterations [Secs. 60-63]

The following changes are required to be registered with the Registrar:

Sec.	Type of Alterations	Who is to sign application for Alteration
60	Alteration in the firm's Name, or in the location of the principal place of business of a registered firm,	All the partners, or by their agents
61	When a branch is closed or a new one is opened,	Any partner or agent of firm
62	Changes in the names and address of partners,	Any partner or agent of firm
63	Changes in the constitution of a registered firm due to admission and retirement of partners. Dissolution of a firm should also be reported,	Any partner before dissolution or agent of such partner
63	Withdrawal or continuation by a minor on attaining majority.	Major partner (who was minor earlier) or his agents.

Point to be noted:—

Registrar of Firm is deemed to be a public servant under section 21 of the Indian Penal Code.

MULTIPLE CHOICE QUESTIONS

1. The Registrar of Firms is appointed by —

(A) Central Government.

(B) State Government.

(C) Central and State Government.

(D) Chief Justice of India.

2. The Registrar of Firms is deemed to be a _____ u/s 21 of the Indian Penal Code.

(A) Government Servant

(B) Civil Servant

(C) Public Servant

(D) Not a Servant at all

3. The _______ is empowered to grant exemption from the application of Chapter VII of the Partnership Act, 1932 (dealing with Registration of Firms).

(A) State Government

(B) Central Government

(C) Central and State Government

(D) Chief Justice of India

4. Registration of Firm may be effected at any time during the continuance of Partnership.

(A) True

(B) Partly True

(C) False

(D) None of the above

5. Application for Registration of Firm should be made to the Registrar of Firms in the area in which the place of business or principal place of business of the Firm is situated/proposed to be situated.

(A) True

(B) Partly True

(C) False

(D) None of the above

6. Which of the following is not required to be given in an application for registration of a Firm?

(A) Place or business or principal place of business

(B) Profits earned by the Firm for the past three financial years

(C) Names in full and permanent address of the Partners

(D) Duration of the Firm, if any

7. Which of the following is not required to be given in an application for registration of a Firm?

(A) Firm Name

(B) Place of business or principal place of business

(C) Names of any other places where the Firm carries on business

(D) Details of Capital Contribution of Partners

8. Which of the following is not required to be given in an application for registration of a Firm?

(A) Date when each Partner joined the Firm

(B) Names in full and permanent address of the Partners

(C) Duration of the Firm, if any

(D) Permanent Account Number under Income Tax Law

9. Which of the following is required to be given in an application for registration of a Firm?

(A) Date when each Partner joined the Firm

(B) Original Partnership Deed

(C) Bank Account of the Firm

(D) Permanent Account Number under Income Tax Law

10. Which of the following is not required to be given in an application for registration of a Firm?

(A) Firm Name

(B) Date when each partner joined the Firm

(C) Date of Birth of each Partner of the Firm

(D) Duration of the Firm, if any

11. Which of the following is required to be given in an application for registration of a Firm?

(A) Names in full and permanent address of the Firm's Auditors

(B) Name in full and permanent address of the Firm's Partners

(C) Names in full and permanent address of the Firm's Lawyers

(D) Names in full and permanent address of the Firm's Advisors.

12. Which of the following details is required to be given in an application for registration of a Firm?

(A) Capital Contribution of Partners

(B) Goodwill of the Firm

(C) Places of business of the Firm

(D) Bank Account of the Firm

13. Chapter VII of the Partnership Act deals with —

(A) Dissolution of Firms.

(B) Rights of Partners.

(C) Registration of Firms.

(D) Preliminaries.

14. Which of the following cannot be altered by Partners by making contract among themselves?

(A) To have access to and to inspect and copy any of the books of the Firm.

(B) To take part in the conduct of the business.

(C) To express opinion on matters connected with the business of the Firm.

(D) To indemnify the Firm for any loss caused to do by his fraud in the conduct of the Firm's business.

15. Registration of Firm is covered by Sec. ______of the Partnership Act, 1932.

(A) 56

(B) 57

(C) 58

(D) 59

16. Which of the following words are not permissible in a Firm's name?

(A) & Co.

(B) Imperial

(C) Business Ventures

(D) Consultants

17. Which of the following words are not permissible in a Firm's name?

(A) Associates

(B) & Co.

(C) & Brothers

(D) Corporation.

18. Section ______ of the Partnership Act, 1932 deals with recording of change in constitution or of dissolution of Registered Firms.

(A) 60

(B) 61

(C) 62

(D) 63

19. Which of the following statements, about the registration of firm, is not true –

(A) It must be done at the time of its formation.

(B) It may be done at the time of formation.

(C) The registration of a firm may be effected by sending by post to the Registrar a statement in the prescribed form.

(D) It may be done at any time after its formation.

20. As per the accepted view, the registration of the firm is considered complete, when–

(A) Complete application for registration is filed with the Registrar of Firms.

(B) Registrar files the statement and makes entries in the Register of Firms.

(C) Registrar is satisfied that all the provisions have been duly complied with.

(D) Court records the statement and certifies the entries in Register of Firms.

21. Registration of a partnership is complete –

(A) Only after the issue of certificate of Registration by the Registrar of Firms.

(B) As soon as an application in the prescribed form with the prescribed fee and other relevant details is delivered to the Registrar of Firms.

(C) Only after the Registrar of Firms records an entry of the statement in the Register of Firms to this effect.

(D) After giving the information to the Central Government in this regard.

22. After the registration of a firm, a change in the firm name and principal place of business required almost a new registration.

(A) True

(B) False

23. An unregistered firm can enforce by suit its dues from a third party.

(A) True

(B) False

24. A Partner of an Unregistered Firm cannot sue the Firm or any other Partner of the Firm to enforce a right –

(A) Arising from a contract

(B) Conferred by the Partnership Act

(C) Either (A) or (B)

(D) Both (A) and (B)

25. A partner of an unregistered firm cannot sue for his dues from the firm or from other partners.

(A) True

(B) False

26. Non-registration of a firm does not affect the right of an Official Assignee. Receiver or Court to realise the property of an insolvent partner.

(A) True

(B) False

27. Neither the firm nor the partners of an unregistered firm, when sued, can claim a set-off exceeding Rs. 100 –

(A) True

(B) False

28. Notice to Registrar, of change in constitution or of dissolution of a registered Firm should specify the date of dissolution.

(A) True

(B) Partly True

(C) False

(D) None of the above

29. Section _________ of the Partnership Act, 1932 deals with recording of withdrawal of a Minor from a Registered Firm.

(A) 60

(B) 61

(C) 62

(D) 63

30. Registration of a partnership firm is—

(A) Compulsory from the beginning.

(B) Not compulsory till first five years of beginning of the partnership.

(C) Not compulsory at all.

(D) Compulsory only if the Registrar of Firms, gives an order in this regard.

31. Registration of a firm is—

(A) Compulsory.

(B) Optional.

(C) Occasional.

(D) None of the above

32. Which of the following is not disability of an unregistered firm?

(A) It cannot file a suit against third parties

(B) Its partners cannot file a suit against a firm.

(C) It cannot claim a set-off exceeding Rs. 100.

(D) It cannot be sued by a third party.

33. Closing and Opening of Branches of Registered Firms in covered by section ______ of the Partnership Act, 1932.

(A) 60

(B) 61

(C) 62

(D) 63

34. Alterations in Firm Name and place of business of Registered Firms is covered by Section ______ of the Partnership Act, 1932

(A) 60

(B) 61

(C) 62

(D) 63

35. Section of the Partnership Act, 1932 deals with changes in names and addresses of Partners of Registered Firms.

(A) 60

(B) 61

(C) 62

(D) 63

36. Every Registered Firm shall file a statement specifying the alteration in its Principal Place of business, signed in the manner under section 58 along with the prescribed fees.

(A) True

(B) Partly True

(C) False

(D) None of the above

37. A Registered Firm need not intimate the alteration in its Firm Name, to the Registrar of Firms.

(A) True

(B) Partly True

(C) False

(D) None of the above

38. Intimation to Registrar, of any change in names and address of partners of Registered Firms, should be signed by —

(A) All the partners or their agents.

(B) Majority of the Partners or their agents.

(C) All Working Partners or their agents.

(D) Any one Partner or his agent.

39. On an application made in this behalf, the Registrar shall furnish a copy of an entry or a portion thereof in the Register of the Firms duly certified under his hand.

(A) True

(B) Partly True

(C) False

(D) None of the above.

40. M and N were in Partnership but did not register their Firm. They borrowed Rs. 20 Lakhs from K but did not repay the loan, K sued the Firm for the amount due. The Firm contests the claim saying the Firm is not registered and hence a suit cannot be filed. Is the Firm's claim valid?

(A) Yes, K cannot recover the amount.

(B) No, K's rights are not affected by non-registration.

(C) No, K has to sue each Partner individually.

(D) No, K has to sue all Partners jointly.

41. Intimation of a change in constitution of Registered Firm, to the Registrar of Firms, may be given by—

(A) Any Incoming, Continuing or Outgoing Partner.

(B) Agent of the person in (A).

(C) Any person specially authorized in this behalf.

(D) Any one of the above

42. P and Q jointly acquired a cyber café on 01.01.2009. Each of them contributed a half of the expenses incurred for the purchase of computers and furniture. They agreed to share Profits equally.

The relationship of P and Q is that of –

(A) Co-owners.

(B) Co-venturers.

(C) Partners, because they agree to share profits.

(D) Not partners, because the firm is unregistered.

43. In *Q. 42* above, Can R (age 17 years) be admitted to their business?

(A) Yes

(B) Yes, if R is admitted with the consent of P & Q, only to share the benefits.

(C) Yes, if the firm is registered.

(D) No

44. In *Q. 42* above, they further decided to register as a partnership firm on 01.03.2009. Will they be registered? If yes, With effect from which date?

(A) Yes, w.e.f. 01.01.2009

(B) Yes, w.e.f. 01.03.2009

(C) Yes, w.e.f. the date on which the registrar makes entries in the register of firms

(D) No

45. In *Q. 42* above, Mr. S is indebted to the firm for a sum of Rs.500 and the firm files a suit against him on 01.03.2009. Will the firm succeed?

(A) No, because the sum does not exceeds Rs. 1,000.

(B) No, because the registration is still pending

(C) No, as Mr. S has not acknowledged the debt

(D) Yes

46. In *Q. 42* above, on 31.12.2009, it was decided to discontinue the business, due to heavy losses.

(A) The firm will be dissolved on receipt of permission from Court.

(B) The firm will be dissolved by mutual consent of all.

(C) The firm cannot be dissolved before 01.01.2009.

(D) The firm will not be dissolved

ANSWERS TO MULTIPLE CHOICE QUESTIONS

1. B	**11.** B	**21.** C	**31.** B	**41.** D
2. C	**12.** C	**22.** Y	**32.** D	**42.** C
3. A	**13.** C	**23.** B	**33.** B	**43.** B
4. A	**14.** D	**24.** D	**34.** A	**44.** C
5. A	**15.** D	**25.** A	**35.** C	**45.** B
6. B	**16.** B	**26.** A	**36.** A	**46.** B
7. D	**17.** D	**27.** A	**37.** C	
8. D	**18.** D	**28.** A	**38.** D	
9. A	**19.** A	**29.** D	**39.** A	
10. C	**20.** B	**30.** C	**40.** B	

Chapter 3

Implied Authorities Of Partner

AUTHORITY OF A PARTNER [Secs. 19 and 22]

☞ **Express Authority:**

An express authority is given to a partner by an agreement. For example, one of the partners may be authorised to operate a bank account on behalf of the firm.

☞ **Implied Authority:**

This is an authority, which is not given to a partner by an agreement, but by law. It flows from the legal relations of the partners and is based on the law of agency. It is also known as apparent, ostensible and ordinary authority.

The act of the partner will be within the implied authority of the partner, if the following conditions are satisfied:

1. **The act must be done in the ordinary course of business.**

   For Example: One partner of a cloth merchant firm places an order to purchase certain quantity of milk in the firm's name. This act will not bind the firm, even if the act is done in the firm's name.

2. **The act must be done in the usual way.** 'What is a usual way?' It is a question of fact and circumstances.

   For Example: In a trading firm, a partner has implied authority to draw and accept a bill of exchange, but in a non-trading firm, a partner has no such implied authority, as it is not usual.

3. **The act must be done in the firm's name.**

   For Example: One of the two partners in a firm executed a pronote in favour of the plaintiff. The partner signed the note describing himself as 'Proprietor'. Held the firm was not liable on the pronote, as it was not executed in the firm's name. —*Punjab United Bank Ltd.* v *Mohandas* (1934)

Acts within the Implied Authority of a Partner

In a trading firm, the implied authority of a partner has been held to include the following:

(1) Purchasing and selling of goods, on behalf of the firm, in which the firm deals,

(2) Receiving payment from the debtors of the firm and giving receipts for the amount received,

(3) Settling accounts with persons dealing with the firm,

(4) Engaging servants for the partnership business,

(5) Borrowing money on the credit of the firm,

(6) Drawing, accepting, indorsing the Negotiable Instruments in the name of the firm,

(7) Pledging any goods of the firm for the purpose of borrowing money, and

(8) Employing a solicitor to defend an action against the firm.

Acts Outside the Implied Authority of a Partner

In the absence of any usage or custom of trade to the contrary, the implied authority of a partner does not empower him to do the following acts—

(1) Submit a dispute relating to the business of the firm to arbitration,

(2) Open a bank account on behalf of the firm in his own name,

(3) Compromise or relinquish any claim or portion of a claim by the firm,

(4) Withdraw a suit or proceeding filed on behalf of the firm,

(5) Admit any liability in a suit or proceeding against the firm,

(6) Acquire immovable property on behalf of the firm,

(7) Transfer immovable property belonging to the firm, or

(8) Enter into partnership on behalf of the firm.

It is to be noted that the above acts can be done by a partner, if any of the following two conditions are satisfied:

1. If he has specific or express authority from the other partners, or
2. The usage or custom of trade permits him.

Implied authority and third parties

1. **Restrictions on implied authority:** Restrictions on the implied authority of a partner may be imposed by the partnership agreement. However, such restrictions are valid only if the third party had their knowledge.
2. **Effect of Representations by a partner (Sec. 23):** If a partner makes any representation relating to the firm, it will be binding on the firm, provided the representation is made in the ordinary course of business.
3. **Effect of notice to active partner (Sec. 24):** Notice to an active partner operates as notice to the firm, except in the case of a fraud on the firm committed by or with the consent of that partner.
4. **Liability of a partner for acts of the firm (Sec. 25):** Every partner is liable, jointly with all the other partners and also severally, for all acts of the firm, done while he is a partner.
5. **Liability of the firm for the wrongful acts of a partner (See. 26):** The firm is liable for any loss caused to a third party by the wrongful act or omission of a partner, while acting in the ordinary course of business or with the authority of his partner.

   For Example: (a) A appointed a firm of B and C to buy and sell wine for him on commission. A left the money with the firm for the purpose. B, the active partner, rendered false accounts of purchase and sale to A and misappropriated the money.

   Held, the firm was liable. *Mellors* v *Shaw* (1861)

6. Liability of firm for misapplication by partners (Sec. 27):

The firm is liable to make good the loss in the following two conditions:

(a) Where a partner acting within his apparent authority receives money or property from a third party and misapplies it, or

(b) Where a firm in the course of its business receives money or property from a third party, and the money or property is misapplied by any of the partners while it is in the custody of the firm.

TYPES OF PARTNERS

1. Active partner/actual partner/ostensible partner/full fledged partner:

A partner is known as an actual partner, if—

(i) he becomes a partner by an agreement, and

(ii) he is actively engaged in the conduct of the business of the partnership firm.

Such a partner has a power to bind the other partners by his acts done in the ordinary course of business. If such partner wants to retire, he has to give a public notice of his retirement; otherwise he will continue to be liable for the acts of the firm.

2. Sleeping or Dormant Partner:

(i) A sleeping partner is one, who does not take an active part in the conduct of the firm's business.

(ii) He invests capital and has a share in the profits of the business.

(iii) It is to be noted that such partner is responsible to third parties for the acts of the firm, even if the third parties had no knowledge of the existence of the sleeping partner. In fact, his position is like an undisclosed principal.

(iv) Further a sleeping partner need not give a public notice of his retirement from the firm.

Types of Partners
1. Active/Actual/Ostensible/ full-fledged Partner
2. Sleeping or Dormant Partner
3. Nominal Partner
4. Partner In Profit Only
5. Partner by Estoppel or Holding Out
6. Sub-Partner
7. Minor Partner

3. Nominal partner:

(i) A nominal partner is one, who does not have any real interest in the business, but lends his name to the firm.

(ii) He does not invest any capital nor he has any share in the profits or loss of the firm.

(iii) He does not participate in the management of the firm.

(iv) Such partner is liable to the outsiders for all the debts of the firm.

4. Partner in profit only:

(i) Such partner shall get a share in the profits, but shall not bear the loss of the firm.

(ii) However, he shall be liable like all other partners, since the liability of the partners is joint and several. So, if the firm incurs any losses and the other partners become insolvent, the third party may hold such a partner liable.

5. Partner by Estoppel/Holding out (Sec. 28):

Sometimes a person is not a partner in a firm. But he may be liable for the debts of the firm, as if he were a partner. Such a partner is called a partner by estoppel or holding out. For this, the following conditions must be fulfilled:

(1) He must have *expressly or impliedly* represented himself to be a partner, or he must have knowingly permitted himself to be represented as a partner to the other person, and

(2) The other person must have acted on the faith of such representation and given credit to the firm.

This rule is based on the principle of equity and natural justice.

For Example: One MW was the manager of B's business. The business was carried in the name of MW & Co.

Held, that MW by permitting his name to be used in the title of the firm had made a representation that he was a partner. As such, he was liable to those who gave credit to the firm on the faith of the representation.

—*Bevan* v *The National Bank Ltd.* (1906)

6. Sub-Partner (Sec. 29): For detail, refer to next chapter.

7. Minor partner (Sec. 30)

☞ **Can a Minor become a partner in a partnership firm?**

➢ As per Sec. 11 of the Indian Contract Act, an agreement by or with a minor is void. He has no capacity to enter into a contract. Following this principle, a minor cannot become a partner (Sec. 30).

➢ However, as per section 30(1), a minor may be admitted to the benefits of partnership with the consent of all the partners. In fact, this provision is based on the rule that a minor cannot be a promisor, but he can be a beneficiary in a contract.

➢ It should, however, be noted that a new partnership cannot be formed with a minor partner. Also, there cannot be a partnership of minors among themselves as they are incapable of entering into a contract.

☞ Position of a minor partner before attaining majority?

1. Rights:

(a) He has a right to share the property and profits of the firm in an agreed proportion.

(b) He has a right to have access to and inspect and copy any of the accounts of the firm, but not books.

(c) When he is not given his due share of profit, he has a right to file a suit for his share of the property of the firm.

2. Liabilities:

(a) The liability of the minor partner is confined only to the extent of his share in the profits and property of the firm. Over and above this, he is neither personally liable nor is his private estate liable.

(b) He cannot be declared insolvent, but if the firm is declared insolvent, his share in the firm vests in the official receiver or official assignee.

☞ Position of a Minor partner after Attaining Majority?

On attaining majority, the minor partner has to decide, whether he shall continue in the firm or leave it. He has to decide the above question within six months—

(a) from the date of his attaining majority, or

(b) from the date when he first comes to know that he had been admitted to the benefits of partnership

Whichever date is later

He has to give a public notice of his choice within the above period.

If he fails to give a public notice, he is deemed to have become a partner after the expiry of the above period.

Where he elects to become a partner:

(a) He becomes personally liable to the third parties for all acts of the firm done since he was admitted to the benefit of the partnership and not from the date he becomes major.

(b) His share in the property and profits of the firm remains the same as before.

(c) Public Notice is not mandatory.

Where he elects not to become a partner:

(a) He continues to be liable as before until the date of the public notice.

(b) His share shall not be liable for any acts of the firm done after the date of the notice.

(c) He shall be entitled to sue the partners for his share of the property and profits.

(d) Public Notice is mandatory.

☑☑☑

MULTIPLE CHOICE QUESTIONS

☞ Implied Authority of Partner

1. A and B are partners. A with the intention of cheating B goes to a shop and purchases such articles on behalf of the firm as might be use in the ordinary course of the partnership business, but converts them to his own separate use. B receives no part of the money and knows nothing of the transaction. Is B liable?

(A) Yes, as the act is covered within the implied authority of a partner.

(B) No, as the act is not covered within the implied authority of a partner.

(C) Either of (A) or (B)

(D) Both (A) and (B)

2. A and B are solicitors in partnership. C, a client of the firm, hands over a sum of money to A to be invested on security. A never invests, it but applies it to his own use. B receives no part of the money and knows nothing of the transaction. Is B liable?

(A) Yes, as the act is covered within the implied authority of partner.

(B) No, as the act is not covered within the implied authority of partner.

(C) Either of (A) or (B)

(D) Both (A) and (B)

3. A, being a partner in a firm of solicitors, draws a bill of exchange in the name of the firm without authority. Are the other partners liable?

(A) Yes, as the act is covered within the implied authority of a partner.

(B) No, as the act is not covered within the implied authority of a partner.

(C) Yes, the firm is always liable for the negotiable instruments drawn by the partner.

(D) Both (A) and (C)

4. Which of the following acts are not included in the implied authority of a partner?

(A) To buy or sell goods on account of partners.

(B) To borrow money for the purposes of a firm.

(C) To enter into partnership on behalf of the firm.

(D) To engage a lawyer to defend actions against firm.

5. Agency by ostensible authority may happen in the following ways –

(A) By estoppel.

(B) By a legal presumption.

(C) By holding-out.

(D) All of the above.

6. The maxim '*delegatus non protest delegare*' means—

(A) A person to whom authority has been given cannot delegate the authority to another.

(B) A person whom authority has been given can delegate the authority to another with prior permission.

(C) A person whom authority has been given to indemnify an agent for injury caused by the principal's neglect can be delegated.

(D) An authority can be delegated under protest by the person to whom the authority has been given.

7. For an effective notice on the Firm, it must be made to—

(A) All the partners jointly.

(B) To any one of the working partners.

(C) Any one of the working partners and all the dormant partners.

(D) Only the dormant Partners.

8. Z, a Partner of a Firm dealing in readymade garments places an order for liquor worth Rs.50,000 in the Firm's name. Can the principle of Z's implied authority be invoked here?

(A) Yes, the act is done by the Partner.

(B) Yes, the act is done in the Firm's name.

(C) No, the act is not related to the Firm's business.

(D) No, dealing in liquor is opposed to public policy.

9. In which of the following cases, the Firm is not bound by the act of the Partner?

(A) Act done by a Partner or his agent of behalf of the Firm.

(B) Act done by a partner in the Firm name.

(C) Act done by a partner in any manner expressing or implying an intention to bind the Firm.

(D) Act done fraudulently or negligently.

10. Partners of a Firm by an express contract decided that no Partner would have the authority to sell goods above value Rs. 1 lakh without consulting the other Partners. Due to unfavourable conditions, prices crashed. One Partner, in order to save the Firm from loss, sold all stock worth Rs. 15 lakhs without consulting any other Partner.

(A) The Firm is bound by the act.

(B) The Firm is not bound by the act.

(C) The Partner has to indemnify the Firm for the loss.

(D) The Partner has to indemnify the other Partners for the loss.

11. Implied authority of the partner does not empower him to –

(A) Submit a dispute relating to the business of the firm to arbitration.

(B) Withdraw a suit or proceeding filed on behalf of the firm.

(C) Both (A) & (B)

(D) None of the above

☞ Types of Partner

12. 'Partner by holding out' is governed by Section of ______ The Indian Partnership Act, 1932.

(A) 28

(B) 17

(C) 30

(D) 11

13. Suppose, A is not a partner in a particular firm. But he represents himself or knowingly permits himself to be represented as a partner in that particular firm to B who on the faith of such representation, gives credit to the firm. Decide –

(A) A is liable, because such partner is know as active partner.

(B) A is liable, because such partner is know as partner by estoppel.

(C) A is not liable.

(D) Both (A) and (B)

14. A person, even if he is not a partner in the firm, may be held liable as partner, if he knowingly permits himself to be represented as a partner.

(A) True, as the principle of holding out applies in such a case.

(B) False, as a person can become a partner only by agreement not otherwise.

15. A minor is—

(A) A partner of a firm.

(B) Representative of the firm.

(C) An active partner of the firm.

(D) Entitled to the benefits of the firm.

16. Active partner is one who—

(A) Takes part in the business of the firm.

(B) Actively participates in co-curricular activities.

(C) Actively shares the profits.

(D) Makes a show of authority.

17. Types of partners includes—

(A) Active Partner.

(B) Sleeping Partner.

(C) Nominal Partner.

(D) All of the above.

18. A partnership at will is one –

(A) Which does not have any deed.

(B) Which does not have any partner.

(C) Where the partnership is not for a fixed period of time.

(D) Which cannot be dissolved.

19. Minor can become a partner in an existing firm.

(A) True

(B) False

20. Is it compulsory for a minor who has attained majority to give public notice that he has elected either to become or not to become a Partner in the firm?

(A) Yes

(B) No

(C) Partly yes

(D) None of the above

21. When a minor is admitted to the benefits of the partnership, the partnership agreement should be–

(A) Written and registered.

(B) Written and not registered.

(C) Stamped as per law.

(D) None of the above.

22. Which of the following statements is not true about minor's position as a partner?

(A) He cannot become a full-fledged partner.

(B) He can become a full-fledged partner in an existing firm.

(C) A minor has the right to receive the agreed share of profits.

(D) He can become partner on becoming a major.

23. A induces B to believe that he (A) is a partner of a Firm PQ & Co. B believing that A is a Partner, gives credit to PQ & Co. What is A's liability?

(A) A is liable to compensate B.

(B) A can plead innocence saying that he is not a Partner of PQ & Co.

(C) A can require B to give credit to him (A) and not the Firm.

(D) A is liable to PQ & Co.

24. The rule of estoppel implies that a person who holds himself out to be a Partner —

(A) Can claim innocence and claim that he was misrepresented as a Partner.

(B) Can claim that he is a real Partner in the Firm.

(C) Is estopped from denying that he was represented as a partner.

(D) Is estopped from admitting liability to third parties.

25. Which of the following statements is not true about minor's position as a partner?

(1) He cannot become a full-fledged partner.

(2) He can become a full-fledged partner in an existing firm.

(3) He has to bear all liabilities, like other partners.

(4) He can become partner on becoming a major.

(A) 1 & 2

(B) 2 & 3

(C) 3 & 4

(A) 1 & 4

26. Failure by a minor to give public notice within six months will have the following effect —

(A) The Partnership Firm stands dissolved.

(B) Minor automatically becomes Partner.

(C) Minor automatically ceases to be a Partner.

(D) The Partnership becomes an illegal association.

27. Which is not true regarding the rights of a minor partner

(A) He has a right such share of the property and profits of the firm as may have been agreed upon.

(B) he has right to have access to and inspect and copy of books of the firm.

(C) He has right to have access to and inspect and copy of any of accounts.

(D) All of these

28. Which of the following is correct—

(A) A minor can be admitted as a partner provided the partnership deed is signed by the guardian of the minor on behalf of and in the best interest of such minor.

(B) A minor can enter into a contract of partnership provided it is a 'necessity' and not a 'luxury'.

(C) A minor cannot be admitted as a partner unless all the partners agree to it.

(D) A minor can be admitted to the benefits of partnership.

29. A, B and C enter into a partnership agreement under which 'C' is not liable for the losses. D filed a suit against A, B, and C. Examine the position of C.

(A) C is liable to D only

(B) C is liable to D, jointly with A and B also

(C) C is not liable to D

(D) C is not liable to D jointly with A and B.

30. On attaining majority, which statement is correct?

(A) A minor cannot become a partner.

(B) He can become a partner at any time.

(C) He has to decide within 6 months, whether he shall remain in the firm or leave it.

(D) None of the above

31. Which of the following statement is incorrect, when the minor elects not to become a partner?

(A) His rights and liabilities continue to be those of a minor upto the date of giving public notice.

(B) His share is not liable for any acts of the Firm done after the date of notice.

(C) His share is not liable for his share in the profits and property.

(D) He becomes personally liable for all acts with retrospective effect from the date of his admission.

ANSWERS TO MULTIPLE CHOICE QUESTIONS

1. A
2. B
3. B
4. C
5. D
6. A
7. B
8. C
9. D
10. A
11. C
12. A
13. B
14. A
15. D
16. A
17. D
18. C
19. A
20. B
21. D
22. B
23. A
24. C
25. B
26. B
27. B
28. D
29. B
30. C
31. D

Chapter 4

Reconstitution And Dissolution Of Firm

RECONSTITUTION OF FIRM

ADMISSION OF A PARTNER [Sec. 31]

☞ **When can a partner be admitted to a partnership firm?**

A person may be admitted as a new partner–

(i) in accordance with the Partnership Deed.

(ii) with the consent of all the existing partners, or

For Example: B and R were partners in a firm. One of the terms of the partnership deed was that B could introduce into the partnership any of his sons on their attaining the age of 21. B's son S attained the age of 21 and he proposed to make him a partner. R refused to give consent to admit S.

Held, R could not prevent S from being a partner as the clause in the partnership agreement operated as a consent.

—*Byrne* v *Reid* (1902)

What is Reconstitution?

A firm is said to be reconstituted when any of the following changes occur and the firm continues:

1. Admission of a partner (Sec. 31)
2. Retirement of a partner (Sec. 32)
3. Expulsion of a partner (Sec. 33)
4. Insolvency of a partner (Sec. 34)
5. Death of a partner (Sec. 35)
6. Transfer of a partner's share (Sec. 29)

☞ **Liability of an Incoming partner:**

A new partner admitted into a firm is not liable for any act of the firm done before his admission. However, an incoming partner may, by an agreement, agree to become liable for the acts done before his admission, provided:

(a) The newly constituted firm has agreed to pay the debts, and

(b) The creditors have agreed to accept the new firm as their debtor and discharge the old firm from its liability.

However, the position will be different, if a minor partner on attaining majority elects to become partner. In this case, a minor partner on attaining maturity shall be liable for all acts of the firm done since he was admitted to the benefit of the partnership and not from the date he becomes a major.

RETIREMENT OF A PARTNER [Sec. 32]

☞ **When can a partner retire from a partnership firm?** A partner may retire—

(i) in accordance with the Partnership Deed, or

(ii) with the consent of all the other partners, or

(iii) where the partnership is at will, by giving notice in writing to all the other partners of his intention to retire.

☞ **Liability of a Retired Partner:**

(i) For the Acts done before retirement: Even after retirement, a partner continues to be liable for all the acts of the firm done before his retirement, unless he is discharged. He may be discharged from liability to any third party for any acts done before his retirement, by an agreement made by him with such third party and continuing partners of the reconstituted firm. The above agreement may be express or implied.

For Example: A, B and C are three partners, A retires and Z joins the firm. The creditors of the firm accept B, C and Z as their debtors and Z also agrees to pay the debts incurred by the old firm. A is discharged from his liability for the acts of the firm.

(ii) For the Acts done after retirement:

- As a general rule, a retired partner cannot be held liable for the acts of a firm done after his retirement.
- But he may be held responsible on the ground of estopple in the following cases:

(a) The public notice of his retirement is not given.

(b) The outsider has given credit to the firm on the *bona fide* belief that he is still the partner of the firm.

(c) The retired partner is not liable to any third party, who deals with the firm without knowing that he was a partner.

☞ **Rights of a retired partner:**

(1) To carry on Competing Business (Sec. 36): A retired partner may carry on a business competing with that of the firm and he may advertise such business, but subject to a contract to the contrary, he will not—

(a) Use the firm name,

(b) Represent himself as carrying of the business of the firm, or

(c) Solicit the custom of persons, who were dealing with the firm before he ceased to be a partner.

(2) To Share Subsequent Profits (Sec. 37): Where the other partners carry on the firm's business without making a final settlement of the outgoing partner, then in the absence of any agreement, the outgoing partner or his legal representative shall be entitled to, **at his option**, to—

(i) such share of the profits as is proportionate to his share in the property of the firm, or

(ii) interest @ 6% p.a. on the amount of his share in the property of the firm.

EXPULSION OF A PARTNER [Sec. 33]

☞ **When can a partner be expelled from a partnership firm?** A partner may be expelled from partnership subject to the following three conditions:

(1) The power of expulsion of a partner should be conferred by the Partnership Deed.

(2) The power should be exercised by a majority of the partners.

(3) The power should be exercised in good faith. The following three criteria are the test of good faith—

(a) The expulsion must be in the interest of the partnership,

(b) A proper notice is served to the expelled partner,

(c) He is given an opportunity of being heard.

☞ **What is irregular expulsion?**

If a partner is expelled without complying with the above conditions, the expulsion is called irregular. In such a case, the expelled partner may—

(1) claim re-instatement as a partner, or

(2) sue for the refund of his share of capital and profits in the firm.

In short, in the case of irregular expulsion, the partner does not cease to be a partner. It is wholly inoperative. Further, irregular expulsion does not give right to damage to expelled partner.

INSOLVENCY OF A PARTNER [Sec. 34]

The legal effects of insolvency of a partner are as follows:

(1) Where a partner in a firm is adjudicated insolvent, he ceases to be a partner on the date on which the order of adjudication is made.

(2) The firm is dissolved on the date of the Order of adjudication, but the partners may specifically provide that on such a contingency, the firm shall not be dissolved.

(3) The estate of the insolvent-partner is not liable for the acts of the firm done after the date of the order of adjudication. A public notice to the effect that a partner has been adjudicated insolvent is not required.

(4) The firm is also not liable for any act of the insolvent partner after the date of the order of adjudication.

DEATH OF A PARTNER [Secs. 35 and 42(c)]

Same as for insolvency of a partner.

For Example: M was a partner in a firm. The firm ordered goods in M's lifetime, but delivery was made after M's death. Held, M's estate was not liable for the price of goods sold and delivered.

—*Bagel* v *Miller* (1903)

Upon the death of a partner, the legal heirs do not become partners. If they want to become partners, a fresh contract has to be made, as the partnership is created by contract.

TRANSFER OF PARTNER'S INTEREST [Sec. 29]

- **Meaning:** When a partner agrees to share his own share in profits and assets with an outsider, it is called sub-partnership and the outsider is called sub-partner.
- **Rights of Transferee:** A partner can assign his share of the profit and his share in the assets of a firm to outsider. In that case, the Transferee is not entitled—

  (i) to interfere in the conduct of the business of the firm, or

  (ii) to ask for the accounts of the firm, or

  (iii) to inspect the books of the firm.

  But, such a transferee is entitled–

  (i) to receive the share of the profit of the transferring partner. He is bound to accept the accounts of the profit as agreed to by the partners;

  (ii) in the case of dissolution, to receive the transferring partner's share in the assets of the firm.
- A partner cannot assign the whole of his rights and interest in the firm to an outsider, so as to make him a partner of the firm.

  Where a partner, *other than the partner suing*, has in any way transferred the whole of his interest in the firm to a third party or where his share has been attached under a decree, or sold for the recovery of arrears of land revenue, the Court may dissolve the firm at the instance of any other partner.
- **Liability**: This sub-partner is not liable for the debts of firm.

Rights and Duties of a partner after Reconstitution (Sec. 17)

Change in constitution due to Admission / Outgoing	**Where the firm constituted for a fixed term continues business after the expiry of that fixed term**	**Where the firm constituted to carry out one or more ventures, carries out other ventures**
In this case, the mutual rights and duties of the partners in the reconstituted firm remain the same as they were before the change.	In this case, the mutual rights and duties of the partners in the reconstituted firm remain the same as they were before the expiry, so far as they may be consistent with the incidents of partnership at will.	In this case, the mutual rights and duties of the partners in respect of the other ventures remain the same as they were in the original ventures.

Revocation of continuing guarantee by change in firm (Sec. 38):

→ Where a continuing guarantee given to a firm or to a third party, and

→ thereafter there is change in constitution of firm,

→ then *in the absence of agreement to the contrary*, the continuing guarantee is revoked as to future transactions from the date of any change in the constitution of the firm.

DISSOLUTION OF FIRM

As per section 39, the dissolution of partnership among all the partners of a firm is called the 'dissolution of the firm'.

☞ **Dissolution of partnership firm:**

It means dissolution of partnership among all the partners of a firm. Thus, in this case, the partnership among all partners comes to an end and therefore, the business of the firm is also closed down. There are two modes of dissolution of a partnership firm:

1. Dissolution without the order of the court,
2. Dissolution with the order of the court.

⇒⇒⇒

DISSOLUTION WITHOUT THE ORDER OF THE COURT [Secs. 40 to 43]

(i) Dissolution by Agreement [Sec. 40]

A firm may be dissolved-

(a) with the consent of all the partners, or

(b) As per Deed

(ii) Compulsory Dissolution [Sec. 41]

(a) When all the partners of a firm are declared insolvent,

(b) When all the partners of a firm except one are declared insolvent,

(c) When the business of the firm becomes unlawful.*

(iii) On Happening Certain Contingencies [Sec. 42]

Subject to the contract between the partners, a firm shall be dissolved in the following cases:

(a) On the expiry of the partnership duration

(b) On the completion of the partnership adventure(s)

(c) On the death of a partner

(d) On the insolvency of a partner.

(iv) Dissolution by notice of partnership-at-will [Sec. 43]

* It should be noted that where two or more separate adventures are carried on by a firm, the illegality of one or more shall not automatically dissolve the lawful business of the firm.

DISSOLUTION WITH THE ORDER OF THE COURT [Sec. 44]

At the suit of a partner, the Court may dissolve a firm on the following grounds:

(i) Insanity of a partner: Where a partner has become a person of unsound mind, the court may dissolve the firm on the petition of any of the other partners or by the next friend of the insane partner.

(ii) Permanent incapacity: Where a partner, other than the partner suing, has become in any way permanently incapable of performing his duties as a partner, the Court may dissolve the firm. For example, a partner becomes blind or is paralysed due to polio.

(iii) Misconduct: Where a partner, other than the partner suing, is guilty of misconduct and it is likely to affect the business prejudicially, the court may dissolve the firm. For example,

(a) Travelling on railway by a partner without ticket,

(b) Gambling by a partner on a stock exchange, though such gambling may in no way be connected with the business of the firm,

(c) Fraudulent breach of trust by a partner.

(iv) Persistent breach of agreement: Where a partner, other than the partner suing, wilfully or persistently commits breach of the partnership agreements or otherwise so conducts himself that it is not reasonably practicable for the other partners to carry on the business of the firm with him, the court may, at the instance of any of the other partners, dissolve the firm. For Example—

(a) A partner having the keys of the shop continuously fails to come to the shop in time,

(b) A partner keeps erroneous accounts,

(c) If there is continued quarreling between the partners or there is such a state of animosity that all mutual confidence is destroyed,

(v) Transfer of Interest: Where a partner, other than the partner suing, has in any way transferred the whole of his interest in the firm to a third party or where his share has been attached under a decree, or sold in the recovery of arrears of land revenue, the Court may dissolve the firm at the instance of any other partner.

(vi) Business Working at a Loss: Where the business of a firm cannot be carried on except at a loss, the Court may dissolve the firm on the suit of a partner.

(vii) Any Other Ground: The Court may dissolve a firm on any other ground, which renders the dissolution of the firm just and equitable. The other just and equitable grounds may be continued quarrelling, deadlock in the management etc.

RIGHTS OF PARTNERS ON DISSOLUTION

1. Right to have Business Wound Up (Sec. 46): On the dissolution of a firm, every partner is entitled to have the property of the firm, applied in payment of outside debts and liabilities of the firm and have the surplus distributed among the partners in accordance with their rights. This right of a partner is called **'partner's lien'**.

2. Right to have the debts of the firm settled out of the property of the Firm (Sec. 49):

(a) Debts of the firm shall be paid first out of the property of the firm and if there is any surplus, it shall be distributed among the partners.

(b) Private debts of the partners shall be paid first out of the private estate of the partner and if there is any surplus and the liabilities of the firm exceed the assets of the firm, it shall be utilised towards the payment of the debts of the firm.

3. Right to share personal profits earned after dissolution [Sec. 50]: If the firm is dissolved due to the death of a partner and the surviving partners or the representative of the deceased partner have earned any personal profit from the use of the firm's property or the firm's name or the firm's business connection before the firm has been completely wound up, a partner has a right to a share in such personal profits.

4. Right to return of Premium on Premature Dissolution [Sec. 51]: Where a partner has paid a premium on entering into partnership for a fixed term and the firm is dissolved before the expiration of the term, he is entitled to repayment of the whole or part of the premium.

However, no refund can be claimed where the dissolution—

(a) is due to the death of a partner, or

(b) is due to the misconduct of the partner who had paid the premium, or

(c) is in pursuance of an agreement which contains no provisions for the refund of the premium or any part thereof.

5. Right where a Partnership Contract is rescinded for Fraud or Misrepresentation (Sec. 52): Where a contract creating a partnership is rescinded on the ground of fraud or misrepresentation of one of the partners, the partner entitled to rescind has the following rights:

(a) Right of lien on the surplus assets: If there is any surplus assets after the debts of the firm have been paid, he has a lien on such surplus assets for any sum paid by him for the purchase of his share in the firm and for any capital contributed by him.

(b) Right of Subrogation: If he pays off any creditor of the firm from his own pocket, he steps into the shoes of that creditor, i.e. he becomes the creditor of the firm for that amount.

(c) Right to be Indemnified: He has also a right to be indemnified by the partner or partners guilty of fraud or misrepresentation against all the debts of the firm.

6. Right to Restrain Partners from Use of Firm Name or Property (Sec. 53): After a firm is dissolved, every partner may restrain any other partner from carrying on a similar business in the firm name or from using any of the property of the firm for his own benefit, until the affairs of the firm have been completely wound up. However, it is to be noted that this restriction does not apply in the following two conditions:

(i) When there is a contract between the partners to the contrary,

(ii) When a partner has bought the goodwill of the firm.

LIABILITIES OF PARTNERS ON DISSOLUTION

1. Liabilities for the acts of Partners done after Dissolution (Sec. 45): If the public notice for dissolution is not given, the partners continue to be liable as such to third parties for any act done by any of them after the dissolution. In such a case, the act is deemed to be an act done before the dissolution.

For Example: A and B, partners in a trade, agree to dissolve the partnership. They execute a deed for that purpose declaring the partnership dissolved as from January 1, but do not give a public notice of the dissolution.

On February 1, A endorses a bill in the partnership name to C. The firm is liable on the bill.

However, the following are not liable for acts done after the dissolution of the firm and no notice of dissolution need be given :

(a) The estate of a deceased partner,

(b) An insolvent partner,

(c) An sleeping partner, who retires.

2. Continuing Authority of Partners for Purposes of Winding Up (Sec. 47): After the dissolution of a firm, the authority of each partner to bind the firm and the other mutual rights and obligations of the partners continue, so far as may be necessary for the following purposes:

(a) To wind up the firm, and

(b) To complete transactions begun, but unfinished at the time of the dissolution.

SETTLEMENT OF ACCOUNTS

The partners are free to lay down the modes in which the accounts will be settled on dissolution of the firm. In the absence of any specific agreement, the provisions of Sections 48 and 55 will apply, which are as follows:

1. Sale of Goodwill [Sec. 55(1)]: In settling the account, goodwill shall be included in the assets and it may be sold either separately or along with the other property of the firm.

Rights on Sale of Goodwill of Firm

Buyer's Right	Rights of Partners after Selling Goodwill
(1) Right to carry on same business under old Name. (2) Right to represent himself as successor of business of old firm.	(1) Right to carry on similar business. (2) Right to compete with purchaser of Goodwill. (3) Advertise their business. (4) But subject to the contract to the contrary, they cannot do the following— — Use firm's Name — Represent themselves as carrying on old Business. — Solicit Customers of old firm.

2. Sharing of Deficiency [Sec. 48(a)]: If at the time of settlement, any deficiency arises, the partners shall bear such deficiency in the profit sharing ratio. Thus, losses shall be paid in the following order:

(a) First out of Profits,

(b) Next out of capital, and

(c) Lastly, if necessary, by the partners individually in the profit sharing ratio.

For Example: A and B are partners in a business sharing profits and losses equally. A dies and on accounts of the partnership being taken, it is found that A had contributed £1929 and B £29 to the capital of the firm. The assets amount to £1400 only. The deficiency of 558 (=1929 +29-1400), must be shared equally by B and the estate of A —*Nowell* v *Nowell* (1869)

3. Application of Assets [Sec. 48(b)]: The assets of the firm shall be applied in the following order:

(a) In paying the debts of the firm to the third parties.

(b) In paying to each partner rateably what is due to him from the firm for advances distinguished from capital,

(c) In paying to each partner rateably what is due to him on account of capital, and

(d) the residue, if any, shall be divided among the partners in the profit sharing ratio.

If the assets are sufficient to pay (1) and (2) above, but insufficient to repay to each partner his full capital, the deficiency in the capital shall be borne by the partners in the proportion in which they are entitled to share profits.

☞ **Garner Vs. Murray (1904) Rule:**

Facts of the case:	G, M and W were partners in a firm on terms that profits should be divided equally. The capital was contributed in unequal shares. The capital contributed by G was more than the capital contributed by M. On the dissolution of the firm, the assets were insufficient to repay the capital in full. W became insolvent.
Decision of the case:	The following decisions were given in this case: 1. The solvent partners should bring the share of their loss in cash. 2. The solvent partners shall bear the deficiency of capital of the insolvent partner in the ratio of their capitals.

It is to be noted that the rule of *Garner* v. *Murray* is applicable only when there is no other agreement between the partners. Again, this rule is not strictly applied in India in as much as the solvent partners are not asked to bring the share of their loss in cash.

4. Settlement of Debt [Sec. 49]:

(a) Debts of the firm shall be paid first out of the property of the firm and if there is any surplus, it shall be distributed among the partners.

(b) Private debts of the partners shall be paid first out of the private estate of the partner and if there is any surplus and the liabilities of the firm exceed the assets of the firm, it shall be utilised towards the payment of the debts of the firm.

RULE OF EVIDENCE [Sec. 68]

(1) Any statement/intimation recorded in the Register of Firms shall, as against any person by whom or on whose behalf such statement, intimation or notice was signed, be conclusive proof of any fact therein stated.

(2) A certified copy of an entry relating to a firm in the Register of Firms may be produced in proof of the fact of the registration of such firm, and of the contents of any statement, intimation or notice recorded or noted therein.

PUBLIC NOTICE [Sec. 72]

☞ **When the Notice is Required?**

A public notice has to be given on the following occasions:

1. Retirement or Expulsion of a partner,
2. Dissolution of Firm,
3. Election to become or not to become a partner in Firm by a minor on his attaining majority.

☞ Mode of Giving Public Notice?

1. In the case of registered firm, the public notice is given by the following modes:

(i) By notice to the Registrar of Firms under section 63.

(ii) By publication in the Official Gazette,

(iii) By publication in at least one vernacular newspaper circulating in the district, where the firm has its place or principal place of business.

2. In other cases, *i.e.* in the case of unregistered firm, where public notice is required to be given, it is given by publication in—

(i) the Official Gazette, and

(ii) at least one vernacular newspaper circulating in the district, where the firm has its place or principal place of business.

☞ Consequences of Failure to Give Public Notice?

1. On Retirement of a partner (Sec. 32):

A retired partner can be held liable for the acts done after his retirement, if the public notice of his retirement is not given. The notice may be given either by the retired partner or any partner of the reconstituted firm.

2. On Expulsion of a partner (Sec. 33):

If a partner is expelled from the firm and a public notice is not given, the expelled partner and the other partners shall continue to be liable to third parties dealing with the firm as in the case of a retired partner.

3. On dissolution of firm (Sec. 45):

If the public notice for dissolution is not given, the partners continue to be liable as such to third parties for any act done by any of them after the dissolution. In such a case, the act is deemed to be an act done before the dissolution.

4. Minor Partner on attaining Majority (Sec. 30):

On attaining majority, the minor partner has to decide, whether he shall continue in the firm or leave it. He has to decide the above question within 6 months—

(a) from the date of his attaining majority, or

(b) from the date when he first comes to know that he had been admitted to the benefits of partnership.

} Whichever date is later

He has to give a public notice of his choice within the above period.

If he fails to give a public notice, he is deemed to have become a partner after the expiry of the above period.

MULTIPLE CHOICE QUESTIONS

☞ Admission

1. The reconstitution of the firm takes place in case–

(A) Admission of a Partner.

(B) Retirement of a partner.

(C) Change in profit sharing ratio.

(D) All of the above

2. A person may be admitted as a new partner –

(A) In accordance with a contract between the existing partners or with the consent of all the existing partners.

(B) In accordance with a contract between the existing partners or with the consent of all the existing partners, subject to the provisions of Section 31 of the Act.

(C) After obtaining specific approval of the Registrar of Firms & Societies to this effect.

(D) By simply taking the consent of the new partner.

3. A new partner can be admitted in the firm with the consent of –

(A) All the partners.

(B) Simple majority of partners.

(C) Partner having major profit share.

(D) New partner only.

4. The liability of a new partner generally commences from –

(A) The date of his admission.

(B) The first date of the financial year in which he was admitted.

(C) Any day after his admission as he so decides.

(D) Any day to be decided by the Registrar of Firms.

5. Any act of the old partners—

(A) can be ratified by the New Partner.

(B) cannot be ratified by the New Partner.

(C) can be compromised by the New Partner.

(D) cannot be condoned by the New Partner.

☛ Retirement

6. P, Q and R are Partners. R is a sleeping Partner who has not been known by creditors to be a Partner or P and Q, R retires without giving a public notice of the retirement. Is R liable for subsequent debts incurred by P and Q?

(A) Yes

(B) No

(C) Partly yes

(D) None of the above

7. A partner may retire from an existing firm–

(A) with consent of all partners.

(B) as per express agreement.

(C) where the partnership is at will, simply by giving a notice of retirement.

(D) all of the above

8. A partner may retire from a firm –

(A) With consent of all other partners.

(B) With the consent of main partner.

(C) With the consent of sleeping partner.

(D) No consent of any partner.

9. After retirement from firm, which of the following partners is not liable by holding out, even if the public notice of retirement is not given?

(A) Active partner.

(B) Sleeping partner.

(C) Representative of deceased partner.

(D) Both (B) and (C)

10. An accepted view is that where the existence of a retiring partner was not known, he is not liable for debts incurred by the firm after his retirement, even if public notice of his retirement was not given.

(A) True

(B) False

11. X, Y and Z are partners, Z who is in active partnership retires without giving public notice of his retirement. X and Y in carrying on old business incurred a liability towards M. Is Z also liable to M?

(A) Yes

(B) No

12. The representatives of a deceased partner cannot claim share in subsequent profit of the firm u/s 37.

(A) True

(B) Partly true

(C) False

(D) None of the above

13. When by a contract between partners, an option to purchase the interest of outgoing partner was exercised by other partners then the outgoing Partner will still be entitled to further share of the profits.

(A) True

(B) Partly true

(C) False

(D) None of the above

14. Section ____ of the Partnership Act, 1932 deals with "Right of Outgoing partner to carry on competing business"

(A) 36

(B) 37

(C) 38

(D) 39

15. Which of the following is not a mode of Retirement of partner?

(A) Retirement with other partners' consent.

(B) Retirement in accordance with an express agreement.

(C) By giving written notice of his intention to retire in a partnership at will.

(D) Transfer of interest by a partner.

16. X, Y and Z are partners. Z who is an active partner retires without giving public notice of his retirement. Will Z be liable for the subsequent debts of the Firm?

(A) Yes

(B) No

(C) Partly yes

(D) None of the above

17. Where the existence of a Retiring partner was not known, he is not liable for debts incurred by the Firm after his retirement even if public notice of his retirement was not given.

(A) True

(B) Partly true

(C) False

(D) None of the above

18. In a partnership firm, having three or more Partners, where a partner decides to retire from the Firm—

(A) The Firm is automatically dissolved.

(B) The Firm's activities are suspended.

(C) The Firm continues with the continuing partner as its members.

(D) The Firm becomes an illegal association.

19. Retiring Partner continues to be liable for acts of the Firm done—

(A) upto the date of admission of a new partner.

(B) upto the date of giving public notice of retirement.

(C) upto the close of the financial year in which he retires.

(D) all of the above

20. To avoid liability to third parties, public notice of retirement should be given. Such public notice must be given by—

(A) Retiring partner only.

(B) Any partner of the reconstituted Firm.

(C) By the retiring partner or any partner of the reconstituted Firm.

(D) All the partners of the reconstituted Firm.

☞ Expulsion

21. A partner may be expelled from partnership subject to which conditions –

(A) The power of expulsion of a partner should be conferred by the contract between the partners

(B) The power should be exercised by majority of partners

(C) The power should be exercised in good faith

(D) All of these

22. A partner may be expelled from the firm on the fulfillment of the condition that the expulsion power is exercised—

(A) is given by express contract,

(B) by majority of partners,

(C) in absolute good faith,

(D) all of the above.

23. In good faith and based on the contract between partners a partner may be expelled from the Firm by —

(A) Unanimous consent of all the partners.

(B) Majority of the partners.

(C) Any of the working partners.

(D) Any of the dormant partners.

24. The test of good faith as required u/s 33(1) includes the following–

(A) That the expulsion must be in the interest of the partnership.

(B) That the partner to be expelled is served with a notice.

(C) That the partner to be expelled is given an opportunity of being heard.

(D) All of the above

25. A third party deals with the Firm without knowledge that K, *sleeping partner*, has been expelled from the Firm. In such a case, K—

(A) Is not liable to the third parties.

(B) Is liable to the third parties.

(C) Is liable to the Firm.

(D) Is liable to the continuing partners.

26. When a Partner is expelled otherwise than in good faith, it is —

(A) Generally valid.

(B) Valid *vis-à-vis* third parties.

(C) in restraint of trade .

(D) null and void.

27. When a partner is expelled otherwise than in good faith, his remedy is—

(A) to request the Continuing partners to take him back.

(B) to request Creditors to deal with him directly.

(C) to seek judicial recourse for dissolution of Firm.

(D) to claim compensation from Continuing partners.

28. A partner can be expelled, if—

(A) Such expulsion is in good faith.

(B) The majority of the partner agree on such expulsion.

(C) The expelled partner is given an opportunity to start a business competing with that of the firm.

(D) Compensation is paid.

29. The invalid expulsion of a partner gives him a right to claim damages.

(A) True

(B) Partly True

(C) False

(D) None of the above

30. In case of invalid expulsion of a partner, the firm automatically gets dissolved.

(A) True

(B) Partly true

(C) False

(D) None of the above

31. 'Expulsion of a partner" is dealt with u/s _____ of the Partnership Act, 1932

(A) 23

(B) 32

(C) 33

(D) 22

☞ Insolvent

32. Insolvent means—

(A) A person when he ceases to pay his debts in ordinary course of business.

(B) A person when he accepts to pay his debts before due date.

(C) A person when he accepts to pay his debts as they become due.

(D) All of these

33. No public notice is required on the death of a Partner.

(A) True

(B) Partly true

(C) False

(D) None of the above

34. After dissolution, the person who has represented himself or knowingly permitted himself to be represented as a partner of the insolvent, after the adjudication, will be liable for the insolvent's acts.

(A) True

(B) Partly true

(C) False

(D) None of the above

35. Where a partner in a firm is adjudicated as insolvent, he ceases to be a partner from the —

(A) Day on which the order of adjudication is made.

(B) First day of the financial year in which the order of adjudication is made.

(C) Day on which the Firm comes to know of his insolvency.

(D) Day as decided by the Registrar of Firms.

☞ Death

36. Death of partner has the effect of—

(A) Dissolving the firm.

(B) Result in continuance of the business of the firm.

(C) Computation of profits upto the date of death.

(D) None of the above

37. A, B and C are partners. An order is placed with D for supplying a certain quantity of goods to the firm on credit. Before D could supply the goods, C died. D supplies the goods after C's death, being totally ignorant about the fact of C's death. A and B subsequently become insolvent. Can D make C's estate liable for his debt?

(A) Yes

(B) No

38. The heir of the deceased partner—

(A) Has a right to become a partner in the firm of the deceased partner.

(B) Does not have a right to become a partner in the firm of the deceased partner.

(C) Can become a partner in the firm of the deceased partner only if the surviving partners give their consent in this regard.

(D) Both (B) & (C).

39. On the insolvency of a partner, the insolvent ceases to be a partner in the firm, whether the firm is dissolved or not –

(A) True

(B) False, as the insolvent partner will cease to be a partner, when a public notice is given.

(C) False, as the insolvent partner will not automatically cease to be a partner. Provision in the partnership deed is necessary.

(D) Both (B) and (C)

40. A, B and C are in partnership. B dies on 26th June, which of the following statement is true?

(A) B's estate is not liable at all.

(B) B's estate is not liable for any acts of the Firm done after 26th June.

(C) B's estate is liable for all acts upto the end of the financial year when the death occurred.

(D) B's estate is liable only upto the previous financial year.

41. X, Y and Z were partners in a Firm. During the course of business, the firm ordered a Textile Machinery with ABC Ltd. After the order was placed, but before delivery of machinery X expired. Thereafter the remaining Partners become insolvent and the Firm was unable to pay for the machine.

(A) X's estate will be liable for the price of the Machinery.

(B) X's estate will not be liable for the price of the Machinery.

(C) ABC Ltd will be liable for the price of the Machinery.

(D) ABC Ltd will not be liable for the price of the Machinery.

42. Unless agreed otherwise, a Firm is dissolved by the death of a partner –

(A) True

(B) Partly True

(C) False

(D) None of the above

43. When under a contract between the partners, the firm is not dissolved by the death of a partner, the estate of deceased partner remains liable for—

(A) Acts as were done during the tenure of his Partnership

(B) acts as were done after the date of his death

(C) Either (A) or (B)

(D) Both (A) and (B)

☞ Transfer of Interest

44. A share in a partnership–

(A) Can be transferred in accordance with the terms and conditions contained in the partnership deed.

(B) Can be transferred only if all the partners agree for such transfer.

(C) Cannot be transferred at all.

(D) Can be transferred through the recognized stock exchanges.

45. Can a share in a Partnership be transferred like any other property?

(A) Yes

(B) No

(C) Partly yes

(D) None of the above

46. Does the Assignees of a Partner's interest by sale, mortgage or otherwise enjoy the same rights and privileges as the original Partner?

(A) Yes

(B) No

(C) Partly yes

(D) None of the above

47. In case of transfer of Partners' interest u/s 29, the Transferee is entitled to interfere with the conduct of the business.

(A) True

(B) Partly true

(C) False

(D) None of the above

48. Which of the following Partners are not liable in relation to the Firm?

(A) Partner by holding out

(B) Working Partner

(C) Sub- Partner

(D) Partner by estoppel

☞ Rights & Duties after re-constitution

49. Where a Firm constituted for a fixed term continues carry on business after the expiry of the said term mutual rights and duties of the partners —

(A) Will be decided by the Registrar of Firms.

(B) Will be decided upon by the working Partners.

(C) Will remain the same as immediately before the expiry, and consistent with Partnership at Will.

(D) Should be compulsorily determined by a new written agreement.

50. Where a Firm constituted to carry out one or more adventures or undertakings carries out other adventures or undertakings, the mutual rights and duties of the Partners—

(A) Will be decided by the Registrar of Firms.

(B) Will be decided upon by the working Partners.

(C) Will remain the same as applicable in respect of the original adventures or undertakings.

(D) Should be compulsorily determined by a new written agreement.

51. In case of change in the constitution of the Firm, the continuing guarantee given to the Firm or the third party in respect to the transactions of the Firm—

(A) Is not affected at all.

(B) Is revoked as to future transactions.

(C) Is revoked with retrospective effect.

(D) Ceases to be continuing guarantee.

52. In case of change in the constitution of the Firm, the ________ given to the Firm or the third party in respect to the transactions of the Firm, is revoked as to future transactions.

(A) Continuing guarantee.

(B) Performance guarantee.

(C) Bank guarantee.

(D) Fidelity guarantee.

53. In case of ________ the continuing guarantee given to the Firm or the third party in respect to the transactions of the Firm, is revoked as to future transactions.

(A) dissolution of the firm.

(B) insolvency of partner.

(C) death of Partner.

(D) change in the constitution of the firm.

☞ Dissolution

54. An accepted view is that where all the partners except one die or become insolvent, the firm is dissolved.

(A) True, as there must be at least two partners to continue the firm.

(B) False, as the firm is dissolved only where all the partners die or become insolvent.

55. A partnership firm is compulsorily dissolved, where—

(A) All partners have become insolvent.

(B) Firm's business has become unlawful.

(C) The fixed term has expired.

(D) In cases (A) and (B) only.

56. Dissolution by agreement is –

(A) Dissolution by the adjudication of all the partners or of all the partners but one as insolvent.

(B) Dissolution as a result of any agreement between all the partners.

(C) Dissolution by the business of the firm becoming unlawful.

(d) All of the above

57. Dissolution of a firm may take place in the following manner –

(A) Compulsory dissolution.

(B) Dissolution by agreement.

(C) By intervention of the court.

(D) All of the above

58. On which of the following grounds, a partner may apply to the court for dissolution of the firm?

(A) Insanity of a partner

(B) Misconduct of a partner

(C) Perpetual losses in business

(D) All of the above

59. Where all the partners except one die or become insolvent, the Firm is dissolved.

(A) True, as there must be at least two Partners to continue the Firm.

(B) False, as the Firm is dissolved only where all the Partners die or become insolvent.

(C) Partly Yes

(D) None of the above

60. Where dissolution of Firm is sought for on the ground that a Partner has in any way transferred the whole of his interest in a Firm to a third party, the suit shall be brought by—

(A) the Transferee.

(B) the Transferor Partner.

(C) any other Partner.

(D) majority of the Partners.

61. In which of the following situations, the firm will not be compulsorily dissolved?

(A) All partners are declared insolvent.

(B) The business of the Firm becomes unlawful.

(C) The Partnership has various adventures and one such adventure becomes illegal.

(D) All partners except one are declared insolvent.

62. The finding that the business of the Firm cannot be carried on except at a loss, is a sufficient ground for the Court to order dissolution of the Firm.

(A) True

(B) Partly true

(C) False

(D) None of the above

63. In the absence of contract to the contrary, which of the following will not result in dissolution of the Firm?

(A) Expiry of the fixed term agreed upon by the partners

(B) Death of a partner

(C) Admission of a new partner

(D) Adjudication of a partner as insolvent.

64. The expression 'Dissolution of Firm' and 'Dissolution of partnership' have the same meaning and are used interchangeably.

(A) True as the Firm as a whole is closed down in both the cases.

(B) False, as the Firm as a whole is not closed down in later case.

(C) Partly true

(D) None of the above

65. Where a partner has become of unsound mind, a suit for dissolution may be brought by—

(A) any other partner.

(B) next friend of the partner who has become of unsound mind.

(C) either (A) or (B)

(D) both (A) and (B)

66. Which of the following do not constitute a ground for dissolution by court?

(A) Misconduct by partner

(B) Transfer of interest by partner

(C) Just and equitable grounds

(D) Suit by the dormant partner

67. If all partners or all but one partner of the Firm are declared insolvent—

(A) Firm is also declared insolvent

(B) Solvent partner has to repay the debts of the firm

(C) Firm is automatically dissolved

(D) None of the above

68. A, B and C are in Partnership. A and C are adjudicated insolvent, while B wants to continue the Firm.

(A) Firm is also declared insolvent.

(B) B has to repay the debts of the Firm.

(C) Firm is automatically dissolved and hence B cannot continue.

(D) The Court has to give order for dissolution.

69. The Court may order dissolution if a partner is guilty of misconduct, which may affect the business of the Firm. Which of these do not constitute such misconduct?

(A) Gambling on stock exchange.

(B) Persistent refusal and neglect by a partner to attend the business.

(C) Non- interference in the Firm's day to day business by a dormant partner.

(D) Taking away of the books of the firm by the partner.

70. Where dissolution of Firm is sought for on the ground that a partner has allowed his share to be sold in the recovery of arrears of land revenue the suit shall be brought by –

(A) all the other partners.

(B) any other partner.

(C) the partner whose share is to be sold.

(D) a majority of the partners.

71. Which of the following do not constitute just and equitable ground for dissolution of Firm?

(A) Deadlock in management

(B) Disappearance of substratum of business

(C) Partners not in talking terms

(D) Substantial business profits are earned

72. Amar, Akbar and Anthony jointly started business of supplying cotton and agreed to share profits equally through oral agreement on 01.03.2009. Amar and Akbar are active partners, while Anthony is a sleeping partner.

Is the Partnership firm valid?

(A) No, as the agreement was not a written one.

(B) No, as Akbar is not participating.

(C) No, as the firm has not been registered.

(D) Yes, because they agree to share profits.

73. In *Q. 72* above, If Amar applies for insolvency on 1.6.2009 and is declared insolvent on 01.08.2009.

(A) The firm would not be dissolved.

(B) The firm would be dissolved on 01.06.2009.

(C) The firm would be dissolved on 01.08.2009, w.e.f. 1.8.2009.

(D) The firm would be dissolved with retrospective effect from 1.1.2009.

74. In *Q. 72* above, If Akbar becomes insane, and Anthony files a suit, can the court pass an order for dissolution?

(A) No, because the suit has not been filed by an active partner.

(B) No, because other partners can still continue.

(C) Yes, if Akbar agrees to it.

(D) Yes

75. In *Q. 72* above, If Amar becomes insane, and his friend files a suit. Can the court pass an order for dissolution?

(A) No, because suit has not been filled by a partner.

(B) No, because other partners are still working.

(C) Yes, if Amar agrees to it.

(D) Yes

76. In *Q. 72* above, If Anthony becomes insane, and Akbar files a suit. Can the court pass an order for dissolution?

(A) Yes

(B) Yes, if Amar agrees to it.

(C) No, because other partners are still working.

(D) The court may not pass, Because such a partner is not an active partner.

☞ Rights & Liabilities of Partner on Disserve

77. Sec. ______ of the Partnership Act deals with personal profits earned after dissolution.

(A) 50

(B) 51

(C) 52

(D) 53

78. Where a Partnership Contract is rescinded on grounds of fraud or misrepresentation, the party entitled to rescind, is also entitled to rank as a Creditor of the Firm in respect of —

(A) His own Capital.

(B) His share of Profits.

(C) Any payment made by him for the Firm's debts.

(D) All of the above

79. When goodwill of the Firm is sold, the Partners agree with the Buyer, not to carry out similar business a specified period or within the specific local limits. This agreement in restraint of trade is valid provided the restrictions imposed are —

(A) Understandable.

(B) Reasonable.

(C) Implementable.

(D) Feasible.

80. On dissolution, the partners remain liable to until–

(A) Accounts are settled.

(B) Partners dues are paid off.

(C) A Public Notice is given.

(D) The registrar strikes off the name.

81. Where a Partnership Contract is rescinded on ground of fraud or misrepresentation, the party entitled to rescind, is entitled to—

(A) A lien on/right of retention of the surplus of assets of the Firm remaining after settlement of Firm's debts, for any sum paid by him for purchase of share or for contribution of capital.

(B) rank as a Creditor of the Firm in respect of any payment made by him for the Firm's debts.

(C) Be indemnified by the Partner(s) guilty of such fraud or misrepresentation against all debts of the Firm.

(D) All of the above

82. Section ______ deals with Sale of Goodwill after Dissolution of Firm.

(A) 52

(B) 53

(C) 54

(D) 55

83. Where a partner has paid premium on entering into partnership for a fixed term, and it is dissolved before the expiry of such term (otherwise than by death) he shall be entitled to–

(A) repayment of the entire premium.

(B) repayment of part of the premium.

(C) both (A) and (B)

(D) either (A) or (B)

84. Section 53 prohibits Partners from carrying on similar business *in their own name*, till that affairs of the Firm are completely wound up.

(A) True

(B) Partly true

(C) False

(D) None of the above

85. Arun paid a premium for entering into partnership for a fixed term. The firm is dissolved before the expiry of such term, due to difference of opinion between partners. Here –

(A) Arun is entitled to the return of the entire premium.

(B) Arun is not entitled to any return of premium.

(C) Arun is entitled to return of entire premium or pro- rata part thereof.

(D) Arun has to pay further premium.

86. B paid a premium for entering into Partnership for a fixed term. The Firm is dissolved before the expiry of such term. In which of these cases is B entitled to return of premium or any part thereof?

(A) Dissolution is caused by death of a Partner.

(B) Dissolution is due to B's misconduct.

(C) Dissolution is based on agreement which contains no provision as to return to the premium.

(D) Dissolution is due to the retirement of another Partner.

87. After dissolution, the authority to bind the Firm, other mutual rights and liabilities of partners continue, in so far as may be necessary—

(A) to wind up the affairs of the firm.

(B) to complete the transaction that had begun but left unfinished at the time of dissolution.

(C) either (A) or (B)

(D) both (A) and (B)

88. D, F and A are partners of Firm, decided to dissolve the firm with effect from 1st April. They do not give any public notice of dissolution while continuing the business. During the course of business, they incur a liability to the third party M. Which of the following true?

(A) The Firm is not liable to M.

(B) Any one of the partners is liable to M.

(C) The Firm is liable to M.

(D) M does not have any remedy.

89. After dissolution of a Firm, any partner or his representative may restrain any other partner or his representative from carrying on similar business ______ for his own benefit, until the affairs are fully wound up.

(A) in the Firm Name

(B) by using Firm's Property

(C) None of the above

(D) Either (A) or (B)

90. After dissolution of a Firm, any partner or his representative may restrain any other partner or his representative from carrying on ______ in the Firm Name or by using Firm's Property for own benefit, until the affairs are fully wound up.

(A) Competing business

(B) Similar business

(C) Incidental business

(D) Related business

91. After dissolution of a Firm, any partner or his representative may restrain any other partner or his representative from carrying on similar business in the Firm Name or by using firm's property from own benefit, until—

(A) the affairs of the Firm are fully wound up.

(B) public notice of dissolution is given.

(C) dissolution deed is signed by all partners.

(D) all of the above

92. After dissolution of a Firm, any partner or his representative may restrain any other partner or his representative from carrying on similar business in the Firm Name or by using firm's property, _____ until the affairs are fully wound up.

(A) for the benefit of all partners

(B) for the benefit of the Firm

(C) for the benefit of continuing partners

(D) for his own benefit

93. Where any partner has bought the Firm's Goodwill, he can use the Firm's name. No partner can restrain him from using the Firm's Name in such case.

(A) True

(B) Partly true

(C) False

(D) None of the above.

94. When Goodwill of the Firm is sold upon dissolution and a partner carries on a competing business, which of the following is permissible?

(A) Use of Firm's Name

(B) Holding out as carrying on the business of the Firm.

(C) Soliciting the custom of the Firm's customers/suppliers etc.

(D) Advertising such competing business.

95. When Goodwill of the Firm is sold upon dissolution, a partner can carry on a competing business and advertise such business. However, he cannot solicit the custom of persons who were dealing with the Firm before its dissolution.

(A) True

(B) Partly true

(C) False

(D) None of the above

96. Upon dissolution of Firm, all or some of the partners agree not to carry on similar business for a specified period or within specified local limits. This agreement in restraint of trade is —

(A) Valid.

(B) Invalid.

(C) Voidable.

(D) Wholly void.

☞ Settlement of Accounts

97. Goodwill is the property of the firm, and like any other property it belongs proportionately to all the partners.

(A) True

(B) False, as Goodwill is a Fictitious Assets

(C) False, as Goodwill is an Intangible Assets

(D) None of above

98. In case of Joint Debts due from Firm and also separate debts due from Partners, where there is any Surplus after payment of the Firm's debts, then the share of each Partner shall be —

(A) Applied in the payment of his separate debts

(B) Paid to him directly

(C) Either (A) or (B)

(D) Neither (A) or (B)

99. Partnership property vests —

(A) In the Partner of the Firm

(B) In the Firm

(C) In the continuing Partners of the Firm

(D) In the retiring Partners of the Firm

100. The principle evolved in the case of *Garner v. Murray* (*1904*) is –

(A) Deficiencies in the capital of the insolvent partner are distributed among the solvent partners in the ratio of their capital.

(B) Partners have a fiduciary relationship with each other.

(C) Partners liability is unlimited.

(D) Partners can make supernatural profits, provided proper disclosures are made in this regard.

101. Upon dissolution of Firm, surplus left after settlement of the debts and liabilities of the Firm shall be –

(A) Credited to the Reserve Account.

(B) Credited to the Government of India A/c.

(C) Distributed among the partners equally.

(D) Distributed among the partners according to their rights.

102. Upon dissolution of firm, Losses, including deficiencies of Capital, shall be paid first out of profits and then —

(A) Out of Profits.

(B) Out of Capital.

(C) By the partners individually in their profit sharing ratio.

(D) By the partners equally.

103. Upon dissolution, the goodwill of the firm—

(A) Must be sold separately.

(B) Must be sold along with the assets of the Firm only.

(C) May be sold either separately or along with the assets of the Firm.

(D) Cannot be sold at all.

104. The accounting rule in respect of loss arising due to insolvency of a partner is dealt with in—

(A) *Derry* v *Peel*

(B) *Carlill* v *Carbolic Smoke Ball Co.*

(C) *Garner* v *Murray*

(D) *Chinnaiah* v *Ramaiya*

☞ Public Notice

105. Intimation of a Dissolution of Registered Firm, to the Registrar of Firms, may be given by —

(A) Any person who was a Partner prior to dissolution.

(B) Agent of the person in (A)

(C) Any person specially authorized in this behalf

(D) Any one of the above.

106. In case of Registered Firms, which of the following is not proper mode of giving Public Notice?

(A) Serving a copy of the notice to the Registrar of Firms

(B) Publishing the Notice in the Official Gazette

(C) Publishing the Notice in one English newspaper circulating in the district where the Firm's principal place of business is situated.

(D) Publishing the Notice in one vernacular newspaper circulating in the district where the Firm's principal place of business is situated.

ANSWERS TO MULTIPLE CHOICE QUESTIONS

1.	D	**23.**	B	**45.**	A	**67.**	C	**89.**	D
2.	B	**24.**	D	**46.**	B	**68.**	C	**90.**	B
3.	A	**25.**	A	**47.**	C	**69.**	C	**91.**	A
4.	A	**26.**	D	**48.**	C	**70.**	B	**92.**	D
5.	B	**27.**	C	**49.**	C	**71.**	D	**93.**	A
6.	B	**28.**	A	**50.**	C	**72.**	D	**94.**	D
7.	D	**29.**	C	**51.**	B	**73.**	C	**95.**	A
8.	A	**30.**	C	**52.**	A	**74.**	D	**96.**	A
9.	D	**31.**	C	**53.**	D	**75.**	D	**97.**	A
10.	A	**32.**	A	**54.**	A	**76.**	A	**98.**	C
11.	A	**33.**	A	**55.**	D	**77.**	A	**99.**	B
12.	C	**34.**	A	**56.**	B	**78.**	C	**100.**	A
13.	C	**35.**	A	**57.**	D	**79.**	B	**101.**	D
14.	A	**36.**	A	**58.**	D	**80.**	C	**102.**	B
15.	D	**37.**	B	**59.**	A	**81.**	D	**103.**	C
16.	A	**38.**	D	**60.**	C	**82.**	D	**104.**	C
17.	A	**39.**	A	**61.**	C	**83.**	D	**105.**	D
18.	C	**40.**	B	**62.**	A	**84.**	C	**106.**	C
19.	B	**41.**	B	**63.**	C	**85.**	C		
20.	C	**42.**	A	**64.**	B	**86.**	D		
21.	D	**43.**	A	**65.**	C	**87.**	D		
22.	D	**44.**	B	**66.**	D	**88.**	C		